The Federal Register Index is issued monthly in cumulative form. This index is based on a consolidation of the "Contents" entries in the daily Federal Register.

A List of CFR Sections Affected (LSA) is published monthly, keyed to the revision dates of the 50 CFR titles.

REPUBLICATION OF MATERIAL

There are no restrictions on the republication of material appearing in the Code of Federal Regulations.

INQUIRIES

For a legal interpretation or explanation of any regulation in this volume, contact the issuing agency. The issuing agency's name appears at the top of odd-numbered pages.

For inquiries concerning CFR reference assistance, call 202–741–6000 or write to the Director, Office of the Federal Register, National Archives and Records Administration, 8601 Adelphi Road, College Park, MD 20740-6001 or e-mail *fedreg.info@nara.gov.*

THIS TITLE

Title 21—FOOD AND DRUGS is composed of nine volumes. The parts in these volumes are arranged in the following order: Parts 1–99, 100–169, 170–199, 200–299, 300–499, 500–599, 600–799, 800–1299 and 1300–end. The first eight volumes, containing parts 1–1299, comprise Chapter I—Food and Drug Administration, Department of Health and Human Services. The ninth volume, containing part 1300 to end, includes Chapter II—Drug Enforcement Administration, Department of Justice, and Chapter III—Office of National Drug Control Policy. The contents of these volumes represent all current regulations codified under this title of the CFR as of April 1, 2023.

For this volume, Robert J. Sheehan, III was Chief Editor. The Code of Federal Regulations publication program is under the direction of John Hyrum Martinez, assisted by Stephen J. Frattini.

Title 21—Food and Drugs

(This book contains parts 600 to 799)

1

CHAPTER I—FOOD AND DRUG ADMINISTRATION, DEPARTMENT OF HEALTH AND HUMAN SERVICES (CONTINUED)

EDITORIAL NOTE: Nomenclature changes to chapter I appear at 59 FR 14366, Mar. 28, 1994, and 66 FR 56035, Nov. 6, 2001.

SUBCHAPTER F—BIOLOGICS

SUBCHAPTER G—COSMETICS

SUBCHAPTER F—BIOLOGICS

PART 600—BIOLOGICAL PRODUCTS: GENERAL

Subpart A—General Provisions

AUTHORITY: 21 U.S.C. 321, 351, 352, 353, 355, 356c, 356e, 360, 360i, 371, 374, 379k–1; 42 U.S.C. 216, 262, 263, 263a, 264.

CROSS REFERENCES: For U.S. Customs Service regulations relating to viruses, serums, and toxins, see 19 CFR 12.21–12.23. For U.S. Postal Service regulations relating to the admissibility to the United States mails see parts 124 and 125 of the Domestic Mail Manual, that is incorporated by reference in 39 CFR part 111.

Subpart A—General Provisions

§ 600.2 Mailing addresses.

(a) *Licensed biological products regulated by the Center for Biologics Evaluation and Research (CBER).* Unless otherwise stated in paragraph (c) of this section, or as otherwise prescribed by FDA regulation, all submissions to CBER referenced in parts 600 through 680 of this chapter, as applicable, must be sent to: Food and Drug Administra-

tion, Center for Biologics Evaluation and Research, Document Control Center, 10903 New Hampshire Ave., Bldg. 71, Rm. G112, Silver Spring, MD 20993–0002. Examples of such submissions include: Biologics license applications (BLAs) and their amendments and supplements, biological product deviation reports, fatality reports, and other correspondence. Biological products samples must not be sent to this address but must be sent to the address in paragraph (c) of this section.

(b) *Licensed biological products regulated by the Center for Drug Evaluation and Research (CDER).* Unless otherwise stated in paragraphs (b)(1), (b)(2), or (c) of this section, or as otherwise prescribed by FDA regulation, all submissions to CDER referenced in parts 600, 601, and 610 of this chapter, as applicable, must be sent to: CDER Central Document Room, Center for Drug Evaluation and Research, Food and Drug Administration, 5901B Ammendale Rd., Beltsville, MD 20705. Examples of such submissions include: BLAs and their amendments and supplements, and other correspondence.

(1) *Biological Product Deviation Reporting (CDER).* All biological product deviation reports required under § 600.14 must be sent to: Division of Compliance Risk Management and Surveillance, Office of Compliance, Center for Drug Evaluation and Research, Food and Drug Administration, 10903 New Hampshire Ave., Silver Spring, MD 20993–0002.

(2) *Advertising and Promotional Labeling (CDER).* All advertising and promotional labeling supplements required under § 601.12(f) of this chapter must be sent to: Division of Drug Marketing, Advertising and Communication, Center for Drug Evaluation and Research, Food and Drug Administration, 5901–B Ammendale Rd., Beltsville, MD 20705–1266.

(c) *Samples and Protocols for licensed biological products regulated by CBER or CDER.* (1) Biological product samples and/or protocols, other than radioactive biological product samples and protocols, required under §§ 600.13, 600.22, 601.15, 610.2, 660.6, 660.36, or 660.46

5

of this chapter must be sent by courier service to: Food and Drug Administration, Center for Biologics Evaluation and Research, ATTN: Sample Custodian, 10903 New Hampshire Ave., Bldg. 75, Rm. G707, Silver Spring, MD 20993–0002. The protocol(s) may be placed in the box used to ship the samples to CBER. A cover letter should not be included when submitting the protocol with the sample unless it contains pertinent information affecting the release of the lot.

(2) Radioactive biological products required under § 610.2 of this chapter must be sent by courier service to: Food and Drug Administration, Center for Biologics Evaluation and Research, ATTN: Sample Custodian, c/o White Oak Radiation Safety Program, 10903 New Hampshire Ave., Bldg. 52–72, Rm. G406A, Silver Spring, MD 20993–0002.

(d) Address information for submissions to° CBER and CDER other than those listed in parts 600 through 680 of this chapter are included directly in the applicable regulations.

(e) Obtain updated mailing address information for biological products regulated by CBER at *http://www.fda.gov/BiologicsBloodVaccines/default.htm*, or for biological products regulated by CDER at *http://www.fda.gov/Drugs/default.htm*.

[70 FR 14981, Mar. 24, 2005, as amended at 74 FR 13114, Mar. 26, 2009; 78 FR 19585, Apr. 2, 2013; 80 FR 18091, Apr. 3, 2015; 79 FR 33090, June 10, 2014]

§ 600.3 Definitions.

As used in this subchapter:

(a) *Act* means the Public Health Service Act (58 Stat. 682), approved July 1, 1944.

(b) *Secretary* means the Secretary of Health and Human Services and any other officer or employee of the Department of Health and Human Services to whom the authority involved has been delegated.

(c) *Commissioner of Food and Drugs* means the Commissioner of the Food and Drug Administration.

(d) *Center for Biologics Evaluation and Research* means Center for Biologics Evaluation and Research of the Food and Drug Administration.

(e) *State* means a State or the District of Columbia, Puerto Rico, or the Virgin Islands.

(f) *Possession* includes among other possessions, Puerto Rico and the Virgin Islands.

(g) *Products* includes biological products and trivalent organic arsenicals.

(h) *Biological product* means a virus, therapeutic serum, toxin, antitoxin, vaccine, blood, blood component or derivative, allergenic product, protein, or analogous product, or arsphenamine or derivative of arsphenamine (or any other trivalent organic arsenic compound), applicable to the prevention, treatment, or cure of a disease or condition of human beings.

(1) A virus is interpreted to be a product containing the minute living cause of an infectious disease and includes but is not limited to filterable viruses, bacteria, rickettsia, fungi, and protozoa.

(2) A therapeutic serum is a product obtained from blood by removing the clot or clot components and the blood cells.

(3) A toxin is a product containing a soluble substance poisonous to laboratory animals or to man in doses of 1 milliliter or less (or equivalent in weight) of the product, and having the property, following the injection of non-fatal doses into an animal, of causing to be produced therein another soluble substance which specifically neutralizes the poisonous substance and which is demonstrable in the serum of the animal thus immunized.

(4) An antitoxin is a product containing the soluble substance in serum or other body fluid of an immunized animal which specifically neutralizes the toxin against which the animal is immune.

(5) A product is analogous:

(i) To a virus if prepared from or with a virus or agent actually or potentially infectious, without regard to the degree of virulence or toxicogenicity of the specific strain used.

(ii) To a therapeutic serum, if composed of whole blood or plasma or containing some organic constituent or product other than a hormone or an amino acid, derived from whole blood, plasma, or serum.

(iii) To a toxin or antitoxin, if intended, irrespective of its source of origin, to be applicable to the prevention, treatment, or cure of disease or injuries of man through a specific immune process.

(6) A protein is any alpha amino acid polymer with a specific, defined sequence that is greater than 40 amino acids in size. When two or more amino acid chains in an amino acid polymer are associated with each other in a manner that occurs in nature, the size of the amino acid polymer for purposes of this paragraph (h)(6) will be based on the total number of amino acids in those chains, and will not be limited to the number of amino acids in a contiguous sequence.

(i) *Trivalent organic arsenicals* means arsphenamine and its derivatives (or any other trivalent organic arsenic compound) applicable to the prevention, treatment, or cure of diseases or injuries of man.

(j) A product is deemed *applicable to the prevention, treatment, or cure of diseases or injuries of man* irrespective of the mode of administration or application recommended, including use when intended through administration or application to a person as an aid in diagnosis, or in evaluating the degree of susceptibility or immunity possessed by a person, and including also any other use for purposes of diagnosis if the diagnostic substance so used is prepared from or with the aid of a biological product.

(k) *Proper name*, as applied to a product, means the name designated in the license for use upon each package of the product.

(l) *Dating period* means the period beyond which the product cannot be expected beyond reasonable doubt to yield its specific results.

(m) *Expiration date* means the calendar month and year, and where applicable, the day and hour, that the dating period ends.

(n) The word *standards* means specifications and procedures applicable to an establishment or to the manufacture or release of products, which are prescribed in this subchapter or established in the biologics license application designed to insure the continued

safety, purity, and potency of such products.

(o) The word *continued* as applied to the safety, purity and potency of products is interpreted to apply to the dating period.

(p) The word *safety* means the relative freedom from harmful effect to persons affected, directly or indirectly, by a product when prudently administered, taking into consideration character of the product in relation to the condition of the recipient at the time.

(q) The word *sterility* is interpreted to mean freedom from viable contaminating microorganisms, as determined by the tests conducted under §610.12 of this chapter.

(r) *Purity* means relative freedom from extraneous matter in the finished product, whether or not harmful to the recipient or deleterious to the product. *Purity* includes but is not limited to relative freedom from residual moisture or other volatile substances and pyrogenic substances.

(s) The word *potency* is interpreted to mean the specific ability or capacity of the product, as indicated by appropriate laboratory tests or by adequately controlled clinical data obtained through the administration of the product in the manner intended, to effect a given result.

(t) *Manufacturer* means any legal person or entity engaged in the manufacture of a product subject to license under the act; "Manufacturer" also includes any legal person or entity who is an applicant for a license where the applicant assumes responsibility for compliance with the applicable product and establishment standards.

(u) *Manufacture* means all steps in propagation or manufacture and preparation of products and includes but is not limited to filling, testing, labeling, packaging, and storage by the manufacturer.

(v) *Location* includes all buildings, appurtenances, equipment and animals used, and personnel engaged by a manufacturer within a particular area designated by an address adequate for identification.

(w) *Establishment* has the same meaning as "facility" in section 351 of the

Public Health Service Act and includes all locations.

(x) *Lot* means that quantity of uniform material identified by the manufacturer as having been thoroughly mixed in a single vessel.

(y) A *filling* refers to a group of final containers identical in all respects, which have been filled with the same product from the same bulk lot without any change that will affect the integrity of the filling assembly.

(z) *Process* refers to a manufacturing step that is performed on the product itself which may affect its safety, purity or potency, in contrast to such manufacturing steps which do not affect intrinsically the safety, purity or potency of the product.

(aa) *Selling agent* or *distributor* means any person engaged in the unrestricted distribution, other than by sale at retail, of products subject to license.

(bb) *Container* (referred to also as "final container") is the immediate unit, bottle, vial, ampule, tube, or other receptacle containing the product as distributed for sale, barter, or exchange.

(cc) *Package* means the immediate carton, receptacle, or wrapper, including all labeling matter therein and thereon, and the contents of the one or more enclosed containers. If no package, as defined in the preceding sentence, is used, the container shall be deemed to be the package.

(dd) *Label* means any written, printed, or graphic matter on the container or package or any such matter clearly visible through the immediate carton, receptacle, or wrapper.

(ee) *Radioactive biological product* means a biological product which is labeled with a radionuclide or intended solely to be labeled with a radionuclide.

(ff) *Amendment* is the submission of information to a pending license application or supplement, to revise or modify the application as originally submitted.

(gg) *Supplement* is a request to approve a change in an approved license application.

(hh) *Distributed* means the biological product has left the control of the licensed manufacturer.

(ii) *Control* means having responsibility for maintaining the continued safety, purity, and potency of the product and for compliance with applicable product and establishment standards, and for compliance with current good manufacturing practices.

(jj) *Assess the effects of the change*, as used in § 601.12 of this chapter, means to evaluate the effects of a manufacturing change on the identity, strength, quality, purity, and potency of a product as these factors may relate to the safety or effectiveness of the product.

(kk) *Specification*, as used in § 601.12 of this chapter, means the quality standard (i.e., tests, analytical procedures, and acceptance criteria) provided in an approved application to confirm the quality of products, intermediates, raw materials, reagents, components, in-process materials, container closure systems, and other materials used in the production of a product. For the purpose of this definition, *acceptance criteria* means numerical limits, ranges, or other criteria for the tests described.

(ll) *Complete response letter* means a written communication to an applicant from FDA usually describing all of the deficiencies that the agency has identified in a biologics license application or supplement that must be satisfactorily addressed before it can be approved.

(mm) *Resubmission* means a submission by the biologics license applicant or supplement applicant of all materials needed to fully address all deficiencies identified in the complete response letter. A biologics license application or supplement for which FDA issued a complete response letter, but which was withdrawn before approval and later submitted again, is not a resubmission.

[38 FR 32048, Nov. 20, 1973, as amended at 40 FR 31313, July 25, 1975; 55 FR 11014, Mar. 26, 1990; 61 FR 24232, May 14, 1996; 62 FR 39901, July 24, 1997; 64 FR 56449, Oct. 20, 1999; 65 FR 66634, Nov. 7, 2000; 69 FR 18766, Apr. 8, 2004; 70 FR 14982, Mar. 24, 2005; 73 FR 39610, July 10, 2008; 77 FR 26174, May 3, 2012; 85 FR 10063, Feb. 21, 2020]

Subpart B—Establishment Standards

§600.10 Personnel.

(a) [Reserved]

(b) *Personnel.* Personnel shall have capabilities commensurate with their assigned functions, a thorough understanding of the manufacturing operations which they perform, the necessary training and experience relating to individual products, and adequate information concerning the application of the pertinent provisions of this subchapter to their respective functions. Personnel shall include such professionally trained persons as are necessary to insure the competent performance of all manufacturing processes.

(c) *Restrictions on personnel*—(1) *Specific duties.* Persons whose presence can affect adversely the safety and purity of a product shall be excluded from the room where the manufacture of a product is in progress.

(2) *Sterile operations.* Personnel performing sterile operations shall wear clean or sterilized protective clothing and devices to the extent necessary to protect the product from contamination.

(3) *Pathogenic viruses and spore-forming organisms.* Persons working with viruses pathogenic for man or with spore-forming microorganisms, and persons engaged in the care of animals or animal quarters, shall be excluded from areas where other products are manufactured, or such persons shall change outer clothing, including shoes, or wear protective covering prior to entering such areas.

(4) *Live vaccine work areas.* Persons may not enter a live vaccine processing area after having worked with other infectious agents in any other laboratory during the same working day. Only persons actually concerned with propagation of the culture, production of the vaccine, and unit maintenance, shall be allowed in live vaccine processing areas when active work is in progress. Casual visitors shall be excluded from such units at all times and all others having business in such areas shall be admitted only under supervision. Street clothing, including shoes, shall be replaced or covered by suitable laboratory clothing before entering a live vaccine processing unit. Persons caring for animals used in the manufacture of live vaccines shall be excluded from other animal quarters and from contact with other animals during the same working day.

[38 FR 32048, Nov. 20, 1973, as amended at 49 FR 23833, June 8, 1984; 55 FR 11014, Mar. 26, 1990; 62 FR 53538, Oct. 15, 1997; 68 FR 75119, Dec. 30, 2003]

§600.11 Physical establishment, equipment, animals, and care.

(a) *Work areas.* All rooms and work areas where products are manufactured or stored shall be kept orderly, clean, and free of dirt, dust, vermin and objects not required for manufacturing. Precautions shall be taken to avoid clogging and back-siphonage of drainage systems. Precautions shall be taken to exclude extraneous infectious agents from manufacturing areas. Work rooms shall be well lighted and ventilated. The ventilation system shall be arranged so as to prevent the dissemination of microorganisms from one manufacturing area to another and to avoid other conditions unfavorable to the safety of the product. Filling rooms, and other rooms where open, sterile operations are conducted, shall be adequate to meet manufacturing needs and such rooms shall be constructed and equipped to permit thorough cleaning and to keep air-borne contaminants at a minimum. If such rooms are used for other purposes, they shall be cleaned and prepared prior to use for sterile operations. Refrigerators, incubators and warm rooms shall be maintained at temperatures within applicable ranges and shall be free of extraneous material which might affect the safety of the product.

(b) *Equipment.* Apparatus for sterilizing equipment and the method of operation shall be such as to insure the destruction of contaminating microorganisms. The effectiveness of the sterilization procedure shall be no less than that achieved by an attained temperature of 121.5 °C maintained for 20 minutes by saturated steam or by an attained temperature of 170 °C maintained for 2 hours with dry heat. Processing and storage containers, filters, filling apparatus, and other pieces of apparatus and accessory equipment, including pipes and tubing, shall be designed and constructed to permit thorough cleaning and, where possible, inspection for cleanliness. All surfaces that come in contact with products shall be clean and free of surface solids, leachable contaminants, and other materials that will hasten the deterioration of the product or otherwise render it less suitable for the intended use. For products for which sterility is a factor, equipment shall be sterile, unless sterility of the product is assured by subsequent procedures.

(c) *Laboratory and bleeding rooms.* Rooms used for the processing of products, including bleeding rooms, shall be effectively fly-proofed and kept free of flies and vermin. Such rooms shall be so constructed as to insure freedom from dust, smoke and other deleterious substances and to permit thorough cleaning and disinfection. Rooms for animal injection and bleeding, and rooms for smallpox vaccine animals, shall be disinfected and be provided with the necessary water, electrical and other services.

(d) *Animal quarters and stables.* Animal quarters, stables and food storage areas shall be of appropriate construction, fly-proofed, adequately lighted and ventilated, and maintained in a clean, vermin-free and sanitary condition. No manure or refuse shall be stored as to permit the breeding of flies on the premises, nor shall the establishment be located in close proximity to off-property manure or refuse storage capable of engendering fly breeding.

(e) *Restrictions on building and equipment use*—(1) *Work of a diagnostic nature.* Laboratory procedures of a clinical diagnostic nature involving materials that may be contaminated, shall not be performed in space used for the manufacture of products except that manufacturing space which is used only occasionally may be used for diagnostic work provided spore-forming pathogenic microorganisms are not involved and provided the space is thoroughly cleaned and disinfected before the manufacture of products is resumed.

(2) *Spore-forming organisms for supplemental sterilization procedure control test.* Spore-forming organisms used as an additional control in sterilization procedures may be introduced into areas used for the manufacture of products, only for the purposes of the test and only immediately before use for such purposes: *Provided,* That (i) the organism is not pathogenic for man or animals and does not produce pyrogens or toxins, (ii) the culture is demonstrated to be pure, (iii) transfer of test cultures to culture media shall be limited to the sterility test area or areas designated for work with spore-forming organisms, (iv) each culture be labeled with the name of the microorganism and the statement "Caution: microbial spores. See directions for storage, use and disposition."; and (v) the container of each culture is designed to withstand handling without breaking.

(3) *Work with spore-forming microorganisms.* (i) Manufacturing processes using spore-forming microorganisms conducted in a multiproduct manufacturing site must be performed under appropriate controls to prevent contamination of other products and areas within the site. Prevention of spore contamination can be achieved by using a separate dedicated building or by using process containment if manufacturing is conducted in a multiproduct manufacturing building. All product and personnel movement between the area where the spore-forming microorganisms are manufactured and other manufacturing areas must be conducted under conditions that will prevent the introduction of spores into other areas of the facility.

(ii) If process containment is employed in a multiproduct manufacturing area, procedures must be in place to demonstrate adequate removal of the spore-forming microorganism(s) from the manufacturing area for subsequent manufacture of other products. These procedures must provide for adequate removal or decontamination of the spore-forming microorganisms on and within manufacturing equipment, facilities, and ancillary room items as well as the removal of disposable or product dedicated items from the manufacturing area. Environmental monitoring specific for the spore-forming microorganism(s) must be conducted in adjacent areas during manufacturing

10

operations and in the manufacturing area after completion of cleaning and decontamination.

(4) *Live vaccine processing.* Live vaccine processing must be performed under appropriate controls to prevent cross contamination of other products and other manufacturing areas within the building. Appropriate controls must include, at a minimum:

(i)(A) Using a dedicated manufacturing area that is either in a separate building, in a separate wing of a building, or in quarters at the blind end of a corridor and includes adequate space and equipment for all processing steps up to, but not including, filling into final containers; and

(B) Not conducting test procedures that potentially involve the presence of microorganisms other than the vaccine strains or the use of tissue culture cell lines other than primary cultures in space used for processing live vaccine; or

(ii) If manufacturing is conducted in a multiproduct manufacturing building or area, using procedural controls, and where necessary, process containment. Process containment is deemed to be necessary unless procedural controls are sufficient to prevent cross contamination of other products and other manufacturing areas within the building. Process containment is a system designed to mechanically isolate equipment or an area that involves manufacturing using live vaccine organisms. All product, equipment, and personnel movement between distinct live vaccine processing areas and between live vaccine processing areas and other manufacturing areas, up to, but not including, filling in final containers, must be conducted under conditions that will prevent cross contamination of other products and manufacturing areas within the building, including the introduction of live vaccine organisms into other areas. In addition, written procedures and effective processes must be in place to adequately remove or decontaminate live vaccine organisms from the manufacturing area and equipment for subsequent manufacture of other products. Written procedures must be in place for verification that processes to remove

or decontaminate live vaccine organisms have been followed.

(5) *Equipment and supplies—contamination.* Equipment and supplies used in work on or otherwise exposed to any pathogenic or potentially pathogenic agent shall be kept separated from equipment and supplies used in the manufacture of products to the extent necessary to prevent cross-contamination.

(f) *Animals used in manufacture*—(1) *Care of animals used in manufacturing.* Caretakers and attendants for animals used for the manufacture of products shall be sufficient in number and have adequate experience to insure adequate care. Animal quarters and cages shall be kept in sanitary condition. Animals on production shall be inspected daily to observe response to production procedures. Animals that become ill for reasons not related to production shall be isolated from other animals and shall not be used for production until recovery is complete. Competent veterinary care shall be provided as needed.

(2) *Quarantine of animals*—(i) *General.* No animal shall be used in processing unless kept under competent daily inspection and preliminary quarantine for a period of at least 7 days before use, or as otherwise provided in this subchapter. Only healthy animals free from detectable communicable diseases shall be used. Animals must remain in overt good health throughout the quarantine periods and particular care shall be taken during the quarantine periods to reject animals of the equine genus which may be infected with glanders and animals which may be infected with tuberculosis.

(ii) *Quarantine of monkeys.* In addition to observing the pertinent general quarantine requirements, monkeys used as a source of tissue in the manufacture of vaccine shall be maintained in quarantine for at least 6 weeks prior to use, except when otherwise provided in this part. Only monkeys that have reacted negatively to tuberculin at the start of the quarantine period and again within 2 weeks prior to use shall be used in the manufacture of vaccine. Due precaution shall be taken to prevent cross-infection from any infected or potentially infected monkeys on the premises. Monkeys to be used in the manufacture of a live vaccine shall be maintained throughout the quarantine period in cages closed on all sides with solid materials except the front.which shall be screened,' with no more than two monkeys housed in one cage. Cage mates shall not be interchanged.

(3) *Immunization against tetanus.* Horses and other animals susceptible to tetanus, that are used in the processing steps of the manufacture of biological products, shall be treated adequately to maintain immunity to tetanus.

(4) *Immunization and bleeding of animals used as a source of products.* Toxins or other nonviable antigens administered in the immunization' of animals used in the manufacture of products shall be sterile. Viable antigens, when so used, shall be free of contaminants, as determined by appropriate tests prior to use. Injections shall not be made into horses within 6 inches of bleeding site. Horses shall not be bled for manufacturing purposes while showing persistent general reaction or local reaction near the site of bleeding. Blood shall not be used if it was drawn within 5 days of injecting the animals with viable microorganisms. Animals shall not be bled for manufacturing purposes when they have an intercurrent disease. Blood intended for use as a source of a biological product shall be collected in clean, sterile vessels. When the product is intended for use by injection, such vessels shall also be pyrogen-free.

(5) [Reserved]

(6) *Reporting of certain diseases.* In cases of actual or suspected infection with foot and mouth disease, glanders, tetanus, anthrax, gas gangrene, equine infectious anemia; equine encephalomyelitis, or any of the pock diseases among animals intended for use or used in the manufacture of products, the manufacturer shall immediately notify the Director, Center for Biologics Evaluation and Research or the Director, Center for Drug Evaluation and Research (see mailing addresses in § 600.2(a) or (b)).

(7) *Monkeys used previously for experimental or test purposes.* Monkeys that have been used previously for experimental or test purposes with live

microbiological agents shall not be used as a source of kidney tissue for the manufacture of vaccine. Except as provided otherwise in this subchapter, monkeys that have been used previously for other experimental or test purposes may be used as a source of kidney tissue upon their return to a normal condition, provided all quarantine requirements have been met.

(8) *Necropsy examination of monkeys.* Each monkey used in the manufacture of vaccine shall be examined at necropsy under the direction of a qualified pathologist, physician, or veterinarian having experience with diseases of monkeys, for evidence of ill health, particularly for (i) evidence of tuberculosis, (ii) presence of herpes-like lesions, including eruptions or plaques on or around the lips, in the buccal cavity or on the gums, and (iii) signs of conjunctivitis. If there are any such signs or other significant gross pathological lesions, the tissue shall not be used in the manufacture of vaccine.

(g) *Filling procedures.* Filling procedures shall be such as will not affect adversely the safety, purity or potency of the product.

(h) *Containers and closures.* All final containers and closures shall be made of material that will not hasten the deterioration of the product or otherwise render it less suitable for the intended use. All final containers and closures shall be clean and free of surface solids, leachable contaminants and other materials that will hasten the deterioration of the product or otherwise render it less suitable for the intended use. After filling, sealing shall be performed in a manner that will maintain the integrity of the product during the dating period. In addition, final containers and closures for products intended for use by injection shall be sterile and free from pyrogens. Except as otherwise provided in the regulations of this subchapter, final containers for products intended for use by injection shall be colorless and sufficiently transparent to permit visual examination of the contents under normal light. As soon as possible after filling final containers shall be labeled as prescribed in § 610.60 *et seq.* of this chapter, except that final containers may be stored without such prescribed labeling provided they are stored in a sealed receptacle labeled both inside and outside with at least the name of the product, the lot number, and the filling identification.

[38 FR 32048, Nov. 20, 1973, as amended at 41 FR 10428, Mar. 11, 1976; 49 FR 23833, June 8, 1984; 55 FR 11013, Mar. 26, 1990; 68 FR 75119, Dec. 30, 2003; 70 FR 14982, Mar. 24, 2005; 72 FR 59003, Oct. 18, 2007; 80 FR 18092, Apr. 3, 2015]

§ 600.12 Records.

(a) *Maintenance of records.* Records shall be made, concurrently with the performance, of each step in the manufacture and distribution of products, in such a manner that at any time successive steps in the manufacture and distribution of any lot may be traced by an inspector. Such records shall be legible and indelible, shall identify the person immediately responsible, shall include dates of the various steps, and be as detailed as necessary for clear understanding of each step by one experienced in the manufacture of products.

(b) *Records retention—*(1) *General.* Records shall be retained for such interval beyond the expiration date as is necessary for the individual product, to permit the return of any clinical report of unfavorable reactions. The retention period shall be no less than five years after the records of manufacture have been completed or six months after the latest expiration date for the individual product, whichever represents a later date.

(2) *Records of recall.* Complete records shall be maintained pertaining to the recall from distribution of any product upon notification by the Director, Center for Biologics Evaluation and Research or the Director, Center for Drug Evaluation and Research, to recall for failure to conform with the standards prescribed in the regulations of this subchapter, because of deterioration of the product or for any other factor by reason of which the distribution of the product would constitute a danger to health.

(3) *Suspension of requirement for retention.* The Director, Center for Biologics Evaluation and Research or the Director, Center for Drug Evaluation and Research, may authorize the suspension of the requirement to retain records of a specific manufacturing step upon a showing that such records no longer have significance for the purposes for which they were made: *Provided,* That a summary of such records shall be retained.

(c) *Records of sterilization of equipment and supplies.* Records relating to the mode of sterilization, date, duration, temperature and other conditions relating to each sterilization of equipment and supplies used in the processing of products shall be made by means of automatic recording devices or by means of a system of recording which gives equivalent assurance of the accuracy and reliability of the record. Such records shall be maintained in a manner that permits an identification of the product with the particular manufacturing process to which the sterilization relates.

(d) *Animal necropsy records.* A necropsy record shall be kept on each animal from which a biological product has been obtained and which dies or is sacrificed while being so used.

(e) *Records in case of divided manufacturing responsibility.* If two or more establishments participate in the manufacture of a product, the records of each such establishment must show plainly the degree of its responsibility. In addition, each participating manufacturer shall furnish to the manufacturer who prepares the product in final form for sale, barter or exchange, a copy of all records relating to the manufacturing operations performed by such participating manufacturer insofar as they concern the safety, purity and potency of the lots of the product involved, and the manufacturer who prepares the product in final form shall retain a complete record of all the manufacturing operations relating to the product.

[38 FR 32048, Nov. 20, 1973, as amended at 49 FR 23833, June 8, 1984; 55 FR 11013, Mar. 26, 1990; 70 FR 14982, Mar. 24, 2005]

§ 600.13 Retention samples.

Manufacturers shall retain for a period of at least 6 months after the expiration date, unless a different time period is specified in additional standards, a quantity of representative material of each lot of each product, sufficient for examination and testing for safety and potency, except Whole Blood, Cryoprecipitated AHF, Platelets, Red Blood Cells, Plasma, and Source Plasma and Allergenic Products prepared to a physician's prescription. Samples so retained shall be selected at random from either final container material, or from bulk and final containers, provided they include at least one final container as a final package, or package-equivalent of such filling of each lot of the product as intended for distribution. Such sample material shall be stored at temperatures and under conditions which will maintain the identity and integrity of the product. Samples retained as required in this section shall be in addition to samples of specific products required to be submitted to the Center for Biologics Evaluation and Research or the Center for Drug Evaluation and Research (see mailing addresses in § 600.2). Exceptions may be authorized by the Director, Center for Biologics Evaluation and Research or the Director, Center for Drug Evaluation and Research, when the lot yields relatively few final containers and when such lots are prepared by the same method in large number and in close succession.

[41 FR 10428, Mar. 11, 1976, as amended at 49 FR 23833, June 8, 1984; 50 FR 4133, Jan. 29, 1985; 55 FR 11013, Mar. 26, 1990; 70 FR 14982, Mar. 24, 2005]

§ 600.14 Reporting of biological product deviations by licensed manufacturers.

(a) *Who must report under this section?* (1) You, the manufacturer who holds the biological product license and who had control over the product when the deviation occurred, must report under this section. If you arrange for another person to perform a manufacturing, holding, or distribution step, while the product is in your control, that step is performed under your control. You must establish, maintain, and follow a procedure for receiving information from that person on all deviations, complaints, and adverse events concerning the affected product.

(2) Exceptions:

(i) Persons who manufacture only in vitro diagnostic products that are not subject to licensing under section 351 of the Public Health Service Act do not

report biological product deviations for those products under this section but must report in accordance with part 803 of this chapter;

(ii) Persons who manufacture blood and blood components, including licensed manufacturers, unlicensed registered blood establishments, and transfusion services, do not report biological product deviations for those products under this section but must report under § 606.171 of this chapter;

(iii) Persons who manufacture Source Plasma or any other blood component and use that Source Plasma or any other blood component in the further manufacture of another licensed biological product must report:

(A) Under § 606.171 of this chapter, if a biological product deviation occurs during the manufacture of that Source Plasma or any other blood component; or

(B) Under this section, if a biological product deviation occurs after the manufacture of that Source Plasma or any other blood component, and during manufacture of the licensed biological product.

(b) *What do I report under this section?* You must report any event, and information relevant to the event, associated with the manufacturing, to include testing, processing, packing, labeling, or storage, or with the holding or distribution, of a licensed biological product, if that event meets all the following criteria:

(1) Either:

(i) Represents a deviation from current good manufacturing practice, applicable regulations, applicable standards, or established specifications that may affect the safety, purity, or potency of that product; or

(ii) Represents an unexpected or unforeseeable event that may affect the safety, purity, or potency of that product; and

(2) Occurs in your facility or another facility under contract with you; and

(3) Involves a distributed biological product.

(c) *When do I report under this section?* You should report a biological product deviation as soon as possible but you must report at a date not to exceed 45-calendar days from the date you, your agent, or another person who performs a manufacturing, holding, or distribution step under your control, acquire information reasonably suggesting that a reportable event has occurred.

(d) *How do I report under this section?* You must report on Form FDA-3486.

(e) *Where do I report under this section?*

(1) For biological products regulated by the Center for Biologics Evaluation and Research (CBER), send the completed Form FDA 3486 to the CBER Document Control Center (see mailing address in § 600.2(a)), or submit electronically using CBER's electronic Web-based application.

(2) For biological products regulated by the Center for Drug Evaluation and Research (CDER), send the completed Form FDA-3486 to the Division of Compliance Risk Management and Surveillance (HFD–330) (see mailing addresses in § 600.2). CDER does not currently accept electronic filings.

(3) If you make a paper filing, you should identify on the envelope that a biological product deviation report (BPDR) is enclosed.

(f) *How does this regulation affect other FDA regulations?* This part supplements and does not supersede other provisions of the regulations in this chapter. All biological product deviations, whether or not they are required to be reported under this section, should be investigated in accordance with the applicable provisions of parts 211 and 820 of this chapter.

[65 FR 66634, Nov. 7, 2000, as amended at 70 FR 14982, Mar. 24, 2005; 80 FR 18092, Apr. 3, 2015]

§ 600.15 Temperatures during shipment.

The following products shall be maintained during shipment at the specified temperatures:

(a) *Products.*

Product	Temperature
Cryoprecipitated AHF	− 18 °C or colder.
Measles and Rubella Virus Vaccine Live	10 °C or colder.
Measles Live and Smallpox Vaccine	Do.
Measles, Mumps, and Rubella Virus Vaccine Live	Do.
Measles and Mumps Virus Vaccine Live	Do.
Measles Virus Vaccine Live	Do.
Mumps Virus Vaccine Live	Do.
Fresh Frozen Plasma	− 18 °C or colder.
Liquid Plasma	1 to 10 °C.
Plasma	− 18 °C or colder.
Platelet Rich Plasma	Between 1 and 10 °C if the label indicates storage between 1 and 6 °C, or all reasonable methods to maintain the temperature as close as possible to a range between 20 and 24 °C, if the label indicates storage between 20 and 24 °C.
Platelets	Between 1 and 10 °C if the label indicates storage between 1 and 6 °C, or all reasonable methods to maintain the temperature as close as possible to a range between 20 to 24 °C, if the label indicates storage between 20 and 24 °C.
Poliovirus Vaccine Live Oral Trivalent	0 °C or colder.
Poliovirus Vaccine Live Oral Type I	Do.
Poliovirus Vaccine Live Oral Type II	Do.
Poliovirus Vaccine Live Oral Type III	Do.
Red Blood Cells (liquid product)	Between 1 and 10 °C.
Red Blood Cells Frozen	− 65 °C or colder.
Rubella and Mumps Virus Vaccine Live	10 °C or colder.
Rubella Virus Vaccine Live	Do.
Smallpox Vaccine (Liquid Product)	0 °C or colder.
Source Plasma	− 5 °C or colder.
Source Plasma Liquid	10 °C or colder.
Whole Blood	Blood that is transported from the collecting facility to the processing facility shall be transported in an environment capable of continuously cooling the blood toward a temperature range of 1 to 10 °C, or at a temperature as close as possible to 20 to 24 °C for a period not to exceed 6 hours. Blood transported from the storage facility shall be placed in an appropriate environment to maintain a temperature range between 1 to 10 °C during shipment.
Yellow Fever Vaccine	0 °C or colder.

15

(b) *Exemptions.* Exemptions or modifications shall be made only upon written approval, in the form of a supplement to the biologics license application, approved by the Director, Center for Biologics Evaluation and Research.

[39 FR 39872, Nov. 12, 1974, as amended at 49 FR 23833, June 8, 1984; 50 FR 4133, Jan. 29, 1985; 50 FR 9000, Mar. 6, 1985; 55 FR 11013, Mar. 26, 1990; 59 FR 49351, Sept. 28, 1994; 64 FR 56449, Oct. 20, 1999]

Subpart C—Establishment Inspection

§ 600.20 Inspectors.

Inspections shall be made by an officer of the Food and Drug Administration having special knowledge of the methods used in the manufacture and control of products and designated for such purposes by the Commissioner of Food and Drugs, or by any officer, agent, or employee of the Department of Health and Human Services specifically designated for such purpose by the Secretary.

[38 FR 32048, Nov. 20, 1973]

§ 600.21 Time of inspection.

The inspection of an establishment for which a biologics license application is pending need not be made until the establishment is in operation and is manufacturing the complete product for which a biologics license is desired.

[38 FR 32048, Nov. 20, 1973, as amended at 48 FR 26314, June 7, 1983; 64 FR 56449, Oct. 20, 1999; 84 FR 12508, Apr. 2, 2019]

§ 600.22 [Reserved]

Subpart D—Reporting of Adverse Experiences

SOURCE: 59 FR 54042, Oct. 27, 1994, unless otherwise noted.

§ 600.80 Postmarketing reporting of adverse experiences.

(a) *Definitions.* The following definitions of terms apply to this section:

Adverse experience. Any adverse event associated with the use of a biological product in humans, whether or not considered product related, including the following: An adverse event occurring in the course of the use of a biological product in professional practice; an adverse event occurring from overdose of the product whether accidental or intentional; an adverse event occurring from abuse of the product; an adverse event occurring from withdrawal of the product; and any failure of expected pharmacological action.

Blood Component. As defined in § 606.3(c) of this chapter.

Disability. A substantial disruption of a person's ability to conduct normal life functions.

Individual case safety report (ICSR). A description of an adverse experience related to an individual patient or subject.

ICSR attachments. Documents related to the adverse experience described in an ICSR, such as medical records, hospital discharge summaries, or other documentation.

Life-threatening adverse experience. Any adverse experience that places the patient, in the view of the initial reporter, at immediate risk of death from the adverse experience as it occurred, i.e., it does not include an adverse experience that, had it occurred in a more severe form, might have caused death.

Serious adverse experience. Any adverse experience occurring at any dose that results in any of the following outcomes: Death, a life-threatening adverse experience, inpatient hospitalization or prolongation of existing hospitalization, a persistent or significant disability/incapacity, or a congenital anomaly/birth defect. Important medical events that may not result in death, be life-threatening, or require hospitalization may be considered a serious adverse experience when, based upon appropriate medical judgment, they may jeopardize the patient or subject and may require medical or surgical intervention to prevent one of the outcomes listed in this definition. Examples of such medical events include allergic bronchospasm requiring intensive treatment in an emergency room or at home, blood dyscrasias or convulsions that do not result in inpatient hospitalization, or the development of drug dependency or drug abuse.

Unexpected adverse experience: Any adverse experience that is not listed in the current labeling for the biological product. This includes events that may be symptomatically and pathophysiologically related to an event listed in the labeling, but differ from the event because of greater severity or specificity. For example, under this definition, hepatic necrosis would be unexpected (by virtue of greater severity) if the labeling only referred to elevated hepatic enzymes or hepatitis. Similarly, cerebral thromboembolism and cerebral vasculitis would be unexpected (by virtue of greater specificity) if the labeling only listed cerebral vascular accidents. "Unexpected," as used in this definition, refers to an adverse experience that has not been previously observed (i.e., included in the labeling) rather than from the perspective of such experience not being anticipated from the pharmacological properties of the pharmaceutical product.

(b) *Review of adverse experiences.* Any person having a biologics license under § 601.20 of this chapter must promptly review all adverse experience information pertaining to its product obtained or otherwise received by the applicant from any source, foreign or domestic, including information derived from commercial marketing experience, postmarketing clinical investigations, postmarketing epidemiological/surveillance studies, reports in the scientific literature, and unpublished scientific papers. Applicants are not required to resubmit to FDA adverse product experience reports forwarded to the applicant by FDA; applicants, however, must submit all followup information on such reports to FDA. Any person subject to the reporting requirements under paragraph (c) of this section must also develop written procedures for the surveillance, receipt, evaluation, and reporting of postmarketing adverse experiences to FDA.

(c) *Reporting requirements.* The applicant must submit to FDA postmarketing 15-day Alert reports and periodic safety reports pertaining to its biological product as described in this section. These reports must be submitted to the Agency in electronic format as described in paragraph (h)(1) of this section, except as provided in paragraph (h)(2) of this section.

(1)(i) *Postmarketing 15-day "Alert reports".* The applicant must report each adverse experience that is both serious and unexpected, whether foreign or domestic, as soon as possible but no later than 15 calendar days from initial receipt of the information by the applicant.

(ii) *Postmarketing 15-day "Alert reports"—followup.* The applicant must promptly investigate all adverse experiences that are the subject of these postmarketing 15-day Alert reports and must submit followup reports within 15 calendar days of receipt of new information or as requested by FDA. If additional information is not obtainable, records should be maintained of the unsuccessful steps taken to seek additional information.

(iii) *Submission of reports.* The requirements of paragraphs (c)(1)(i) and (c)(1)(ii) of this section, concerning the submission of postmarketing 15-day Alert reports, also apply to any person whose name appears on the label of a licensed biological product as a manufacturer, packer, distributor, shared manufacturer, joint manufacturer, or any other participant involved in divided manufacturing. To avoid unnecessary duplication in the submission to FDA of reports required by paragraphs (c)(1)(i) and (c)(1)(ii) of this section, obligations of persons other than the applicant of the final biological product may be met by submission of all reports of serious adverse experiences to the applicant of the final product. If a person elects to submit adverse experience reports to the applicant rather than to FDA, the person must submit, by any appropriate means, each report to the applicant within 5 calendar days of initial receipt of the information by the person, and the applicant must then comply with the requirements of this section. Under this circumstance, a person who elects to submit reports to the applicant of the final product shall maintain a record of this action which must include:

(A) A copy of all adverse biological product experience reports submitted to the applicant of the final product;

(B) The date the report was received by the person;

(C) The date the report was submitted to the applicant of the final product; and—

(D) The name and address of the applicant of the final product.

(2) *Periodic adverse experience reports.* (i) The applicant must report each adverse experience not reported under paragraph (c)(1)(i) of this section at quarterly intervals, for 3 years from the date of issuance of the biologics license, and then at annual intervals. The applicant must submit each quarterly report within 30 days of the close of the quarter (the first quarter beginning on the date of issuance of the biologics license) and each annual report within 60 days of the anniversary date of the issuance of the biologics license. Upon written notice, FDA may extend or reestablish the requirement that an applicant submit quarterly reports, or require that the applicant submit reports under this section at different times than those stated. Followup information to adverse experiences submitted in a periodic report may be submitted in the next periodic report.

(ii) Each periodic report is required to contain:

(A) *Descriptive information.* (*1*) A narrative summary and analysis of the information in the report;

(*2*) An analysis of the 15-day Alert reports submitted during the reporting interval (all 15-day Alert reports being appropriately referenced by the applicant's patient identification code for nonvaccine biological product reports or by the unique case identification number for vaccine reports, adverse reaction term(s), and date of submission to FDA);

(*3*) A history of actions taken since the last report because of adverse experiences (for example, labeling changes or studies initiated);

(*4*) An index consisting of a line listing of the applicant's patient identification code for nonvaccine biological product reports or by the unique case identification number for vaccine reports and adverse reaction term(s) for ICSRs submitted under paragraph (c)(2)(ii)(B) of this section; and

(B) *ICSRs for serious, expected and, nonserious adverse experiences.* An ICSR for each adverse experience not reported under paragraph (c)(1)(i) of this section (all serious, expected and nonserious adverse experiences). All such ICSRs must be submitted to FDA (either individually or in one or more batches) within the timeframe specified in paragraph (c)(2)(i) of this section. ICSRs must only be submitted to FDA once.

(iii) Periodic reporting, except for information regarding 15-day Alert reports, does not apply to adverse experience information obtained from postmarketing studies (whether or not conducted under an investigational new drug application), from reports in the scientific literature, and from foreign marketing experience.

(d) *Scientific literature.* A 15-day Alert report based on information in the scientific literature must be accompanied by a copy of the published article. The 15-day Alert reporting requirements in paragraph (c)(1)(i) of this section (i.e., serious, unexpected adverse experiences) apply only to reports found in scientific and medical journals either as case reports or as the result of a formal clinical trial.

(e) *Postmarketing studies.* Applicants are not required to submit a 15-day Alert report under paragraph (c) of this section for an adverse experience obtained from a postmarketing clinical study (whether or not conducted under a biological investigational new drug application) unless the applicant concludes that there is a reasonable possibility that the product caused the adverse experience.

(f) *Information reported on ICSRs for nonvaccine biological products.* ICSRs for nonvaccine biological products include the following information:

(1) *Patient information.*

(i) Patient identification code;

(ii) Patient age at the time of adverse experience, or date of birth;

(iii) Patient gender; and

(iv) Patient weight.

(2) *Adverse experience.*

(i) Outcome attributed to adverse experience;

(ii) Date of adverse experience;

(iii) Date of report;

(iv) Description of adverse experience (including a concise medical narrative);

(v) Adverse experience term(s);

(vi) Description of relevant tests, including dates and laboratory data; and

(vii) Other relevant patient history, including preexisting medical conditions.

(3) *Suspect medical product(s).*

(i) Name;

(ii) Dose, frequency, and route of administration used;

(iii) Therapy dates;

(iv) Diagnosis for use (indication);

(v) Whether the product is a combination product as defined in §3.2(e) of this chapter;

(vi) Whether the product is a prescription or nonprescription product;

(vii) Whether adverse experience abated after product use stopped or dose reduced;

(viii) Whether adverse experience reappeared after reintroduction of the product;

(ix) Lot number;

(x) Expiration date;

(xi) National Drug Code (NDC) number, or other unique identifier; and

(xii) Concomitant medical products and therapy dates.

(4) *Initial reporter information.*

(i) Name, address, and telephone number;

(ii) Whether the initial reporter is a health care professional; and

(iii) Occupation, if a health care professional.

(5) *Applicant information.*

(i) Applicant name and contact office address;

(ii) Telephone number;

(iii) Report source, such as spontaneous, literature, or study;

(iv) Date the report was received by applicant;

(v) Application number and type;

(vi) Whether the ICSR is a 15-day "Alert report";

(vii) Whether the ICSR is an initial report or followup report; and

(viii) Unique case identification number, which must be the same in the initial report and any subsequent followup report(s).

(g) *Information reported on ICSRs for vaccine products.* ICSRs for vaccine products include the following information:

(1) *Patient information.*

(i) Patient name, address, telephone number;

(ii) Patient age at the time of vaccination, or date of birth;

(iii) Patient gender; and

(iv) Patient birth weight for children under age 5.

(2) *Adverse experience.*

(i) Outcome attributed to adverse experience;

(ii) Date and time of adverse experience;

(iii) Date of report;

(iv) Description of adverse experience (including a concise medical narrative);

(v) Adverse experience term(s);

(vi) Illness at the time of vaccination;

(vii) Description of relevant tests, including dates and laboratory data; and

(viii) Other relevant patient history, including preexisting medical conditions.

(3) *Suspect medical product(s), including vaccines administered on the same date.*

(i) Name;

(ii) Dose, frequency, and route or site of administration used;

(iii) Number of previous vaccine doses;

(iv) Vaccination date(s) and time(s);

(v) Diagnosis for use (indication);

(vi) Whether the product is a combination product (as defined in §3.2(e) of this chapter);

(vii) Whether the adverse experience abated after product use stopped or dose reduced;

(viii) Whether the adverse experience reappeared after reintroduction of the product;

(ix) Lot number;

(x) Expiration date;

(xi) National Drug Code (NDC) number, or other unique identifier; and

(xii) Concomitant medical products and therapy dates.

(4) *Vaccine(s) administered in the 4 weeks prior to the vaccination date.*

(i) Name of vaccine;

(ii) Manufacturer;

(iii) Lot number;

(iv) Route or site of administration;

(v) Date given; and

(vi) Number of previous doses.

(5) *Initial reporter information.*

(i) Name, address, and telephone number;

(ii) Whether the initial reporter is a health care professional; and

(iii) Occupation, if a health care professional.

(6) *Facility and personnel where vaccine was administered.*

(i) Name of person who administered vaccine;

(ii) Name of responsible physician at facility where vaccine was administered; and

(iii) Name, address (including city, county, and state), and telephone number of facility where vaccine was administered.

(7) *Applicant information.*

(i) Applicant name and contact office address;

(ii) Telephone number;

(iii) Report source, such as spontaneous, literature, or study;

(iv) Date received by applicant;

(v) Application number and type;

(vi) Whether the ICSR is a 15-day "Alert report";

(vii) Whether the ICSR is an initial report or followup report; and

(viii) Unique case identification number, which must be the same in the initial report and any subsequent followup report(s).

(h) *Electronic format for submissions.* (1) Safety report submissions, including ICSRs, ICSR attachments, and the descriptive information in periodic reports, must be in an electronic format that FDA can process, review, and archive. FDA will issue guidance on how to provide the electronic submission (e.g., method of transmission, media, file formats, preparation and organization of files).

(2) Persons subject to the requirements of paragraph (c) of this section may request, in writing, a temporary waiver of the requirements in paragraph (h)(1) of this section. These waivers will be granted on a limited basis for good cause shown. FDA will issue guidance on requesting a waiver of the requirements in paragraph (h)(1) of this section. Requests for waivers must be submitted in accordance with § 600.90.

(i) *Multiple reports.* An applicant should not include in reports under this section any adverse experience that occurred in clinical trials if they were previously submitted as part of the biologics license application. If a report refers to more than one biological product marketed by an applicant,

the applicant should submit the report to the biologics license application for the product listed first in the report.

(j) *Patient privacy.* For nonvaccine biological products, an applicant should not include in reports under this section the names and addresses of individual patients; instead, the applicant should assign a unique code for identification of the patient. The applicant should include the name of the reporter from whom the information was received as part of the initial reporter information, even when the reporter is the patient. The names of patients, health care professionals, hospitals, and geographical identifiers in adverse experience reports are not releasable to the public under FDA's public information regulations in part 20 of this chapter. For vaccine adverse experience reports, these data will become part of the CDC Privacy Act System 09–20–0136, "Epidemiologic Studies and Surveillance of Disease Problems." Information identifying the person who received the vaccine or that person's legal representative will not be made available to the public, but may be available to the vaccinee or legal representative.

(k) *Recordkeeping.* The applicant must maintain for a period of 10 years records of all adverse experiences known to the applicant, including raw data and any correspondence relating to the adverse experiences.

(1) *Revocation of biologics license.* If an applicant fails to establish and maintain records and make reports required under this section with respect to a licensed biological product, FDA may revoke the biologics license for such a product in accordance with the procedures of § 601.5 of this chapter.

(m) *Exemptions.* Manufacturers of the following listed products are not required to submit adverse experience reports under this section:

(1) Whole blood or components of whole blood.

(2) In vitro diagnostic products, including assay systems for the detection of antibodies or antigens to retroviruses. These products are subject to the reporting requirements for devices.

(n) *Disclaimer.* A report or information submitted by an applicant under this section (and any release by FDA of that report or information) does not necessarily reflect a conclusion by the applicant or FDA that the report or information constitutes an admission that the biological product caused or contributed to an adverse effect. An applicant need not admit, and may deny, that the report or information submitted under this section constitutes an admission that the biological product caused or contributed to an adverse effect. For purposes of this provision, this paragraph also includes any person reporting under paragraph (c)(1)(iii) of this section.

[59 FR 54042, Oct. 27, 1994, as amended at 62 FR 34168, June 25, 1997; 62 FR 52252, Oct. 7, 1997; 63 FR 14612, Mar. 26, 1998; 64 FR 56449, Oct. 20, 1999; 70 FR 14982, Mar. 24, 2005; 79 FR 33090, June 10, 2014]

§ 600.81 Distribution reports.

(a) *Reporting requirements.* The applicant must submit to the Center for Biologics Evaluation and Research or the Center for Drug Evaluation and Research, information about the quantity of the product distributed under the biologics license, including the quantity distributed to distributors. The interval between distribution reports must be 6 months. Upon written notice, FDA may require that the applicant submit distribution reports under this section at times other than every 6 months. The distribution report must consist of the bulk lot number (from which the final container was filled), the fill lot numbers for the total number of dosage units of each strength or potency distributed (e.g., fifty thousand per 10-milliliter vials), the label lot number (if different from fill lot number), labeled date of expiration, number of doses in fill lot/label lot, date of release of fill lot/label lot for distribution at that time. If any significant amount of a fill lot/label lot is returned, include this information. Disclosure of financial or pricing data is not required. As needed, FDA may require submission of more detailed product distribution information. Upon written notice, FDA may require that the applicant submit reports under this section at times other than those stated. Requests by an applicant to submit reports at times other than those stat-

ed should be made as a request for a waiver under §600.90.

(b)(1) *Electronic format.* Except as provided for in paragraph (b)(2) of this section, the distribution reports required under paragraph (a) of this section must be submitted to the Agency in an electronic format that FDA can process, review, and archive. FDA will issue guidance on how to provide the electronic submission (e.g., method of transmission, media, file formats, preparation and organization of files).

(2) *Waivers.* An applicant may request, in writing, a temporary waiver of the requirements in paragraph (b)(1) of this section. These waivers will be granted on a limited basis for good cause shown. FDA will issue guidance on requesting a waiver of the requirements in paragraph (b)(1) of this section. Requests for waivers must be submitted in accordance with §600.90.

[59 FR 54042, Oct. 27, 1994, as amended at 64 FR 56449, Oct. 20, 1999; 70 FR 14983, Mar. 24, 2005; 79 FR 33091, June 10, 2014]

§ 600.82 Notification of a permanent discontinuance or an interruption in manufacturing.

(a) *Notification of a permanent discontinuance or an interruption in manufacturing.* (1) An applicant of a biological product, other than blood or blood components for transfusion, which is licensed under section 351 of the Public Health Service Act, and which may be dispensed only under prescription under section 503(b)(1) of the Federal Food, Drug, and Cosmetic Act (21 U.S.C. 353(b)(1)), must notify FDA in writing of a permanent discontinuance of manufacture of the biological product or an interruption in manufacturing of the biological product that is likely to lead to a meaningful disruption in supply of that biological product in the United States if:

(i) The biological product is life supporting, life sustaining, or intended for use in the prevention or treatment of a debilitating disease or condition, including any such biological product used in emergency medical care or during surgery; and

(ii) The biological product is not a radiopharmaceutical biological product.

21

(2) An applicant of blood or blood components for transfusion, which is licensed under section 351 of the Public Health Service Act, and which may be dispensed only under prescription under section 503(b) of the Federal Food, Drug, and Cosmetic Act, must notify FDA in writing of a permanent discontinuance of manufacture of any product listed in its license or an interruption in manufacturing of any such product that is likely to lead to a significant disruption in supply of that product in the United States if:

(i) The product is life supporting, life sustaining, or intended for use in the prevention or treatment of a debilitating disease or condition, including any such product used in emergency medical care or during surgery; and

(ii) The applicant is a manufacturer of a significant percentage of the U.S. blood supply.

(b) *Submission and timing of notification.* Notifications required by paragraph (a) of this section must be submitted to FDA electronically in a format that FDA can process, review, and archive:

(1) At least 6 months prior to the date of the permanent discontinuance or interruption in manufacturing; or

(2) If 6 months' advance notice is not possible because the permanent discontinuance or interruption in manufacturing was not reasonably anticipated 6 months in advance, as soon as practicable thereafter, but in no case later than 5 business days after such a permanent discontinuance or interruption in manufacturing occurs.

(c) *Information included in notification.* Notifications required by paragraph (a) of this section must include the following information:

(1) The name of the biological product subject to the notification, including the National Drug Code for such biological product, or an alternative standard for identification and labeling that has been recognized as acceptable by the Center Director;

(2) The name of the applicant of the biological product;

(3) Whether the notification relates to a permanent discontinuance of the biological product or an interruption in manufacturing of the biological product;

(4) A description of the reason for the permanent discontinuance or interruption in manufacturing; and

(5) The estimated duration of the interruption in manufacturing.

(d)(1) *Public list of biological product shortages.* FDA will maintain a publicly available list of biological products that are determined by FDA to be in shortage. This biological product shortages list will include the following information:

(i) The names and National Drug Codes for such biological products, or the alternative standards for identification and labeling that have been recognized as acceptable by the Center Director;

(ii) The name of each applicant for such biological products;

(iii) The reason for the shortage, as determined by FDA, selecting from the following categories: Requirements related to complying with good manufacturing practices; regulatory delay; shortage of an active ingredient; shortage of an inactive ingredient component; discontinuation of the manufacture of the biological product; delay in shipping of the biological product; demand increase for the biological product; or other reason; and

(iv) The estimated duration of the shortage.

(2) *Confidentiality.* FDA may choose not to make information collected to implement this paragraph available on the biological product shortages list or available under section 506C(c) of the Federal Food, Drug, and Cosmetic Act (21 U.S.C. 356c(c)) if FDA determines that disclosure of such information would adversely affect the public health (such as by increasing the possibility of hoarding or other disruption of the availability of the biological product to patients). FDA will also not provide information on the public shortages list or under section 506C(c) of the Federal Food, Drug, and Cosmetic Act that is protected by 18 U.S.C. 1905 or 5 U.S.C. 552(b)(4), including trade secrets and commercial or financial information that is considered confidential or privileged under § 20.61 of this chapter.

(e) *Noncompliance letters.* If an applicant fails to submit a notification as required under paragraph (a) of this section and in accordance with paragraph (b) of this section, FDA will issue a letter to the applicant informing it of such failure.

(1) Not later than 30 calendar days after the issuance of such a letter, the applicant must submit to FDA a written response setting forth the basis for noncompliance and providing the required notification under paragraph (a) of this section and including the information required under paragraph (c) of this section; and

(2) Not later than 45 calendar days after the issuance of a letter under this paragraph, FDA will make the letter and the applicant's response to the letter public, unless, after review of the applicant's response, FDA determines that the applicant had a reasonable basis for not notifying FDA as required under paragraph (a) of this section.

(f) *Definitions.* The following definitions of terms apply to this section:

Biological product shortage or *shortage* means a period of time when the demand or projected demand for the biological product within the United States exceeds the supply of the biological product.

Intended for use in the prevention or treatment of a debilitating disease or condition means a biological product intended for use in the prevention or treatment of a disease or condition associated with mortality or morbidity that has a substantial impact on day-to-day functioning.

Life supporting or life sustaining means a biological product that is essential to, or that yields information that is essential to, the restoration or continuation of a bodily function important to the continuation of human life.

Meaningful disruption means a change in production that is reasonably likely to lead to a reduction in the supply of a biological product by a manufacturer that is more than negligible and affects the ability of the manufacturer to fill orders or meet expected demand for its product, and does not include interruptions in manufacturing due to matters such as routine maintenance or insignificant changes in manufacturing so long as the manufacturer expects to resume operations in a short period of time.

Significant disruption means a change in production that is reasonably likely to lead to a reduction in the supply of blood or blood components by a manufacturer that substantially affects the ability of the manufacturer to fill orders or meet expected demand for its product, and does not include interruptions in manufacturing due to matters such as routine maintenance or insignificant changes in manufacturing so long as the manufacturer expects to resume operations in a short period of time.

[80 FR 38939, July 8, 2015]

§ 600.90   Waivers.

(a) An applicant may ask the Food and Drug Administration to waive under this section any requirement that applies to the applicant under §§ 600.80 and 600.81. A waiver request under this section is required to be submitted with supporting documentation. The waiver request is required to contain one of the following:

(1) An explanation why the applicant's compliance with the requirement is unnecessary or cannot be achieved,

(2) A description of an alternative submission that satisfies the purpose of the requirement, or

(3) Other information justifying a waiver.

(b) FDA may grant a waiver if it finds one of the following:

(1) The applicant's compliance with the requirement is unnecessary or cannot be achieved,

(2) The applicant's alternative submission satisfies the requirement, or

(3) The applicant's submission otherwise justifies a waiver.

[59 FR 54042, Oct. 27, 1994, as amended at 79 FR 33092, June 10, 2014]

PART 601—LICENSING

Subpart A—General Provisions

601.8   Publication of revocation.
601.9   Licenses; reissuance. .

Subpart B [Reserved]

Subpart C—Biologics Licensing

601.12   Changes to an approved application.
601.14   Regulatory submissions in electronic format.
601.15   Foreign establishments and products: Samples for each importation.
601.20   Biologics licenses; issuance and conditions.
601.21   Products under development.
601.22   Products in short supply; initial manufacturing at other than licensed location.
601.27   Pediatric studies.
601.28   Annual reports of postmarketing pediatric studies.
601.29   Guidance documents.

Subpart D—Diagnostic Radiopharmaceuticals

601.30   Scope.
601.31   Definition.
601.32   General factors relevant to safety and effectiveness.
601.33   Indications.
601.34   Evaluation of effectiveness.
601.35   Evaluation of safety.

Subpart E—Accelerated Approval of Biological Products for Serious or Life-Threatening Illnesses

601.40   Scope.
601.41   Approval based on a surrogate endpoint or on an effect on a clinical endpoint other than survival or irreversible morbidity.
601.42   Approval with restrictions to assure safe use.
601.43   Withdrawal procedures.
601.44   Postmarketing safety reporting.
601.45   Promotional materials.
601.46   Termination of requirements.

Subpart F—Confidentiality of Information

601.50   Confidentiality of data and information in an investigational new drug notice for a biological product.
601.51   Confidentiality of data and information in applications for biologics licenses.

Subpart G—Postmarketing Studies

601.70   Annual progress reports of postmarketing studies.

Subpart H—Approval of Biological Products When Human Efficacy Studies Are Not Ethical or Feasible

601.90   Scope.
601.91   Approval based on evidence of effectiveness from studies in animals.
601.92   Withdrawal procedures.
601.93   Postmarketing safety reporting.
601.94   Promotional materials.
601.95   Termination of requirements.

AUTHORITY: 15 U.S.C. 1451–1561; 21 U.S.C. 321, 351, 352, 353, 355, 356b, 360, 360c–360f, 360h–360j, 371, 374, 379e, 381; 42 U.S.C. 216, 241, 262, 263, 264; sec 122, Pub. L. 105–115, 111 Stat. 2322 (21 U.S.C. 355 note).

SOURCE: 38 FR 32052, Nov. 20, 1973, unless otherwise noted.

CROSS REFERENCES: For U.S. Customs Service regulations relating to viruses, serums, and toxins, see 19 CFR 12.21–12.23. For U.S. Postal Service regulations relating to the admissibility in the United States mails see parts 124 and 125 of the Domestic Mail Manual, that is incorporated by reference in 39 CFR part 111.

Subpart A—General Provisions

§ 601.2   Applications for biologics licenses; procedures for filing.

(a) *General.* To obtain a biologics license under section 351 of the Public Health Service Act for any biological product, the manufacturer shall submit an application to the Director, Center for Biologics Evaluation and Research or the Director, Center for Drug Evaluation and Research (see mailing addresses in § 600.2(a) or (b) of this chapter), on forms prescribed for such purposes, and shall submit data derived from nonclinical laboratory and clinical studies which demonstrate that the manufactured product meets prescribed requirements of safety, purity, and potency; with respect to each nonclinical laboratory study, either a statement that the study was conducted in compliance with the requirements set forth in part 58 of this chapter, or, if the study was not conducted in compliance with such regulations, a brief statement of the reason for the noncompliance; statements regarding each clinical investigation involving human subjects contained in the application, that it either was conducted in compliance with the requirements for institutional review set forth in part 56 of this chapter; or was not subject to such requirements in accordance with §56.104 or §56.105, and was conducted in compliance with requirements for informed consent set forth in part 50 of this chapter. A full description of manufacturing methods; data establishing stability of the product through the dating period; sample(s) representative of the product for introduction or delivery for introduction into interstate commerce; summaries of results of tests performed on the lot(s) represented by the submitted sample(s); specimens of the labels, enclosures, and containers, and if applicable, any Medication Guide required under part 208 of this chapter proposed to be used for the product; and the address of each location involved in the manufacture of the biological product shall be listed in the biologics license application. The applicant shall also include a financial certification or disclosure statement(s) or both for clinical investigators as required by part 54 of this chapter. An application for a biologics license shall not be considered as filed until all pertinent information and data have been received by the Food and Drug Administration. The applicant shall also include either a claim for categorical exclusion under §25.30 or §25.31 of this chapter or an environmental assessment under §25.40 of this chapter. The applicant, or the applicant's attorney, agent, or other authorized official shall sign the application. An application for any of the following specified categories of biological products subject to licensure shall be handled as set forth in paragraph (c) of this section:

(1) Therapeutic DNA plasmid products;

(2) Therapeutic synthetic peptide products of 40 or fewer amino acids;

(3) Monoclonal antibody products for in vivo use; and

(4) Therapeutic recombinant DNA-derived products.

(b) [Reserved]

(c)(1) To obtain marketing approval for a biological product subject to licensure which is a therapeutic DNA plasmid product, therapeutic synthetic peptide product of 40 or fewer amino acids, monoclonal antibody product for in vivo use, or therapeutic recombinant DNA-derived product, an applicant shall submit a biologics license application in accordance with paragraph (a) of this section except that the following sections in parts 600 through 680 of this chapter shall not be applicable to such products: §§600.10(b) and (c), 600.11, 600.12, 600.13, 610.53, and 610.62 of this chapter.

(2) To the extent that the requirements in this paragraph (c) conflict with other requirements in this subchapter, this paragraph (c) shall supersede other requirements.

(d) Approval of a biologics license application or issuance of a biologics license shall constitute a determination that the establishment(s) and the product meet applicable requirements to ensure the continued safety, purity, and potency of such products. Applicable requirements for the maintenance of establishments for the manufacture of a product subject to this section shall include but not be limited to the good manufacturing practice requirements set forth in parts 210, 211, 600, 606, and 820 of this chapter.

(e) Any establishment and product license for a biological product issued under section 351 of the Public Health Service Act (42 U.S.C. 201 et seq.) that has not been revoked or suspended as of December 20, 1999, shall constitute an approved biologics license application in effect under the same terms and conditions set forth in such product license and such portions of the establishment license relating to such product.

(f) *Withdrawal from sale of approved biological products.* A holder of a biologics license application (BLA) must report to FDA, in accordance with the requirements of §§207.61 and 207.65, the withdrawal from sale of an approved biological product. The information must be submitted to FDA within 30 working days of the biological product's withdrawal from sale. The following information must be submitted: The holder's name; product name; BLA number; the National Drug Code; and the date on which the product is expected to be no longer in commercial distribution. The reason for the withdrawal of the biological product is requested but not required to be submitted.

[64 FR 56450, Oct. 20, 1999, as amended at 70 FR 14983, Mar. 24, 2005; 80 FR 18092, Apr. 3, 2015; 80 FR 37974, July 2, 2015; 81 FR 60221, Aug. 31, 2016]

§ 601.3　Complete response letter to the applicant.

(a) *Complete response letter.* The Food and Drug Administration will send the biologics license applicant or supplement applicant a complete response letter if the agency determines that it will not approve the biologics license application or supplement in its present form.

(1) *Description of specific deficiencies.* A complete response letter will describe all of the deficiencies that the agency has identified in a biologics license application or supplement, except as stated in paragraph (a)(2) of this section.

(2) *Inadequate data.* If FDA determines, after a biologics license application or supplement is filed, that the data submitted are inadequate to support approval, the agency might issue a complete response letter without first conducting required inspections, testing submitted product lots, and/or reviewing proposed product labeling.

(3) *Recommendation of actions for approval.* When possible, a complete response letter will recommend actions that the applicant might take to place its biologics license application or supplement in condition for approval.

(b) *Applicant actions.* After receiving a complete response letter, the biologics license applicant or supplement applicant must take either of the following actions:

(1) *Resubmission.* Resubmit the application or supplement, addressing all deficiencies identified in the complete response letter.

(2) *Withdrawal.* Withdraw the application or supplement. A decision to withdraw the application or supplement is without prejudice to a subsequent submission.

(c) *Failure to take action.* (1) FDA may consider a biologics license applicant or supplement applicant's failure to either resubmit or withdraw the application or supplement within 1 year after issuance of a complete response letter to be a request by the applicant to

withdraw the application or supplement, unless the applicant has requested an extension of time in which to resubmit the application or supplement. FDA will grant any reasonable request for such an extension. FDA may consider an applicant's failure to resubmit the application or supplement within the extended time period or request an additional extension to be a request by the applicant to withdraw the application.

(2) If FDA considers an applicant's failure to take action in accordance with paragraph (c)(1) of this section to be a request to withdraw the application, the agency will notify the applicant in writing. The applicant will have 30 days from the date of the notification to explain why the application or supplement should not be withdrawn and to request an extension of time in which to resubmit the application or supplement. FDA will grant any reasonable request for an extension. If the applicant does not respond to the notification within 30 days, the application or supplement will be deemed to be withdrawn.

[73 FR 39611, July 10, 2008]

§ 601.4　Issuance and denial of license.

(a) A biologics license shall be issued upon a determination by the Director, Center for Biologics Evaluation and Research or the Director, Center for Drug Evaluation and Research that the establishment(s) and the product meet the applicable requirements established in this chapter. A biologics license shall be valid until suspended or revoked.

(b) If the Commissioner determines that the establishment or product does not meet the requirements established in this chapter, the biologics license application shall be denied and the applicant shall be informed of the grounds for, and of an opportunity for a hearing on, the decision. If the applicant so requests, the Commissioner shall issue a notice of opportunity for hearing on the matter pursuant to § 12.21(b) of this chapter.

[42 FR 4718, Jan. 25, 1977, as amended at 42 FR 15676, Mar. 22, 1977; 42 FR 19142, Apr. 12, 1977; 64 FR 56450, Oct. 20, 1999; 70 FR 14983, Mar. 24, 2005]

§601.5 Revocation of license.

(a) A biologics license shall be revoked upon application of the manufacturer giving notice of intention to discontinue the manufacture of all products manufactured under such license or to discontinue the manufacture of a particular product for which a license is held and waiving an opportunity for a hearing on the matter.

(b)(1) The Commissioner shall notify the licensed manufacturer of the intention to revoke the biologics license, setting forth the grounds for, and offering an opportunity for a hearing on the proposed revocation if the Commissioner finds any of the following:

(i) Authorized Food and Drug Administration employees after reasonable efforts have been unable to gain access to an establishment or a location for the purpose of carrying out the inspection required under §600.21 of this chapter,

(ii) Manufacturing of products or of a product has been discontinued to an extent that a meaningful inspection or evaluation cannot be made,

(iii) The manufacturer has failed to report a change as required by §601.12 of this chapter,

(iv) The establishment or any location thereof, or the product for which the license has been issued, fails to conform to the applicable standards established in the license and in this chapter designed to ensure the continued safety, purity, and potency of the manufactured product,

(v) The establishment or the manufacturing methods have been so changed as to require a new showing that the establishment or product meets the requirements established in this chapter in order to protect the public health, or

(vi) The licensed product is not safe and effective for all of its intended uses or is misbranded with respect to any such use.

(2) Except as provided in §601.6 of this chapter, or in cases involving willfulness, the notification required in this paragraph shall provide a reasonable period for the licensed manufacturer to demonstrate or achieve compliance with the requirements of this chapter, before proceedings will be instituted for the revocation of the license. If compliance is not demonstrated or achieved and the licensed manufacturer does not waive the opportunity for a hearing, the Commissioner shall issue a notice of opportunity for hearing on the matter under §12.21(b) of this chapter.

[64 FR 56451, Oct. 20, 1999]

§601.6 Suspension of license.

(a) Whenever the Commissioner has reasonable grounds to believe that any of the grounds for revocation of a license exist and that by reason thereof there is a danger to health, the Commissioner may notify the licensed manufacturer that the biologics license is suspended and require that the licensed manufacturer do the following:

(1) Notify the selling agents and distributors to whom such product or products have been delivered of such suspension, and

(2) Furnish to the Center for Biologics Evaluation and Research or the Center for Drug Evaluation and Research, complete records of such deliveries and notice of suspension.

(b) Upon suspension of a license, the Commissioner shall either:

(1) Proceed under the provisions of §601.5(b) of this chapter to revoke the license, or

(2) If the licensed manufacturer agrees, hold revocation in abeyance pending resolution of the matters involved.

[64 FR 56451, Oct. 20, 1999, as amended at 70 FR 14983, Mar. 24, 2005]

§601.7 Procedure for hearings.

(a) A notice of opportunity for hearing, notice of appearance and request for hearing, and grant or denial of hearing for a biological drug pursuant to this part, for which the exemption from the Federal Food, Drug, and Cosmetic Act in §310.4 of this chapter has been revoked, shall be subject to the provisions of §314.200 of this chapter except to the extent that the notice of opportunity for hearing on the matter issued pursuant to §12.21(b) of this chapter specifically provides otherwise.

(b) Hearings pursuant to §§601.4 through 601.6 shall be governed by part 12 of this chapter.

(c) When a license has been suspended pursuant to § 601.6 and a hearing request has been granted, the hearing shall proceed on an expedited basis.

[42 FR 4718, Jan. 25, 1977, as amended at 42 FR 15676, Mar. 22, 1977; 42 FR 19143, Apr. 12, 1977]

§ 601.8 Publication of revocation.

The Commissioner, following revocation of a biologics license under 21 CFR 601.5(b), will publish a notice in the FEDERAL REGISTER with a statement of the specific grounds for the revocation.

[74 FR 20585, May 5, 2009]

§ 601.9 Licenses; reissuance.

(a) *Compliance with requirements.* A biologics license, previously suspended or revoked, may be reissued or reinstated upon a showing of compliance with requirements and upon such inspection and examination as may be considered necessary by the Director, Center for Biologics Evaluation and Research or the Director, Center for Drug Evaluation and Research.

(b) *Exclusion of noncomplying location.* A biologics license, excluding a location or locations that fail to comply with the requirements in this chapter, may be issued without further application and concurrently with the suspension or revocation of the license for noncompliance at the excluded location or locations.

(c) *Exclusion of noncomplying product(s).* In the case of multiple products included under a single biologics license application, a biologics license may be issued, excluding the noncompliant product(s), without further application and concurrently with the suspension or revocation of the biologics license for a noncompliant product(s).

[64 FR 56451, Oct. 20, 1999, as amended at 70 FR 14983, Mar. 24, 2005]

Subpart B [Reserved]

Subpart C—Biologics Licensing

§ 601.12 Changes to an approved application.

(a) *General.* (1) As provided by this section, an applicant must inform the Food and Drug Administration (FDA) (see mailing addresses in § 600.2 of this chapter) about each change in the product, production process, quality controls, equipment, facilities, responsible personnel, or labeling established in the approved license application(s).

(2) Before distributing a product made using a change, an applicant must assess the effects of the change and demonstrate through appropriate validation and/or other clinical and/or nonclinical laboratory studies the lack of adverse effect of the change on the identity, strength, quality, purity, or potency of the product as they may relate to the safety or effectiveness of the product.

(3) Notwithstanding the requirements of paragraphs (b), (c), and (f) of this section, an applicant must make a change provided for in those paragraphs in accordance with a regulation or guidance that provides for a less burdensome notification of the change (for example, by submission of a supplement that does not require approval prior to distribution of the product or in an annual report).

(4) The applicant must promptly revise all promotional labeling and advertising to make it consistent with any labeling change implemented in accordance with paragraphs (f)(1) and (f)(2) of this section.

(5) A supplement or annual report must include a list of all changes contained in the supplement or annual report. For supplements, this list must be provided in the cover letter.

(b) *Changes requiring supplement submission and approval prior to distribution of the product made using the change (major changes).* (1) A supplement shall be submitted for any change in the product, production process, quality controls, equipment, facilities, or responsible personnel that has a substantial potential to have an adverse effect on the identity, strength, quality, purity, or potency of the product as they may relate to the safety or effectiveness of the product.

(2) These changes include, but are not limited to:

(i) Except as provided in paragraphs (c) and (d) of this section, changes in the qualitative or quantitative formulation, including inactive ingredients,

28

or in the specifications provided in the approved application;

(ii) Changes requiring completion of an appropriate human study to demonstrate the equivalence of the identity, strength, quality, purity, or potency of the product as they may relate to the safety or effectiveness of the product;

(iii) Changes in the virus or adventitious agent removal or inactivation method(s);

(iv) Changes in the source material or cell line;

(v) Establishment of a new master cell bank or seed; and

(vi) Changes which may affect product sterility assurance, such as changes in product or component sterilization method(s), or an addition, deletion, or substitution of steps in an aseptic processing operation.

(3) The applicant must obtain approval of the supplement from FDA prior to distribution of the product made using the change. Except for submissions under paragraph (e) of this section, the following shall be contained in the supplement:

(i) A detailed description of the proposed change;

(ii) The product(s) involved;

(iii) The manufacturing site(s) or area(s) affected;

(iv) A description of the methods used and studies performed to evaluate the effect of the change on the identity, strength, quality, purity, or potency of the product as they may relate to the safety or effectiveness of the product;

(v) The data derived from such studies;

(vi) Relevant validation protocols and data; and

(vii) A reference list of relevant standard operating procedures (SOP's).

(4) An applicant may ask FDA to expedite its review of a supplement for public health reasons or if a delay in making the change described in it would impose an extraordinary hardship on the applicant. Such a supplement and its mailing cover should be plainly marked: "Prior Approval Supplement-Expedited Review Requested.

(c) *Changes requiring supplement submission at least 30 days prior to distribution of the product made using the*

change. (1) A supplement shall be submitted for any change in the product, production process, quality controls, equipment, facilities, or responsible personnel that has a moderate potential to have an adverse effect on the identity, strength, quality, purity, or potency of the product as they may relate to the safety or effectiveness of the product. The supplement shall be labeled "Supplement—Changes Being Effected in 30 Days" or, if applicable under paragraph (c)(5) of this section, "Supplement—Changes Being Effected."

(2) These changes include, but are not limited to:

(i) [Reserved]

(ii) An increase or decrease in production scale during finishing steps that involves different equipment; and

(iii) Replacement of equipment with that of similar, but not identical, design and operating principle that does not affect the process methodology or process operating parameters.

(iv) Relaxation of an acceptance criterion or deletion of a test to comply with an official compendium that is consistent with FDA statutory and regulatory requirements.

(3) Pending approval of the supplement by FDA, and except as provided in paragraph (c)(5) of this section, distribution of the product made using the change may begin not less than 30 days after receipt of the supplement by FDA. The information listed in paragraph (b)(3)(i) through (b)(3)(vii) of this section shall be contained in the supplement.

(4) If within 30 days following FDA's receipt of the supplement, FDA informs the applicant that either:

(i) The change requires approval prior to distribution of the product in accordance with paragraph (b) of this section; or

(ii) Any of the information required under paragraph (c)(3) of this section is missing; the applicant shall not distribute the product made using the change until FDA determines that compliance with this section is achieved.

(5) In certain circumstances, FDA may determine that, based on experience with a particular type of change,

29

the supplement for such change is usually complete and provides the proper information, and on particular assurances that the proposed change has been appropriately submitted, the product made using the change may be distributed immediately upon receipt of the supplement by FDA. These circumstances may include substantial similarity with a type of change regularly involving a "Supplement—Changes Being Effected" supplement or a situation in which the applicant presents evidence that the proposed change has been validated in accordance with an approved protocol for such change under paragraph (e) of this section.

(6) If the agency disapproves the supplemental application, it may order the manufacturer to cease distribution of the products made with the manufacturing change.

(d) *Changes to be described in an annual report (minor changes).* (1) Changes in the product, production process, quality controls, equipment, facilities, or responsible personnel that have a minimal potential to have an adverse effect on the identity, strength, quality, purity, or potency of the product as they may relate to the safety or effectiveness of the product shall be documented by the applicant in an annual report submitted each year within 60 days of the anniversary date of approval of the application. The Director, Center for Biologics Evaluation and Research or the Director, Center for Drug Evaluation and Research, may approve a written request for an alternative date to combine annual reports for multiple approved applications into a single annual report submission.

(2) These changes include, but are not limited to:

(i) Any change made to comply with a change to an official compendium, except a change described in paragraph (c)(2)(iv) of this section, that is consistent with FDA statutory and regulatory requirements.

(ii) The deletion or reduction of an ingredient intended only to affect the color of the product, except that a change intended only to affect Blood Grouping Reagents requires supplement submission and approval prior to distribution of the product made using the change in accordance with the requirements set forth in paragraph (b) of this section;

(iii) An extension of an expiration dating period based upon full shelf life data on production batches obtained from a protocol approved in the application;

(iv) A change within the container closure system for a nonsterile product, based upon a showing of equivalency to the approved system under a protocol approved in the application or published in an official compendium;

(v) A change in the size and/or shape of a container containing the same number of dosage units for a nonsterile solid dosage form product, without a change from one container closure system to another;

(vi) The addition by embossing, debossing, or engraving of a code imprint to a solid dosage form biological product other than a modified release dosage form, or a minor change in an existing code imprint; and

(vii) The addition or revision of an alternative analytical procedure that provides the same or increased assurance of the identity, strength, quality, purity, or potency of the material being tested as the analytical procedure described in the approved application, or deletion of an alternative analytical procedure.

(3) The following information for each change shall be contained in the annual report:

(i) A list of all products involved; and

(ii) A full description of the manufacturing and controls changes including: the manufacturing site(s) or area(s) involved; the date the change was made; a cross-reference to relevant validation protocols and/or SOP's; and relevant data from studies and tests performed to evaluate the effect of the change on the identity, strength, quality, purity, or potency of the product as they may relate to the safety or effectiveness of the product.

(iii) A statement by the holder of the approved application or license that the effects of the change have been assessed.

(4) The applicant shall submit the report to the FDA office responsible for reviewing the application. The report

shall include all the information required under this paragraph for each change made during the annual reporting interval which ends on the anniversary date in the order in which they were implemented.

(e) An applicant may submit one or more protocols describing the specific tests and validation studies and acceptable limits to be achieved to demonstrate the lack of adverse effect for specified types of manufacturing changes on the identity, strength, quality, purity, or potency of the product as they may relate to the safety or effectiveness of the product. Any such protocols, or change to a protocol, shall be submitted as a supplement requiring approval from FDA prior to distribution of the product which, if approved, may justify a reduced reporting category for the particular change because the use of the protocol for that type of change reduces the potential risk of an adverse effect.

(f) *Labeling changes.* (1) Labeling changes requiring supplement submission—FDA approval must be obtained before distribution of the product with the labeling change. Except as described in paragraphs (f)(2) and (f)(3) of this section, an applicant shall submit a supplement describing a proposed change in the package insert, package label, container label, or, if applicable, a Medication Guide required under part 208 of this chapter, and include the information necessary to support the proposed change. An applicant cannot use paragraph (f)(2) of this section to make any change to the information required in §201.57(a) of this chapter. An applicant may report the minor changes to the information specified in paragraph (f)(3)(i)(D) of this section in an annual report. The supplement shall clearly highlight the proposed change in the labeling. The applicant shall obtain approval from FDA prior to distribution of the product with the labeling change.

(2) *Labeling changes requiring supplement submission—product with a labeling change that may be distributed before FDA approval.* (i) An applicant shall submit, at the time such change is made, a supplement for any change in the package insert, package label, or container label to reflect newly ac-

quired information, except for changes to the package insert required in §201.57(a) of this chapter (which must be made under paragraph (f)(1) of this section), to accomplish any of the following:

(A) To add or strengthen a contraindication, warning, precaution, or adverse reaction for which the evidence of a causal association satisfies the standard for inclusion in the labeling under §201.57(c) of this chapter;

(B) To add or strengthen a statement about abuse, dependence, psychological effect, or overdosage;

(C) To add or strengthen an instruction about dosage and administration that is intended to increase the safety of the use of the product; and

(D) To delete false, misleading, or unsupported indications for use or claims for effectiveness.

(E) Any labeling change normally requiring a supplement submission and approval prior to distribution of the product that FDA specifically requests be submitted under this provision.

(ii) Pending approval of the supplement by FDA, the applicant may distribute a product with a package insert, package label, or container label bearing such change at the time the supplement is submitted. The supplement shall clearly identify the change being made and include necessary supporting data. The supplement and its mailing cover shall be plainly marked: "Special Labeling Supplement—Changes Being Effected."

(3) *Labeling changes requiring submission in an annual report.* (i) An applicant shall submit any final printed package insert, package label, container label, or Medication Guide required under part 208 of this chapter incorporating the following changes in an annual report submitted to FDA each year as provided in paragraph (d)(1) of this section:

(A) Editorial or similar minor changes;

(B) A change in the information on how the product is supplied that does not involve a change in the dosage strength or dosage form;

(C) A change in the information specified in §208.20(b)(8)(iii) and (b)(8)(iv) of this chapter for a Medication Guide; and

31

(D) A change to the information required in § 201.57(a) of this chapter as follows:

(1) Removal of a listed section(s) specified in § 201.57(a)(5) of this chapter; and

(2) Changes to the most recent revision date of the labeling as specified in § 201.57(a)(15) of this chapter.

(E) A change made pursuant to an exception or alternative granted under § 201.26 or § 610.68 of this chapter.

(ii) The applicant may distribute a product with a package insert, package label, or container label bearing such change at the time the change is made.

(4) *Advertisements and promotional labeling.* Advertisements and promotional labeling shall be submitted to the Center for Biologics Evaluation and Research or Center for Drug Evaluation and Research in accordance with the requirements set forth in § 314.81(b)(3)(i) of this chapter.

(5) The submission and grant of a written request for an exception or alternative under § 201.26 or § 610.68 of this chapter satisfies the requirements in paragraphs (f)(1) through (f)(2) of this section.

(6) For purposes of paragraph (f)(2) of this section, information will be considered newly acquired if it consists of data, analyses, or other information not previously submitted to the agency, which may include (but are not limited to) data derived from new clinical studies, reports of adverse events, or new analyses of previously submitted data (e.g., meta-analyses) if the studies, events or analyses reveal risks of a different type or greater severity or frequency than previously included in submissions to FDA.

(g) *Failure to comply.* In addition to other remedies available in law and regulations, in the event of repeated failure of the applicant to comply with this section, FDA may require that the applicant submit a supplement for any proposed change and obtain approval of the supplement by FDA prior to distribution of the product made using the change.

(h) *Administrative review.* Under § 10.75 of this chapter, an applicant may request internal FDA review of FDA employee decisions under this section.

[62 FR 39901, July 24, 1997, as amended at 63 FR 66399, Dec. 1, 1998. Redesignated at 65 FR 59718, Oct. 6, 2000, and amended at 69 FR 18766, Apr. 8, 2004; 70 FR 14983, Mar. 24, 2005; 71 FR 3997, Jan. 24, 2006; 72 FR 73600, Dec. 28, 2007; 73 FR 49609, Aug. 22, 2008; 73 FR 68333, Nov. 18, 2008; 80 FR 18092, Apr. 3, 2015]

§ 601.14 Regulatory submissions in electronic format.

(a) *General.* Electronic format submissions must be in a form that FDA can process, review, and archive. FDA will periodically issue guidance on how to provide the electronic submission (e.g., method of transmission, media, file formats, preparation and organization of files.)

(b) *Labeling.* The content of labeling required under § 201.100(d)(3) of this chapter (commonly referred to as the package insert or professional labeling), including all text, tables, and figures, must be submitted to the agency in electronic format as described in paragraph (a) of this section. This requirement is in addition to the provisions of §§ 601.2(a) and 601.12(f) that require applicants to submit specimens of the labels, enclosures, and containers, or to submit other final printed labeling. Submissions under this paragraph must be made in accordance with part 11 of this chapter except for the requirements of § 11.10(a), (c) through (h), and (k), and the corresponding requirements of § 11.30.

[68 FR 69020, Dec. 11, 2003]

§ 601.15 Foreign establishments and products: samples for each importation.

Random samples of each importation, obtained by the District Director of Customs and forwarded to the Director, Center for Biologics Evaluation and Research or the Director, Center for Drug Evaluation and Research (see mailing addresses in § 600.2(c) of this chapter) must be at least two final containers of each lot of product. A copy of the associated documents which describe and identify the shipment must accompany the shipment for forwarding with the samples to the Director, Center for Biologics Evaluation and Research or the Director, Center for Drug Evaluation and Research (see mailing addresses in §600.2(c)). For shipments of 20 or less final containers, samples need not be forwarded, provided a copy of an official release from the Center for Biologics Evaluation and Research or Center for Drug Evaluation and Research accompanies each shipment.

[70 FR 14983, Mar. 24, 2005, as amended at 80 FR 18092, Apr. 3, 2015]

§601.20 Biologics licenses; issuance and conditions.

(a) *Examination—compliance with requirements.* A biologics license application shall be approved only upon examination of the product and upon a determination that the product complies with the standards established in the biologics license application and the requirements prescribed in the regulations in this chapter including but not limited to the good manufacturing practice requirements set forth in parts 210, 211, 600, 606, and 820 of this chapter.

(b) *Availability of product.* No biologics license shall be issued unless:

(1) The product intended for introduction into interstate commerce is available for examination, and

(2) Such product is available for inspection during all phases of manufacture.

(c) *Manufacturing process—impairment of assurances.* No product shall be licensed if any part of the process of or relating to the manufacture of such product, in the judgment of the Director, Center for Biologics Evaluation and Research or the Director, Center for Drug Evaluation and Research, would impair the assurances of continued safety, purity, and potency as provided by the regulations contained in this chapter.

(d) *Inspection—compliance with requirements.* A biologics license shall be issued or a biologics license application approved only after inspection of the establishment(s) listed in the biologics license application and upon a determination that the establishment(s) complies with the standards established in the biologics license application and the requirements prescribed in applicable regulations.

(e) *One biologics license to cover all locations.* One biologics license shall be issued to cover all locations meeting the establishment standards identified in the approved biologics license application and each location shall be subject to inspection by FDA officials.

[64 FR 56451, Oct. 20, 1999, as amended at 70 FR 14983, Mar. 24, 2005]

§601.21 Products under development.

A biological product undergoing development, but not yet ready for a biologics license, may be shipped or otherwise delivered from one State or possession into another State or possession provided such shipment or delivery is not for introduction or delivery for introduction into interstate commerce, except as provided in sections 505(i) and 520(g) of the Federal Food, Drug, and Cosmetic Act, as amended, and the regulations thereunder (21 CFR parts 312 and 812).

[64 FR 56451, Oct. 20, 1999]

§601.22 Products in short supply; initial manufacturing at other than licensed location.

A biologics license issued to a manufacturer and covering all locations of manufacture shall authorize persons other than such manufacturer to conduct at places other than such locations the initial, and partial manufacturing of a product for shipment solely to such manufacturer only to the extent that the names of such persons and places are registered with the Commissioner of Food and Drugs and it is found upon application of such manufacturer, that the product is in short supply due either to the peculiar growth requirements of the organism involved or to the scarcity of the animal required for manufacturing purposes, and such manufacturer has established with respect to such persons and places such procedures, inspections, tests or other arrangements as will ensure full compliance with the applicable regulations of this subchapter related to continued safety, purity, and potency. Such persons and places shall be subject to all regulations of this subchapter except §§601.2 to 601.6, 601.9, 601.10, 601.20, 601.21 to

601.33, and 610.60 to 610.65 of this chapter. For persons and places authorized under this section to conduct the initial and partial manufacturing of a product for shipment solely to a manufacturer of a product subject to licensure under § 601.2(c), the following additional regulations shall not be applicable: §§ 600.10(b) and (c), 600.11, 600.12, 600.13, and 610.53 of this chapter. Failure of such manufacturer to maintain such procedures, inspections, tests, or other arrangements, or failure of any person conducting such partial manufacturing to comply with applicable regulations shall constitute a ground for suspension or revocation of the authority conferred pursuant to this section on the same basis as provided in §§ 601.6 to 601.8 with respect to the suspension and the revocation of licenses.

[42 FR 4718, Jan. 25, 1977, as amended at 61 FR 24233, May 14, 1996; 64 FR 56452, Oct. 20, 1999; 80 FR 37974, July 2, 2015]

§ 601.27 Pediatric studies.

(a) *Required assessment.* Except as provided in paragraphs (b), (c), and (d) of this section, each application for a new active ingredient, new indication, new dosage form, new dosing regimen, or new route of administration shall contain data that are adequate to assess the safety and effectiveness of the product for the claimed indications in all relevant pediatric subpopulations, and to support dosing and administration for each pediatric subpopulation for which the product is safe and effective. Where the course of the disease and the effects of the product are similar in adults and pediatric patients, FDA may conclude that pediatric effectiveness can be extrapolated from adequate and well-controlled effectiveness studies in adults, usually supplemented with other information in pediatric patients, such as pharmacokinetic studies. In addition, studies may not be needed in each pediatric age group, if data from one age group can be extrapolated to another. Assessments required under this section for a product that represents a meaningful therapeutic benefit over existing treatments must be carried out using appropriate formulations for the age group(s) for which the assessment is required.

(b) *Deferred submission.* (1) FDA may, on its own initiative or at the request of an applicant, defer submission of some or all assessments of safety and effectiveness described in paragraph (a) of this section until after licensing of the product for use in adults. Deferral may be granted if, among other reasons, the product is ready for approval in adults before studies in pediatric patients are complete, pediatric studies should be delayed until additional safety or effectiveness data have been collected. If an applicant requests deferred submission, the request must provide an adequate justification for delaying pediatric studies, a description of the planned or ongoing studies, and evidence that the studies are being or will be conducted with due diligence and at the earliest possible time.

(2) If FDA determines that there is an adequate justification for temporarily delaying the submission of assessments of pediatric safety and effectiveness, the product may be licensed for use in adults subject to the requirement that the applicant submit the required assessments within a specified time.

(c) *Waivers*—(1) *General.* FDA may grant a full or partial waiver of the requirements of paragraph (a) of this section on its own initiative or at the request of an applicant. A request for a waiver must provide an adequate justification.

(2) *Full waiver.* An applicant may request a waiver of the requirements of paragraph (a) of this section if the applicant certifies that:

(i) The product does not represent a meaningful therapeutic benefit over existing therapies for pediatric patients and is not likely to be used in a substantial number of pediatric patients;

(ii) Necessary studies are impossible or highly impractical because, e.g., the number of such patients is so small or geographically dispersed; or

(iii) There is evidence strongly suggesting that the product would be ineffective or unsafe in all pediatric age groups.

(3) *Partial waiver.* An applicant may request a waiver of the requirements of

paragraph (a) of this section with respect to a specified pediatric age group, if the applicant certifies that:

(i) The product does not represent a meaningful therapeutic benefit over existing therapies for pediatric patients in that age group, and is not likely to be used in a substantial number of patients in that age group;

(ii) Necessary studies are impossible or highly impractical because, e.g., the number of patients in that age group is so small or geographically dispersed;

(iii) There is evidence strongly suggesting that the product would be ineffective or unsafe in that age group; or

(iv) The applicant can demonstrate that reasonable attempts to produce a pediatric formulation necessary for that age group have failed.

(4) *FDA action on waiver.* FDA shall grant a full or partial waiver, as appropriate, if the agency finds that there is a reasonable basis on which to conclude that one or more of the grounds for waiver specified in paragraphs (c)(2) or (c)(3) of this section have been met. If a waiver is granted on the ground that it is not possible to develop a pediatric formulation, the waiver will cover only those pediatric age groups requiring that formulation. If a waiver is granted because there is evidence that the product would be ineffective or unsafe in pediatric populations, this information will be included in the product's labeling.

(5) *Definition of "meaningful therapeutic benefit".* For purposes of this section, a product will be considered to offer a meaningful therapeutic benefit over existing therapies if FDA estimates that:

(i) If approved, the product would represent a significant improvement in the treatment, diagnosis, or prevention of a disease, compared to marketed products adequately labeled for that use in the relevant pediatric population. Examples of how improvement might be demonstrated include, e.g., evidence of increased effectiveness in treatment, prevention, or diagnosis of disease; elimination or substantial reduction of a treatment-limiting drug reaction; documented enhancement of compliance; or evidence of safety and effectiveness in a new subpopulation; or

(ii) The product is in a class of products or for an indication for which there is a need for additional therapeutic options.

(d) *Exemption for orphan drugs.* This section does not apply to any product for an indication or indications for which orphan designation has been granted under part 316, subpart C, of this chapter.

[63 FR 66671, Dec. 2, 1998]

§ 601.28 Annual reports of postmarketing pediatric studies.

Sponsors of licensed biological products shall submit the following information each year within 60 days of the anniversary date of approval of each product under the license to the Director, Center for Biologics Evaluation and Research or the Director, Center for Drug Evaluation and Research (see mailing addresses in §600.2(a) or (b) of this chapter):

(a) *Summary.* A brief summary stating whether labeling supplements for pediatric use have been submitted and whether new studies in the pediatric population to support appropriate labeling for the pediatric population have been initiated. Where possible, an estimate of patient exposure to the drug product, with special reference to the pediatric population (neonates, infants, children, and adolescents) shall be provided, including dosage form.

(b) *Clinical data.* Analysis of available safety and efficacy data in the pediatric population and changes proposed in the labeling based on this information. An assessment of data needed to ensure appropriate labeling for the pediatric population shall be included.

(c) *Status reports.* A statement on the current status of any postmarketing studies in the pediatric population performed by, or on behalf of, the applicant. The statement shall include whether postmarketing clinical studies in pediatric populations were required or agreed to, and, if so, the status of these studies shall be reported to FDA in annual progress reports of postmarketing studies under §601.70 rather than under this section.

[65 FR 59718, Oct. 6, 2000, as amended at 65 FR 64618, Oct. 30, 2000; 70 FR 14984, Mar. 24, 2005; 80 FR 18092, Apr. 3, 2015]

§ 601.29 Guidance documents.

(a) FDA has made available guidance documents under § 10.115 of this chapter to help you comply with certain requirements of this part.

(b) The Center for Biologics Evaluation and Research (CBER) maintains a list of guidance documents that apply to the center's regulations. The lists are maintained on the Internet and are published annually in the FEDERAL REGISTER. You may request a copy of the CBER list from the Food and Drug Administration, Center for Biologics Evaluation and Research, Office of Communication, Outreach and Development, 10903 New Hampshire Ave., Bldg. 71, Rm. 3103, Silver Spring, MD 20993-0002.

[65 FR 56480, Sept. 19, 2000, as amended at 70 FR 14984, Mar. 24, 2005; 80 FR 18092, Apr. 3, 2015]

Subpart D—Diagnostic Radiopharmaceuticals

SOURCE: 64 FR 26668, May 17, 1999, unless otherwise noted.

§ 601.30 Scope.

This subpart applies to radiopharmaceuticals intended for in vivo administration for diagnostic and monitoring use. It does not apply to radiopharmaceuticals intended for therapeutic purposes. In situations where a particular radiopharmaceutical is proposed for both diagnostic and therapeutic uses, the radiopharmaceutical must be evaluated taking into account each intended use.

§ 601.31 Definition.

For purposes of this part, *diagnostic radiopharmaceutical* means:

(a) An article that is intended for use in the diagnosis or monitoring of a disease or a manifestation of a disease in humans and that exhibits spontaneous disintegration of unstable nuclei with the emission of nuclear particles or photons; or

(b) Any nonradioactive reagent kit or nuclide generator that is intended to be used in the preparation of such article as defined in paragraph (a) of this section.

§ 601.32 General factors relevant to safety and effectiveness.

FDA's determination of the safety and effectiveness of a diagnostic radiopharmaceutical includes consideration of the following:

(a) The proposed use of the diagnostic radiopharmaceutical in the practice of medicine;

(b) The pharmacological and toxicological activity of the diagnostic radiopharmaceutical (including any carrier or ligand component of the diagnostic radiopharmaceutical); and

(c) The estimated absorbed radiation dose of the diagnostic radiopharmaceutical.

§ 601.33 Indications.

(a) For diagnostic radiopharmaceuticals, the categories of proposed indications for use include, but are not limited to, the following:

(1) Structure delineation;

(2) Functional, physiological, or biochemical assessment;

(3) Disease or pathology detection or assessment; and

(4) Diagnostic or therapeutic patient management.

(b) Where a diagnostic radiopharmaceutical is not intended to provide disease-specific information, the proposed indications for use may refer to a biochemical, physiological, anatomical, or pathological process or to more than one disease or condition.

§ 601.34 Evaluation of effectiveness.

(a) The effectiveness of a diagnostic radiopharmaceutical is assessed by evaluating its ability to provide useful clinical information related to its proposed indications for use. The method of this evaluation varies depending upon the proposed indication(s) and may use one or more of the following criteria:

(1) The claim of structure delineation is established by demonstrating in a defined clinical setting the ability to locate anatomical structures and to characterize their anatomy.

(2) The claim of functional, physiological, or biochemical assessment is established by demonstrating in a defined clinical setting reliable measurement of function(s) or physiological, biochemical, or molecular process(es).

(3) The claim of disease or pathology detection or assessment is established by demonstrating in a defined clinical setting that the diagnostic radiopharmaceutical has sufficient accuracy in identifying or characterizing the disease or pathology.

(4) The claim of diagnostic or therapeutic patient management is established by demonstrating in a defined clinical setting that the test is useful in diagnostic or therapeutic patient management.

(5) For a claim that does not fall within the indication categories identified in §601.33, the applicant or sponsor should consult FDA on how to establish the effectiveness of the diagnostic radiopharmaceutical for the claim.

(b) The accuracy and usefulness of the diagnostic information is determined by comparison with a reliable assessment of actual clinical status. A reliable assessment of actual clinical status may be provided by a diagnostic standard or standards of demonstrated accuracy. In the absence of such diagnostic standard(s), the actual clinical status must be established in another manner, e.g., patient followup.

§601.35 Evaluation of safety.

(a) Factors considered in the safety assessment of a diagnostic radiopharmaceutical include, among others, the following:

(1) The radiation dose;

(2) The pharmacology and toxicology of the radiopharmaceutical, including any radionuclide, carrier, or ligand;

(3) The risks of an incorrect diagnostic determination;

(4) The adverse reaction profile of the drug;

(5) Results of human experience with the radiopharmaceutical for other uses; and

(6) Results of any previous human experience with the carrier or ligand of the radiopharmaceutical when the same chemical entity as the carrier or ligand has been used in a previously studied product.

(b) The assessment of the adverse reaction profile includes, but is not limited to, an evaluation of the potential of the diagnostic radiopharmaceutical, including the carrier or ligand, to elicit the following:

(1) Allergic or hypersensitivity responses,

(2) Immunologic responses,

(3) Changes in the physiologic or biochemical function of the target and nontarget tissues, and

(4) Clinically detectable signs or symptoms.

(c)(1) To establish the safety of a diagnostic radiopharmaceutical, FDA may require, among other information, the following types of data:

(A) Pharmacology data,

(B) Toxicology data,

(C) Clinical adverse event data, and

(D) Radiation safety assessment.

(2) The amount of new safety data required will depend on the characteristics of the product and available information regarding the safety of the diagnostic radiopharmaceutical, and its carrier or ligand, obtained from other studies and uses. Such information may include, but is not limited to, the dose, route of administration, frequency of use, half-life of the ligand or carrier, half-life of the radionuclide, and results of clinical and preclinical studies. FDA will establish categories of diagnostic radiopharmaceuticals based on defined characteristics relevant to risk and will specify the amount and type of safety data that are appropriate for each category (e.g., required safety data may be limited for diagnostic radiopharmaceuticals with a well established, low-risk profile). Upon reviewing the relevant product characteristics and safety information, FDA will place each diagnostic radiopharmaceutical into the appropriate safety risk category.

(d) *Radiation safety assessment.* The radiation safety assessment must establish the radiation dose of a diagnostic radiopharmaceutical by radiation dosimetry evaluations in humans and appropriate animal models. The maximum tolerated dose need not be established.

Subpart E—Accelerated Approval of Biological Products for Serious or Life-Threatening Illnesses

SOURCE: 57 FR 58959, Dec. 11, 1992, unless otherwise noted.

37

§ 601.40 Scope.

This subpart applies to certain biological products that have been studied for their safety and effectiveness in treating serious or life-threatening illnesses and that provide meaningful therapeutic benefit to patients over existing treatments (e.g., ability to treat patients unresponsive to, or intolerant of, available therapy, or improved patient response over available therapy).

§ 601.41 Approval based on a surrogate endpoint or on an effect on a clinical endpoint other than survival or irreversible morbidity.

FDA may grant marketing approval for a biological product on the basis of adequate and well-controlled clinical trials establishing that the biological product has an effect on a surrogate endpoint that is reasonably likely, based on epidemiologic, therapeutic, pathophysiologic, or other evidence, to predict clinical benefit or on the basis of an effect on a clinical endpoint other than survival or irreversible morbidity. Approval under this section will be subject to the requirement that the applicant study the biological product further, to verify and describe its clinical benefit, where there is uncertainty as to the relation of the surrogate endpoint to clinical benefit, or of the observed clinical benefit to ultimate outcome. Postmarketing studies would usually be studies already underway. When required to be conducted, such studies must also be adequate and well-controlled. The applicant shall carry out any such studies with due diligence.

§ 601.42 Approval with restrictions to assure safe use.

(a) If FDA concludes that a biological product shown to be effective can be safely used only if distribution or use is restricted, FDA will require such postmarketing restrictions as are needed to assure safe use of the biological product, such as:

(1) Distribution restricted to certain facilities or physicians with special training or experience; or

(2) Distribution conditioned on the performance of specified medical procedures.

(b) The limitations imposed will be commensurate with the specific safety concerns presented by the biological product.

§ 601.43 Withdrawal procedures.

(a) For biological products approved under § 601.41 or § 601.42, FDA may withdraw approval, following a hearing as provided in part 15 of this chapter, as modified by this section, if:

(1) A postmarketing clinical study fails to verify clinical benefit;

(2) The applicant fails to perform the required postmarketing study with due diligence;

(3) Use after marketing demonstrates that postmarketing restrictions are inadequate to ensure safe use of the biological product;

(4) The applicant fails to adhere to the postmarketing restrictions agreed upon;

(5) The promotional materials are false or misleading; or

(6) Other evidence demonstrates that the biological product is not shown to be safe or effective under its conditions of use.

(b) *Notice of opportunity for a hearing.* The Director of the Center for Biologics Evaluation and Research or the Director of the Center for Drug Evaluation and Research will give the applicant notice of an opportunity for a hearing on the Center's proposal to withdraw the approval of an application approved under § 601.41 or § 601.42. The notice, which will ordinarily be a letter, will state generally the reasons for the action and the proposed grounds for the order.

(c) *Submission of data and information.* (1) If the applicant fails to file a written request for a hearing within 15 days of receipt of the notice, the applicant waives the opportunity for a hearing.

(2) If the applicant files a timely request for a hearing, the agency will publish a notice of hearing in the FEDERAL REGISTER in accordance with §§ 12.32(e) and 15.20 of this chapter.

(3) An applicant who requests a hearing under this section must, within 30 days of receipt of the notice of opportunity for a hearing, submit the data and information upon which the applicant intends to rely at the hearing.

(d) *Separation of functions.* Separation of functions (as specified in §10.55 of this chapter) will not apply at any point in withdrawal proceedings under this section.

(e) *Procedures for hearings.* Hearings held under this section will be conducted in accordance with the provisions of part 15 of this chapter, with the following modifications:

(1) An advisory committee duly constituted under part 14 of this chapter will be present at the hearing. The committee will be asked to review the issues involved and to provide advice and recommendations to the Commissioner of Food and Drugs.

(2) The presiding officer, the advisory committee members, up to three representatives of the applicant, and up to three representatives of the Center may question any person during or at the conclusion of the person's presentation. No other person attending the hearing may question a person making a presentation. The presiding officer may, as a matter of discretion, permit questions to be submitted to the presiding officer for response by a person making a presentation.

(f) *Judicial review.* The Commissioner's decision constitutes final agency action from which the applicant may petition for judicial review. Before requesting an order from a court for a stay of action pending review, an applicant must first submit a petition for a stay of action under §10.35 of this chapter.

[57 FR 58959, Dec. 11, 1992, as amended at 68 FR 34797, June 11, 2003; 70 FR 14984, Mar. 24, 2005]

§601.44 **Postmarketing safety reporting.**

Biological products approved under this program are subject to the postmarketing recordkeeping and safety reporting applicable to all approved biological products.

§601.45 **Promotional materials.**

For biological products being considered for approval under this subpart, unless otherwise informed by the agency, applicants must submit to the agency for consideration during the preapproval review period copies of all promotional materials, including promotional labeling as well as advertisements, intended for dissemination or publication within 120 days following marketing approval. After 120 days following marketing approval, unless otherwise informed by the agency, the applicant must submit promotional materials at least 30 days prior to the intended time of initial dissemination of the labeling or initial publication of the advertisement.

§601.46 **Termination of requirements.**

If FDA determines after approval that the requirements established in §601.42, §601.43, or §601.45 are no longer necessary for the safe and effective use of a biological product, it will so notify the applicant. Ordinarily, for biological products approved under §601.41, these requirements will no longer apply when FDA determines that the required postmarketing study verifies and describes the biological product's clinical benefit and the biological product would be appropriate for approval under traditional procedures. For biological products approved under §601.42, the restrictions would no longer apply when FDA determines that safe use of the biological product can be assured through appropriate labeling. FDA also retains the discretion to remove specific postapproval requirements upon review of a petition submitted by the sponsor in accordance with §10.30.

Subpart F—Confidentiality of Information

§601.50 **Confidentiality of data and information in an investigational new drug notice for a biological product.**

(a) The existence of an IND notice for a biological product will not be disclosed by the Food and Drug Administration unless it has previously been publicly disclosed or acknowledged.

(b) The availability for public disclosure of all data and information in an IND file for a biological product shall be handled in accordance with the provisions established in §601.51.

(c) Notwithstanding the provisions of §601.51, the Food and Drug Administration shall disclose upon request to an individual on whom an investigational biological product has been used a copy of any adverse reaction report relating to such use.

[39 FR 44656, Dec. 24, 1974]

§ 601.51 Confidentiality of data and information in applications for biologics licenses.

(a) For purposes of this section the biological product file includes all data and information submitted with or incorporated by reference in any application for a biologics license, IND's incorporated into any such application, master files, and other related submissions. The availability for public disclosure of any record in the biological product file shall be handled in accordance with the provisions of this section.

(b) The existence of a biological product file will not be disclosed by the Food and Drug Administration before a biologics license application has been approved unless it has previously been publicly disclosed or acknowledged. The Food and Drug Administration will maintain a list available for public disclosure of biological products for which a license application has been approved.

(c) If the existence of a biological product file has not been publicly disclosed or acknowledged, no data or information in the biological product file is available for public disclosure.

(d)(1) If the existence of a biological product file has been publicly disclosed or acknowledged before a license has been issued, no data or information contained in the file is available for public disclosure before such license is issued, but the Commissioner may, in his discretion, disclose a summary of such selected portions of the safety and effectiveness data as are appropriate for public consideration of a specific pending issue, e.g., at an open session of a Food and Drug Administration advisory committee or pursuant to an exchange of important regulatory information with a foreign government.

(2) Notwithstanding paragraph (d)(1) of this section, FDA will make available to the public upon request the information in the IND that was required to be filed in Docket Number 95S–0158 in the Division of Dockets Management (HFA–305), Food and Drug Administration, 5630 Fishers Lane, rm. 1061, Rock-

ville, MD 20852, for investigations involving an exception from informed consent under § 50.24 of this chapter. Persons wishing to request this information shall submit a request under the Freedom of Information Act.

(e) After a license has been issued, the following data and information in the biological product file are immediately available for public disclosure unless extraordinary circumstances are shown:

(1) All safety and effectiveness data and information.

(2) A protocol for a test or study, unless it is shown to fall within the exemption established for trade secrets and confidential commercial or financial information in § 20.61 of this chapter.

(3) Adverse reaction reports, product experience reports, consumer complaints, and other similar data and information, after deletion of:

(i) Names and any information that would identify the person using the product.

(ii) Names and any information that would identify any third party involved with the report, such as a physician or hospital or other institution.

(4) A list of all active ingredients and any inactive ingredients previously disclosed to the public, as defined in § 20.81 of this chapter.

(5) An assay method or other analytical method, unless it serves no regulatory or compliance purpose and it is shown to fall within the exemption established in § 20.61 of this chapter.

(6) All correspondence and written summaries of oral discussions relating to the biological product file, in accordance with the provisions of part 20 of this chapter.

(7) All records showing the manufacturer's testing of a particular lot, after deletion of data or information that would show the volume of the drug produced, manufacturing procedures and controls, yield from raw materials, costs, or other material falling within § 20.61 of this chapter.

(8) All records showing the testing of and action on a particular lot by the Food and Drug Administration.

(f) The following data and information in a biological product file are not available for public disclosure unless

40

they have been previously disclosed to the public as defined in §20.81 of this chapter or they relate to a product or ingredient that has been abandoned and they no longer represent a trade secret or confidential commercial or financial information as defined in §20.61 of this chapter:

(1) Manufacturing methods or processes, including quality control procedures.

(2) Production, sales, distribution, and similar data and information, except that any compilation of such data and information aggregated and prepared in a way that does not reveal data or information which is not available for public disclosure under this provision is available for public disclosure.

(3) Quantitative or semiquantitative formulas.

(g) For purposes of this regulation, safety and effectiveness data include all studies and tests of a biological product on animals and humans and all studies and tests on the drug for identity, stability, purity, potency, and bioavailability.

[39 FR 44656, Dec. 24, 1974, as amended at 42 FR 15676, Mar. 22, 1977; 49 FR 23833, June 8, 1984; 55 FR 11013, Mar. 26, 1990; 61 FR 51530, Oct. 2, 1996; 64 FR 56452, Oct. 20, 1999; 68 FR 24879, May 9, 2003; 69 FR 13717, Mar. 24, 2004; 70 FR 14984, Mar. 24, 2005]

Subpart G—Postmarketing Studies

SOURCE: 65 FR 64618, Oct. 30, 2000, unless otherwise noted.

§601.70 Annual progress reports of postmarketing studies.

(a) *General requirements.* This section applies to all required postmarketing studies (e.g., accelerated approval clinical benefit studies, pediatric studies) and postmarketing studies that an applicant has committed, in writing, to conduct either at the time of approval of an application or a supplement to an application, or after approval of an application or a supplement. Postmarketing studies within the meaning of this section are those that concern:

(1) Clinical safety;

(2) Clinical efficacy;

(3) Clinical pharmacology; and

(4) Nonclinical toxicology.

(b) *What to report.* Each applicant of a licensed biological product shall submit a report to FDA on the status of postmarketing studies for each approved product application. The status of these postmarketing studies shall be reported annually until FDA notifies the applicant, in writing, that the agency concurs with the applicant's determination that the study commitment has been fulfilled, or that the study is either no longer feasible or would no longer provide useful information. Each annual progress report shall be accompanied by a completed transmittal Form FDA–2252, and shall include all the information required under this section that the applicant received or otherwise obtained during the annual reporting interval which ends on the U.S. anniversary date. The report must provide the following information for each postmarketing study:

(1) *Applicant's name.*

(2) *Product name.* Include the approved product's proper name and the proprietary name, if any.

(3) *Biologics license application (BLA) and supplement number.*

(4) *Date of U.S. approval of BLA.*

(5) *Date of postmarketing study commitment.*

(6) *Description of postmarketing study commitment.* The description must include sufficient information to uniquely describe the study. This information may include the purpose of the study, the type of study, the patient population addressed by the study and the indication(s) and dosage(s) that are to be studied.

(7) *Schedule for completion and reporting of the postmarketing study commitment.* The schedule should include the actual or projected dates for submission of the study protocol to FDA, completion of patient accrual or initiation of an animal study, completion of the study, submission of the final study report to FDA, and any additional milestones or submissions for which projected dates were specified as part of the commitment. In addition, it should include a revised schedule, as appropriate. If the schedule has been previously revised, provide both the original schedule and the most recent, previously submitted revision.

(8) *Current status of the postmarketing study commitment.* The status of each postmarketing study should be categorized using one of the following terms that describes the study's status on the anniversary date of U.S. approval of the application or other agreed upon date:

(i) *Pending.* The study has not been initiated, but does not meet the criterion for delayed.

(ii) *Ongoing.* The study is proceeding according to or ahead of the original schedule described under paragraph (b)(7) of this section.

(iii) *Delayed.* The study is behind the original schedule described under paragraph (b)(7) of this section.

(iv) *Terminated.* The study was ended before completion but a final study report has not been submitted to FDA.

(v) *Submitted.* The study has been completed or terminated and a final study report has been submitted to FDA.

(9) *Explanation of the study's status.* Provide a brief description of the status of the study, including the patient accrual rate (expressed by providing the number of patients or subjects enrolled to date, and the total planned enrollment), and an explanation of the study's status identified under paragraph (b)(8) of this section. If the study has been completed, include the date the study was completed and the date the final study report was submitted to FDA, as applicable. Provide a revised schedule, as well as the reason(s) for the revision, if the schedule under paragraph (b)(7) of this section has changed since the previous report.

(c) *When to report.* Annual progress reports for postmarketing study commitments entered into by applicants shall be reported to FDA within 60 days of the anniversary date of the U.S. approval of the application for the product.

(d) *Where to report.* Submit two copies of the annual progress report of postmarketing studies to the Center for Biologics Evaluation and Research or Center for Drug Evaluation and Research (see mailing addresses in § 600.2(a) or (b) of this chapter).

(e) *Public disclosure of information.* Except for the information described in this paragraph, FDA may publicly dis-

close any information concerning a postmarketing study, within the meaning of this section, if the agency determines that the information is necessary to identify an applicant or to establish the status of the study including the reasons, if any, for failure to conduct, complete, and report the study. Under this section, FDA will not publicly disclose trade secrets, as defined in § 20.61 of this chapter, or information, described in § 20.63 of this chapter, the disclosure of which would constitute an unwarranted invasion of personal privacy.

[65 FR 64618, Oct. 30, 2000, as amended at 70 FR 14984, Mar. 24, 2005; 80 FR 18092, Apr. 3, 2015]

Subpart H—Approval of Biological Products When Human Efficacy Studies Are Not Ethical or Feasible

Source: 67 FR 37996, May 31, 2002, unless otherwise noted.

§ 601.90 Scope.

This subpart applies to certain biological products that have been studied for their safety and efficacy in ameliorating or preventing serious or life-threatening conditions caused by exposure to lethal or permanently disabling toxic biological, chemical, radiological, or nuclear substances. This subpart applies only to those biological products for which: Definitive human efficacy studies cannot be conducted because it would be unethical to deliberately expose healthy human volunteers to a lethal or permanently disabling toxic biological, chemical, radiological, or nuclear substance; and field trials to study the product's efficacy after an accidental or hostile exposure have not been feasible. This subpart does not apply to products that can be approved based on efficacy standards described elsewhere in FDA's regulations (e.g., accelerated approval based on surrogate markers or clinical endpoints other than survival or irreversible morbidity), nor does it address the safety evaluation for the products to which it does apply.

§ 601.91 Approval based on evidence of effectiveness from studies in animals.

(a) FDA may grant marketing approval for a biological product for which safety has been established and for which the requirements of § 601.90 are met based on adequate and well-controlled animal studies when the results of those animal studies establish that the biological product is reasonably likely to produce clinical benefit in humans. In assessing the sufficiency of animal data, the agency may take into account other data, including human data, available to the agency. FDA will rely on the evidence from studies in animals to provide substantial evidence of the effectiveness of these products only when:

(1) There is a reasonably well-understood pathophysiological mechanism of the toxicity of the substance and its prevention or substantial reduction by the product;

(2) The effect is demonstrated in more than one animal species expected to react with a response predictive for humans, unless the effect is demonstrated in a single animal species that represents a sufficiently well-characterized animal model for predicting the response in humans;

(3) The animal study endpoint is clearly related to the desired benefit in humans, generally the enhancement of survival or prevention of major morbidity; and

(4) The data or information on the kinetics and pharmacodynamics of the product or other relevant data or information, in animals and humans, allows selection of an effective dose in humans.

(b) Approval under this subpart will be subject to three requirements:

(1) *Postmarketing studies.* The applicant must conduct postmarketing studies, such as field studies, to verify and describe the biological product's clinical benefit and to assess its safety when used as indicated when such studies are feasible and ethical. Such postmarketing studies would not be feasible until an exigency arises. When such studies are feasible, the applicant must conduct such studies with due diligence. Applicants must include as part of their application a plan or approach to postmarketing study commitments in the event such studies become ethical and feasible.

(2) *Approval with restrictions to ensure safe use.* If FDA concludes that a biological product shown to be effective under this subpart can be safely used only if distribution or use is restricted, FDA will require such postmarketing restrictions as are needed to ensure safe use of the biological product, commensurate with the specific safety concerns presented by the biological product, such as:

(i) Distribution restricted to certain facilities or health care practitioners with special training or experience;

(ii) Distribution conditioned on the performance of specified medical procedures, including medical followup; and

(iii) Distribution conditioned on specified recordkeeping requirements.

(3) *Information to be provided to patient recipients.* For biological products or specific indications approved under this subpart, applicants must prepare, as part of their proposed labeling, labeling to be provided to patient recipients. The patient labeling must explain that, for ethical or feasibility reasons, the biological product's approval was based on efficacy studies conducted in animals alone and must give the biological product's indication(s), directions for use (dosage and administration), contraindications, a description of any reasonably foreseeable risks, adverse reactions, anticipated benefits, drug interactions, and any other relevant information required by FDA at the time of approval. The patient labeling must be available with the product to be provided to patients prior to administration or dispensing of the biological product for the use approved under this subpart, if possible.

§ 601.92 Withdrawal procedures.

(a) *Reasons to withdraw approval.* For biological products approved under this subpart, FDA may withdraw approval, following a hearing as provided in part 15 of this chapter, as modified by this section, if:

(1) A postmarketing clinical study fails to verify clinical benefit;

(2) The applicant fails to perform the postmarketing study with due diligence;

43

(3) Use after marketing demonstrates that postmarketing restrictions are inadequate to ensure safe use of the biological product;

(4) The applicant fails to adhere to the postmarketing restrictions applied at the time of approval under this subpart;

(5) The promotional materials are false or misleading; or

(6) Other evidence demonstrates that the biological product is not shown to be safe or effective under its conditions of use.

(b) *Notice of opportunity for a hearing.* The Director of the Center for Biologics Evaluation and Research or the Director of the Center for Drug Evaluation and Research will give the applicant notice of an opportunity for a hearing on the proposal to withdraw the approval of an application approved under this subpart. The notice, which will ordinarily be a letter, will state generally the reasons for the action and the proposed grounds for the order.

(c) *Submission of data and information.* (1) If the applicant fails to file a written request for a hearing within 15 days of receipt of the notice, the applicant waives the opportunity for a hearing.

(2) If the applicant files a timely request for a hearing, the agency will publish a notice of hearing in the FEDERAL REGISTER in accordance with §§ 12.32(e) and 15.20 of this chapter.

(3) An applicant who requests a hearing under this section must, within 30 days of receipt of the notice of opportunity for a hearing, submit the data and information upon which the applicant intends to rely at the hearing.

(d) *Separation of functions.* Separation of functions (as specified in § 10.55 of this chapter) will not apply at any point in withdrawal proceedings under this section.

(e) *Procedures for hearings.* Hearings held under this section will be conducted in accordance with the provisions of part 15 of this chapter, with the following modifications:

(1) An advisory committee duly constituted under part 14 of this chapter will be present at the hearing. The committee will be asked to review the issues involved and to provide advice and recommendations to the Commissioner of Food and Drugs.

(2) The presiding officer, the advisory committee members, up to three representatives of the applicant, and up to three representatives of CBER may question any person during or at the conclusion of the person's presentation. No other person attending the hearing may question a person making a presentation. The presiding officer may, as a matter of discretion, permit questions to be submitted to the presiding officer for response by a person making a presentation.

(f) *Judicial review.* The Commissioner of Food and Drugs' decision constitutes final agency action from which the applicant may petition for judicial review. Before requesting an order from a court for a stay of action pending review, an applicant must first submit a petition for a stay of action under § 10.35 of this chapter.

[67 FR 37996, May 31, 2002, as amended at 70 FR 14984, Mar. 24, 2005]

§ 601.93 Postmarketing safety reporting.

Biological products approved under this subpart are subject to the postmarketing recordkeeping and safety reporting applicable to all approved biological products.

§ 601.94 Promotional materials.

For biological products being considered for approval under this subpart, unless otherwise informed by the agency, applicants must submit to the agency for consideration during the preapproval review period copies of all promotional materials, including promotional labeling as well as advertisements, intended for dissemination or publication within 120 days following marketing approval. After 120 days following marketing approval, unless otherwise informed by the agency, the applicant must submit promotional materials at least 30 days prior to the intended time of initial dissemination of the labeling or initial publication of the advertisement.

§ 601.95 Termination of requirements.

If FDA determines after approval under this subpart that the requirements established in §§ 601.91(b)(2), 601.92, and 601.93 are no longer necessary for the safe and effective use of a biological product, FDA will so notify the applicant. Ordinarily, for biological products approved under § 601.91, these requirements will no longer apply when FDA determines that the postmarketing study verifies and describes the biological product's clinical benefit. For biological products approved under § 601.91, the restrictions would no longer apply when FDA determines that safe use of the biological product can be ensured through appropriate labeling. FDA also retains the discretion to remove specific postapproval requirements upon review of a petition submitted by the sponsor in accordance with § 10.30 of this chapter.

PART 606—CURRENT GOOD MANUFACTURING PRACTICE FOR BLOOD AND BLOOD COMPONENTS

Subpart A—General Provisions

Sec.
606.3 Definitions.

Subpart B—Organization and Personnel

606.20 Personnel.

Subpart C—Plant and Facilities

606.40 Facilities.

Subpart D—Equipment

606.60 Equipment.
606.65 Supplies and reagents.

Subpart E [Reserved]

Subpart F—Production and Process Controls

606.100 Standard operating procedures.
606.110 Plateletpheresis, leukapheresis, and plasmapheresis.

Subpart G—Additional Labeling Standards for Blood and Blood Components

606.120 Labeling, general requirements.
606.121 Container label.
606.122 Circular of information.

Subpart H—Laboratory Controls

606.140 Laboratory controls.
606.145 Control of bacterial contamination of platelets.
606.151 Compatibility testing.

Subpart I—Records and Reports

606.160 Records.
606.165 Distribution and receipt; procedures and records.
606.170 Adverse reaction file.
606.171 Reporting of product deviations by licensed manufacturers, unlicensed registered blood establishments, and transfusion services.

AUTHORITY: 21 U.S.C. 321, 331, 351, 352, 355, 360, 360j, 371, 374; 42 U.S.C. 216, 262, 263a, 264.

SOURCE: 40 FR 53532, Nov. 18, 1975, unless otherwise noted.

Subpart A—General Provisions

§ 606.3 Definitions.

As used in this part:

(a) *Blood* means a product that is a fluid containing dissolved and suspended elements which was collected from the vascular system of a human.

(b) *Unit* means the volume of blood or one of its components in a suitable volume of anticoagulant obtained from a single collection of blood from one donor.

(c) *Blood component* means a product containing a part of human blood separated by physical or mechanical means.

(d) *Plasma for further manufacturing* means that liquid portion of blood separated and used as material to prepare another product.

(e) *Plasmapheresis* means the procedure in which blood is removed from the donor, the plasma is separated from the formed elements and at least the red blood cells are returned to the donor.

(f) *Plateletpheresis* means the procedure in which blood is removed from a donor, a platelet concentrate is separated, and the remaining formed elements are returned to the donor along with a portion of the residual plasma.

(g) *Leukapheresis* means the procedure in which blood is removed from the donor, a leukocyte concentrate is separated, and the remaining formed elements and residual plasma are returned to the donor.

(h) *Facilities* means any area used for the collection, processing, compatibility testing, storage or distribution of blood and blood components.

(i) *Processing* means any procedure employed after collection, and before or after compatibility testing of blood,

45

and includes the identification of a unit of donor blood, the preparation of components from such unit of donor blood, serological testing, labeling and associated recordkeeping.

(j) *Compatibility testing* means the procedures performed to establish the matching of a donor's blood or blood components with that of a potential recipient.

(k) *Distributed* means:

(1) The blood or blood components have left the control of the licensed manufacturer, unlicensed registered blood establishment, or transfusion service; or

(2) The licensed manufacturer has provided Source Plasma or any other blood component for use in the manufacture of a licensed biological product.

(l) *Control* means having responsibility for maintaining the continued safety, purity, and potency of the product and for compliance with applicable product and establishment standards, and for compliance with current good manufacturing practices.

[40 FR 53532, Nov. 18, 1975, as amended at 64 FR 45370, Aug. 19, 1999; 65 FR 66635, Nov. 7, 2000; 66 FR 1835, Jan. 10, 2001; 66 FR 40889, Aug. 6, 2001; 72 FR 45886, Aug. 16, 2007; 80 FR 29894, May 22, 2015]

Subpart B—Organization and Personnel

§ 606.20 Personnel.

(a) [Reserved]

(b) The personnel responsible for the collection, processing, compatibility testing, storage or distribution of blood or blood components shall be adequate in number, educational background, training and experience, including professional training as necessary, or combination thereof, to assure competent performance of their assigned functions, and to ensure that the final product has the safety, purity, potency, identity and effectiveness it purports or is represented to possess. All personnel shall have capabilities commensurate with their assigned functions, a thorough understanding of the procedures or control operations they perform, the necessary training or experience, and adequate information concerning the application of pertinent

provisions of this part to their respective functions.

(c) Persons whose presence can adversely affect the safety and purity of the products shall be excluded from areas where the collection, processing, compatibility testing, storage or distribution of blood or blood components is conducted.

[40 FR 53532, Nov. 18, 1975, as amended at 49 FR 23833, June 8, 1984; 55 FR 11014, Mar. 26, 1990; 62 FR 53538, Oct. 15, 1997]

Subpart C—Plant and Facilities

§ 606.40 Facilities.

Facilities shall be maintained in a clean and orderly manner, and shall be of suitable size, construction and location to facilitate adequate cleaning, maintenance and proper operations. The facilities shall:

(a) Provide adequate space for the following when applicable:

(1) Private and accurate examinations of individuals to determine their eligibility as blood donors.

(2) The withdrawal of blood from donors with minimal risk of contamination, or exposure to activities and equipment unrelated to blood collection.

(3) The storage of blood or blood components pending completion of tests.

(4) The quarantine storage of blood or blood components in a designated location pending repetition of those tests that initially gave questionable serological results.

(5) The storage of finished products prior to distribution.

(6) The quarantine storage, handling and disposition of products and reagents not suitable for use.

(7) The orderly collection, processing, compatibility testing, storage and distribution of blood and blood components to prevent contamination.

(8) The adequate and proper performance of all steps in plasmapheresis, plateletpheresis and leukapheresis procedures.

(9) The orderly conduct of all packaging, labeling and other finishing operations.

(b) Provide adequate lighting, ventilation and screening of open windows and doors.

(c) Provide adequate, clean, and convenient handwashing facilities for personnel, and adequate, clean, and convenient toilet facilities for donors and personnel. Drains shall be of adequate size and, where connected directly to a sewer, shall be equipped with traps to prevent back-siphonage.

(d) Provide for safe and sanitary disposal for the following:

(1) Trash and items used during the collection, processing and compatibility testing of blood and blood components.

(2) Blood and blood components not suitable for use or distribution.

[40 FR 53532, Nov. 18, 1975, as amended at 80 FR 29895, May 22, 2015]

Subpart D—Equipment

§606.60 Equipment.

(a) Equipment used in the collection, processing, compatibility testing, storage and distribution of blood and blood components shall be maintained in a clean and orderly manner and located so as to facilitate cleaning and maintenance. The equipment shall be observed, standardized and calibrated on a regularly scheduled basis as prescribed in the Standard Operating Procedures Manual and shall perform in the manner for which it was designed so as to assure compliance with the official requirements prescribed in this chapter for blood and blood products.

(b) Equipment that shall be observed, standardized and calibrated with at least the following frequency, include but are not limited to:

Equipment	Performance check	Frequency	Frequency of calibration
Temperature recorder	Compare against thermometer	Daily	As necessary.
Refrigerated centrifuge ..	Observe speed and temperature	Each day of use	Do.
Hematocrit centrifuge	....	....	Standardize before initial use, after repairs or adjustments, and annually. Timer every 3 mo.
General lab centrifuge ...	....	....	Tachometer every 6 mo.
Automated blood-typing machine.	Observe controls for correct results	Each day of use.	
Hemoglobinometer	Standardize against cyanmethemoglobin standard.	......do.	
Refractometer	Standardize against distilled water	......do.	
Blood container scale	Standardize against container of known weight.	......do	As necessary.
Water bath	Observe temperature	......do	Do.
Rh view box	.....do	......do	Do.
Autoclave	.....do	Each time of use	Do.
Serologic rotators	Observe controls for correct results	Each day of use	Speed as necessary.
Laboratory thermometers.	....	....	Before initial use.
Electronic thermometers	....	....	Monthly.
Vacuum blood agitator ..	Observe weight of the first container of blood filled for correct results.	Each day of use	Standardize with container of known mass or volume before initial use, and after repairs or adjustments.

(c) Equipment employed in the sterilization of materials used in blood collection or for disposition of contaminated products shall be designed, maintained and utilized to ensure the destruction of contaminating microorganisms. The effectiveness of the sterilization procedure shall be no less than that achieved by an attained temperature of 121.5 °C (251 °F) maintained for 20 minutes by saturated steam or by an attained temperature of 170 °C (338 °F) maintained for 2 hours with dry heat.

[40 FR 53532, Nov. 18, 1975; 40 FR 55849, Dec. 2, 1975, as amended at 45 FR 9261, Feb. 12, 1980; 57 FR 11263, Apr. 2, 1992; 57 FR 12862, Apr. 13, 1992]

§606.65 Supplies and reagents.

All supplies and reagents used in the collection, processing, compatibility testing, storage and distribution of blood and blood components shall be stored in a safe, sanitary and orderly manner.

(a) All surfaces coming in contact with blood and blood components intended for transfusion shall be sterile, pyrogen-free, and shall not interact with the product in such a manner as to have an adverse effect upon the safety, purity, potency or effectiveness of the product. All final containers and closures for blood and blood components not intended for transfusion shall be clean and free of surface solids and other contaminants.

(b) Each blood collecting container and its satellite container(s), if any, shall be examined visually for damage or evidence of contamination prior to its use and immediately after filling. Such examination shall include inspection for breakage of seals, when indicated, and abnormal discoloration. Where any defect is observed, the container shall not be used, or, if detected after filling, shall be properly discarded.

(c) Representative samples of each lot of the following reagents or solutions shall be tested on a regularly scheduled basis by methods described in the Standard Operating Procedures Manual to determine their capacity to perform as required:

Reagent or solution	Frequency of testing
Anti-human globulin	Each day of use.
Blood grouping reagents	Do.
Lectins	Do.
Antibody screening and reverse grouping cells.	Do.
Hepatitis test reagents	Each run.
Syphilis serology reagents	Do.
Enzymes	Each day of use.

(d) Supplies and reagents that do not bear an expiration date shall be stored in such a manner that the oldest is used first.

(e) Supplies and reagents shall be used in a manner consistent with instructions provided by the manufacturer.

(f) Items that are required to be sterile and come into contact with blood should be disposable whenever possible.

[40 FR 53532, Nov. 18, 1975, as amended at 59 FR 23636, May 6, 1994]

Subpart E [Reserved]

Subpart F—Production and Process Controls

§ 606.100 Standard operating procedures.

(a) In all instances, except clinical investigations, standard operating procedures shall comply with published additional standards in part 640 of this chapter for the products being processed; except that, references in part 640 relating to licenses, licensed establishments and submission of material or data to or approval by the Director, Center for Biologics Evaluation and Research, are not applicable to establishments not subject to licensure under section 351 of the Public Health Service Act.

(b) Establishments must establish, maintain, and follow written standard operating procedures for all steps in the collection, processing, compatibility testing, storage, and distribution of blood and blood components for allogeneic transfusion, autologous transfusion, and further manufacturing purposes; for all steps in the investigation of product deviations related to § 606.171; and for all steps in recordkeeping related to current good manufacturing practice and other applicable requirements and standards. Such procedures must be available to the personnel for use in the areas where the procedures are performed. The written standard operating procedures must include, but are not limited to, descriptions of the following, when applicable:

(1) Criteria used to determine donor eligibility, including acceptable medical history criteria.

(2) Methods of performing donor qualifying tests and measurements, including minimum and maximum values for a test or procedure when a factor in determining acceptability.

(3) Solutions and methods used to prepare the site of phlebotomy to give maximum assurance of a sterile container of blood.

(4) Method of accurately relating the product(s) to the donor.

(5) Blood collection procedure, including in-process precautions taken to measure accurately the quantity of blood removed from the donor.

(6) Methods of component preparation, including any time restrictions for specific steps in processing.

(7) All tests and repeat tests performed on blood and blood components during manufacturing.

(8) Pretransfusion testing, where applicable, including precautions to be taken to identify accurately the recipient blood samples and crossmatched donor units.

(9) Procedures for investigating adverse donor and recipient reactions.

(10) Storage temperatures and methods of controlling storage temperatures for all blood products and reagents as prescribed in §§ 600.15 and 610.53 of this chapter.

(11) Length of expiration dates, if any, assigned for all final products as prescribed in § 610.53 of this chapter.

(12) Criteria for determining whether returned blood is suitable for reissue.

(13) Procedures used for relating a unit of blood or blood component from the donor to its final disposition.

(14) Quality control procedures for supplies and reagents employed in blood collection, processing and pretransfusion testing.

(15) Schedules and procedures for equipment maintenance and calibration.

(16) Labeling procedures, including safeguards to avoid labeling mixups.

(17) Procedures of plasmapheresis, plateletpheresis, and leukapheresis, if performed, including precautions to be taken to ensure reinfusion of a donor's own cells.

(18) Procedures for preparing recovered plasma, if performed, including details of separation, pooling, labeling, storage, and distribution.

(19) Procedures under §§ 610.46 and 610.47 of this chapter:

(i) To identify previously donated blood and blood components from a donor who later tests reactive for evidence of human immunodeficiency virus (HIV) infection or hepatitis C virus (HCV) infection when tested under § 610.40 of this chapter, or when a blood establishment is made aware of other reliable test results or information indicating evidence of HIV or HCV infection;

(ii) To quarantine in-date blood and blood components previously donated by such a donor that are intended for use in another person or further manufacture into injectable products, except pooled components intended solely for further manufacturing into products that are manufactured using validated viral clearance procedures;

(iii) To notify consignees to quarantine in-date blood and blood components previously donated by such a donor intended for use in another person or for further manufacture into injectable products, except pooled components intended solely for further manufacturing into products that are manufactured using validated viral clearance procedures;

(iv) To determine the suitability for release, destruction, or relabeling of quarantined in-date blood and blood components;

(v) To notify consignees of the results of the HIV or HCV testing performed on the donors of such blood and blood components;

(vi) To notify the transfusion recipient, the recipient's physician of record, or the recipient's legal representative that the recipient received blood or blood components at increased risk of transmitting HIV or HCV, respectively.

(20) Procedures for donor deferral as prescribed in § 610.41 of this chapter.

(21) Procedures for donor notification and notification of the referring physician of an autologous donor, including procedures for the appropriate followup if the initial attempt at notification fails, as prescribed in § 630.40 of this chapter.

(22) Procedures to control the risks of bacterial contamination of platelets, including all steps required under § 606.145.

(c) All records pertinent to the lot or unit maintained pursuant to these regulations shall be reviewed before the release or distribution of a lot or unit of final product. The review or portions of the review may be performed at appropriate periods during or after blood collecting, processing, compatibility testing and storing. A thorough investigation, including the conclusions and followup, of any unexplained discrepancy or the failure of a lot or unit to meet any of its specifications shall be made and recorded.

(d) In addition to the requirements of this subpart and in conformity with this section, any facility may utilize current standard operating procedures such as the manuals of the organizations, as long as such specific procedures are consistent with, and at least as stringent as, the requirements contained in this part.

(1) American Association of Blood Banks.

(2) American National Red Cross.

(3) Other organizations or individual blood banks, subject to approval by the Director, Center for Biologics Evaluation and Research.

[40 FR 53532, Nov. 18, 1975, as amended at 49 FR 23833, June 8, 1984; 55 FR 11013, Mar. 26, 1990; 61 FR 47422, Sept. 9, 1996; 64 FR 45370, Aug. 19, 1999; 66 FR 31176, June 11, 2001; 72 FR 48798, Aug. 24, 2007; 80 FR 80651, Dec. 28, 2015; 80 FR 29895, May 22, 2015]

§ 606.110 Plateletpheresis, leukapheresis, and plasmapheresis.

(a) The use of plateletpheresis and leukapheresis procedures to obtain a product for a specific recipient may be at variance with the additional standards for specific products prescribed in this part provided that: (1) A physician has determined that the recipient must be transfused with the leukocytes or platelets from a specific donor, and (2) the procedure is performed under the supervision of a responsible physician who is aware of the health status of the donor, and the physician has determined and documented that the donor's health permits plateletpheresis or leukapheresis.

(b) Plasmapheresis of donors who do not meet the donor requirements of §§ 630.10, 630.15, 640.64 and 640.65 of this chapter for the collection of plasma containing rare antibodies shall be permitted only with the prior approval of the Director, Center for Biologics Evaluation and Research.

[40 FR 53532, Nov. 18, 1975, as amended at 49 FR 23833, June 8, 1984; 55 FR 11013, Mar. 26, 1990; 80 FR 29895, May 22, 2015]

Subpart G—Additional Labeling Standards for Blood and Blood Components

§ 606.120 Labeling, general requirements.

(a) Labeling operations shall be separated physically or spatially from other operations in a manner adequate to prevent mixups.

(b) The labeling operation shall include the following labeling controls:

(1) Labels shall be held upon receipt, pending review and proofing against an approved final copy, to ensure accuracy regarding identity, content, and conformity with the approved copy.

(2) Each type of label representing different products shall be stored and maintained in a manner to prevent mixups, and stocks of obsolete labels shall be destroyed.

(3) All necessary checks in labeling procedures shall be utilized to prevent errors in translating test results to container labels.

(c) All labeling shall be clear and legible.

[50 FR 35469, Aug. 30, 1985]

§ 606.121 Container label.

(a) The container label requirements are designed to facilitate the use of a uniform container label for blood and blood components intended for use in transfusion or further manufacture by all blood establishments.

(b) The label provided by the collecting facility and the initial processing facility must not be removed, altered, or obscured, except that the label may be altered to indicate the proper name of the product, with any appropriate modifiers and attributes, and other information required to identify accurately the contents of a container after blood components considered finished products have been prepared.

(c) The container label must include the following information, as well as other specialized information as required in this section for specific products:

(1) The proper name of the product in a prominent position, with any appropriate modifiers and attributes.

(2) The name, address, unique facility identifier, and, if a licensed product, the license number of each manufacturer; except the container label for blood and blood components for further manufacture is not required to include a unique facility identifier.

(3) The donor or lot number relating the unit to the donor. If pooled, all donor numbers, all donation numbers, or a pool number that is traceable to each individual unit comprising the pool.

(4)(i) The expiration date, including the day, month, and year, and, if the dating period for the product is 72 hours or less, including any product prepared in a system that might compromise sterility, the hour of expiration.

(ii) If Source Plasma intended for manufacturing into noninjectable products is pooled, the expiration date for the pool is determined from the collection date of the oldest unit in the pool, and the pooling records must show the collection date for each unit in the pool.

(5) For Whole Blood, Plasma, Platelets, and partial units of Red Blood Cells, the volume of the product, accurate to within ±10 percent; or optionally for Platelets, the volume or volume range within reasonable limits.

(6) Where applicable, the name and volume of source material.

(7) The recommended storage temperature (in degrees Celsius).

(8) If the product is intended for transfusion, the statements:

(i) "Rx only."

(ii) "See circular of information for indications, contraindications, cautions, and methods of infusion."

(iii) "Properly identify intended recipient."

(iv) "This product may transmit infectious agents."

(v) The appropriate donor classification statement, i.e., "paid donor" or "volunteer donor," in no less prominence than the proper name of the product.

(A) A paid donor is a person who receives monetary payment for a blood donation.

(B) A volunteer donor is a person who does not receive monetary payment for a blood donation.

(C) Benefits, such as time off from work, membership in blood assurance programs, and cancellation of non-replacement fees that are not readily convertible to cash, do not constitute monetary payment within the meaning of this paragraph.

(9) If the product is intended for transfusion or as is otherwise appropriate, the ABO group and Rh type of the donor must be designated conspicuously. For Cryoprecipitated Antihemophiliac Factor (AHF), the Rh type may be omitted. The Rh type must be designated as follows:

(i) If the test using Anti-D Blood Grouping Reagent is positive, the product must be labeled: "Rh positive."

(ii) If the test using Anti-D Blood Grouping Reagent is negative, but the test for weak D (formerly D_u) is positive, the product must be labeled: "Rh positive."

(iii) If the test using Anti-D Blood Grouping Reagent is negative and the test for weak D (formerly D_u) is negative, the product must be labeled: "Rh negative."

(10) If the product is not intended for transfusion, a statement as applicable: "Caution: For Manufacturing Use Only," or "Caution: For Use in Manufacturing Noninjectable Products Only," or other cautionary statement as approved by the Director, Center for Biologics Evaluation and Research (CBER).

(11) If the product is intended for further manufacturing use, a statement listing the results of all the tests for relevant transfusion-transmitted infections required under §610.40 of this chapter for which the donation has been tested and found negative; except that the container label for Source Plasma is not required to list the negative results of serological syphilis testing under §640.65(b) of this chapter.

(12) The blood and blood components must be labeled in accordance with §610.40 of this chapter, when the donation is tested and demonstrates evidence of infection due to a relevant transfusion-transmitted infection(s).

(13) The container label of blood or blood components intended for transfusion must bear encoded information in a format that is machine-readable

and approved for use by the Director, CBER.

(i) *Who is subject to this machine-readable requirement?* All blood establishments that manufacture, process, repack, or relabel blood or blood components intended for transfusion and regulated under the Federal Food, Drug, and Cosmetic Act or the Public Health Service Act.

(ii) *What blood products are subject to this machine-readable requirement?* All blood and blood components intended for transfusion are subject to the machine-readable information label requirement in this section.

(iii) *What information must be machine-readable?* Each label must have machine-readable information that contains, at a minimum:

(A) A unique facility identifier;

(B) Lot number relating to the donor;

(C) Product code; and

(D) ABO and Rh of the donor, except as described in paragraphs (c)(9) and (i)(5) of this section.

(iv) *How must the machine-readable information appear?* The machine-readable information must:

(A) Be unique to the blood or blood component;

(B) Be surrounded by sufficient blank space so that the machine-readable information can be scanned correctly; and

(C) Remain intact under normal conditions of use.

(v) *Where does the machine-readable information go?* The machine-readable information must appear on the label of any blood or blood component which is or can be transfused to a patient or from which the blood or blood component can be taken and transfused to a patient.

(d) Unless otherwise approved by the Director, CBER, the container label for blood and blood components intended for transfusion must be white and print must be solid black, with the following additional exceptions:

(1) The ABO and Rh blood groups must be printed as follows:

(i) Rh positive: Use black print on white background and use solid black or other solid color for ABO.

(ii) Rh negative: Use white print on black background for Rh and use black

outline on a white background for ABO.

(2) The proper name of the product, with any appropriate modifiers and attributes, the donor classification statement, and the statement "properly identify intended recipient" may be printed in solid red or in solid black.

(3) The following color scheme may be used for differentiating ABO Blood groups:

Blood group	Color of label
O	Blue
A	Yellow
B	Pink
AB	White

(4) Special labels, such as those described in paragraphs (h) and (i) of this section, may be color-coded.

(e) Container label requirements for particular products or groups of products.

(1) Whole Blood labels must include:

(i) The name of the applicable anticoagulant approved for use by the Director, CBER.

(ii) The volume of anticoagulant.

(iii) If tests for unexpected antibodies are positive, blood intended for transfusion must be labeled: "Contains (name of antibody)."

(2) Except for frozen, deglycerolized, or washed Red Blood Cell products, Red Blood Cell labels must include:

(i) The type of anticoagulant, and if applicable, the volume of Whole Blood and type of additive solution, with which the product was prepared.

(ii) If tests for unexpected antibodies are positive and the product is intended for transfusion, the statement: "Contains (name of antibody)."

(3) If tests for unexpected antibodies are positive, Plasma intended for transfusion must be labeled: "Contains (name of antibody)."

(4) Recovered plasma labels must include:

(i) In lieu of an expiration date, the date of collection of the oldest material in the container.

(ii) For recovered plasma not meeting the requirements for manufacture into licensable products, the statement: "Not for Use in Products Subject to License Under Section 351 of the Public Health Service Act."

(iii) The type of anticoagulant with which the product was prepared.

(5) Source Plasma labels must include the following information:

(i) The cautionary statement, as specified in paragraph (c)(10) of this section, must follow the proper name with any appropriate modifiers and attributes and be of similar prominence as the proper name.

(ii) The statement "Store at −20 °C or colder," provided, that where plasma is intended for manufacturing into noninjectable products, this statement may be replaced by a statement of the temperature appropriate for manufacture of the final product to be prepared from the plasma.

(iii) The total volume or weight of plasma and total quantity and type of anticoagulant used.

(iv) When plasma collected from a donor is reactive for a serologic test for syphilis, a statement that the plasma is reactive and must be used only for the manufacturing of positive control reagents for the serologic test for syphilis.

(v) Source Plasma diverted for Source Plasma Salvaged must be relabeled "Source Plasma Salvaged" as prescribed in §640.76 of this chapter. Immediately following the proper name of the product, with any appropriate modifiers and attributes, the labeling must prominently state as applicable, "STORAGE TEMPERATURE EXCEEDED −20 °C" or "SHIPPING TEMPERATURE EXCEEDED −5 °C."

(vi) A statement as to whether the plasma was collected from normal donors, or from donors in specific collection programs approved by the Director, CBER. In the case of specific collection programs, the label must state the defining characteristics of the plasma. In the case of immunized donors, the label must state the immunizing antigen.

(f) Blood and blood components determined to be unsuitable for transfusion must be prominently labeled "NOT FOR TRANSFUSION," and the label must state the reason the unit is considered unsuitable. The provision does not apply to blood and blood components intended solely for further manufacture.

(g) [Reserved]

(h) The following additional information must appear on the label for blood and blood components shipped in an emergency prior to completion of required tests, in accordance with §610.40(g) of this chapter:

(1) The statement: "FOR EMERGENCY USE ONLY BY __ ."

(2) Results of any tests prescribed under §§610.40 and 640.5(b) or (c) of this chapter completed before shipment.

(3) Indication of any tests prescribed under §§610.40 and 640.5(b) or (c) of this chapter not completed before shipment.

(i) The following additional information must appear on the label for blood and blood components intended for autologous transfusion:

(1) Information adequately identifying the patient, e.g., name, date of birth, hospital, and identification number.

(2) Date of donation.

(3) The statement: "AUTOLOGOUS DONOR."

(4) The ABO and Rh blood group and type, except as provided in paragraph (c)(9) of this section.

(5) Each container of blood and blood component intended for autologous use and obtained from a donor who fails to meet any of the donor eligibility requirements under §630.10 of this chapter or who is reactive to or positive for one or more tests for evidence of infection due to relevant transfusion-transmitted infections under §610.40 of this chapter must be prominently and permanently labeled "FOR AUTOLOGOUS USE ONLY" and as otherwise required under §610.40 of this chapter. Such units also may have the ABO and Rh blood group and type on the label.

(6) Units of blood and blood components originally intended for autologous use, except those labeled as prescribed under paragraph (i)(5) of this section, may be issued for allogeneic transfusion provided the container label complies with all applicable provisions of paragraphs (b) through (e) of this section. In such case, the special label required under paragraphs (i)(1), (i)(2), and (i)(3) of this section must be removed or otherwise obscured.

(j) A tie-tag attached to the container may be used for providing the information required by paragraphs (e)(1)(iii), (e)(2)(ii), and (e)(3), (h), or (i)(1), (i)(2), and (i)(3) of this section.

[77 FR 16, Jan. 3, 2012, as amended at 80 FR 29895, May 22, 2015]

§ 606.122 Circular of information.

A circular of information must be available for distribution if the product is intended for transfusion. The circular of information must provide adequate directions for use, including the following information:

(a) Instructions to mix the product before use.

(b) Instructions to use a filter in the administration equipment.

(c) The statement "Do Not Add Medications" or an explanation concerning allowable additives.

(d) A description of the product, its source, and preparation, including the name and proportion of the anticoagulant used in collecting the Whole Blood from each product is prepared.

(e) A statement that the product was prepared from blood that was found negative when tested for relevant transfusion-transmitted infections, as required under § 610.40 of this chapter (include each test that was performed).

(f) The statement: "Warning: The risk of transmitting infectious agents is present. Careful donor selection and available laboratory tests do not eliminate the hazard."

(g) The names of cryoprotective agents and other additives that may still be present in the product.

(h) The names and results of all tests performed when necessary for safe and effective use.

(i) The use of the product, indications, contradications, side effects and hazards, dosage and administration recommendations.

(j) [Reserved]

(k) For Red Blood Cells, the circular of information must contain:

(1) Instructions to administer a suitable plasma volume expander if Red Blood Cells are substituted when Whole Blood is the indicated product.

(2) A warning not to add Lactated Ringer's Injection U.S.P. solution to Red Blood Cell products.

(l) For Platelets, the circular of information must contain:

(1) The approximate volume of plasma from which a sample unit of Platelets is prepared.

(2) Instructions to begin administration as soon as possible, but not more than 4 hours after entering the container.

(m) For Plasma, the circular of information must contain:

(1) A warning against further processing of the frozen product if there is evidence of breakage or thawing.

(2) Instructions to thaw the frozen product at a temperature appropriate for the product.

(3) When applicable, instructions to begin administration of the product within a specified time after thawing.

(4) Instructions to administer to ABO-group-compatible recipients.

(5) A statement that this product has the same risk of transmitting infectious agents as Whole Blood; other plasma volume expanders without this risk are available for treating hypovolemia.

(n) For Cryoprecipitated AHF, the circular of information must contain:

(1) A statement that the average potency is 80 or more International Units of antihemophilic factor.

(2) The statement: "Usually contains at least 150 milligrams of fibrinogen"; or, alternatively, the average fibrinogen level determined by assay of representative units.

(3) A warning against further processing of the product if there is evidence of breakage or thawing.

(4) Instructions to thaw the product for no more than 15 minutes at a temperature of between 30 and 37 °C.

(5) Instructions to store at room temperature after thawing and to begin administration as soon as possible but no more than 4 hours after entering the container or after pooling and within 6 hours after thawing.

(6) A statement that 0.9 percent Sodium Chloride Injection U.S.P. is the preferred diluent.

(7) Adequate instructions for pooling to ensure complete removal of all concentrated material from each container.

(8) The statement: "Good patient management requires monitoring treatment responses to Cryoprecipitated AHF transfusions

with periodic plasma factor VIII or fibrinogen assays in hemophilia A and hypofibrinogenemic recipients, respectively."

[50 FR 35470, Aug. 30, 1985, as amended at 53 FR 116, Jan. 5, 1988; 64 FR 45371, Aug. 19, 1999; 77 FR 18, Jan. 3, 2012; 80 FR 29895, May 22, 2015]

Subpart H—Laboratory Controls

§ 606.140 Laboratory controls.

Laboratory control procedures shall include:

(a) The establishment of scientifically sound and appropriate specifications, standards and test procedures to assure that blood and blood components are safe, pure, potent and effective.

(b) Adequate provisions for monitoring the reliability, accuracy, precision and performance of laboratory test procedures and instruments.

(c) Adequate identification and handling of all test samples so that they are accurately related to the specific unit of product being tested, or to its donor, or to the specific recipient, where applicable.

§ 606.145 Control of bacterial contamination of platelets.

(a) Blood collection establishments and transfusion services must assure that the risk of bacterial contamination of platelets is adequately controlled using FDA approved or cleared devices or other adequate and appropriate methods found acceptable for this purpose by FDA.

(b) In the event that a blood collection establishment identifies platelets as bacterially contaminated, that establishment must not release for transfusion the product or any other component prepared from the same collection, and must take appropriate steps to identify the organism.

(c) In the event that a transfusion service identifies platelets as bacterially contaminated, the transfusion service must not release the product and must notify the blood collection establishment that provided the platelets. The transfusion service must take appropriate steps to identify the organism; these steps may include contracting with the collection estab-

lishment or a laboratory to identify the organism. The transfusion service must further notify the blood collection establishment either by providing information about the species of the contaminating organism when the transfusion service has been able to identify it, or by advising the blood collection establishment when the transfusion service has determined that the species cannot be identified.

(d) In the event that a contaminating organism is identified under paragraph (b) or (c) of this section, the collection establishment's responsible physician, as defined in § 630.3(i) of this chapter, must determine whether the contaminating organism is likely to be associated with a bacterial infection that is endogenous to the bloodstream of the donor, in accordance with a standard operating procedure developed under § 606.100(b)(22). This determination may not be further delegated.

[80 FR 29895, May 22, 2015]

§ 606.151 Compatibility testing.

Standard operating procedures for compatibility testing shall include the following:

(a) A method of collecting and identifying the blood samples of recipients to ensure positive identification.

(b) The use of fresh recipient serum or plasma samples less than 3 days old for all pretransfusion testing if the recipient has been pregnant or transfused within the previous 3 months.

(c) Procedures to demonstrate incompatibility between the donor's cell type and the recipient's serum or plasma type.

(d) A provision that, if the unit of donor's blood has not been screened by a method that will demonstrate agglutinating, coating and hemolytic antibodies, the recipient's cells shall be tested with the donor's serum (minor crossmatch) by a method that will so demonstrate.

(e) Procedures to expedite transfusion in life-threatening emergencies. Records of all such incidents shall be maintained, including complete documentation justifying the emergency

55

action, which shall be signed by a physician.

[40 FR 53532, Nov. 18, 1975, as amended at 64 FR 45371, Aug. 19, 1999; 66 FR 1835, Jan. 10, 2001; 66 FR 40889, Aug. 6, 2001]

Subpart I—Records and Reports

§ 606.160 Records.

(a)(1) Records shall be maintained concurrently with the performance of each significant step in the collection, processing, compatibility testing, storage and distribution of each unit of blood and blood components so that all steps can be clearly traced. All records shall be legible and indelible, and shall identify the person performing the work, include dates of the various entries, show test results as well as the interpretation of the results, show the expiration date assigned to specific products, and be as detailed as necessary to provide a complete history of the work performed.

(2) Appropriate records shall be available from which to determine lot numbers of supplies and reagents used for specific lots or units of the final product.

(b) Records shall be maintained that include, but are not limited to, the following when applicable:

(1) Donor records:

(i) Donor selection, including medical interview and examination and where applicable, informed consent.

(ii) Permanent and temporary deferrals for health reasons including reason(s) for deferral.

(iii) Donor adverse reaction complaints and reports, including results of all investigations and followup.

(iv) Therapeutic bleedings, including signed requests from attending physicians, the donor's disease and disposition of units.

(v) Immunization, including informed consent, identification of the antigen, dosage and route of administration.

(vi) Blood collection, including identification of the phlebotomist.

(vii) Records to relate the donor with the unit number of each previous donation from that donor.

(viii) Records concerning the following activities performed under §§ 610.46 and 610.47 of this chapter: Quarantine; consignee notification; testing;

notification of a transfusion recipient, the recipient's physician of record, or the recipient's legal representative; and disposition.

(ix) The donor's postal address provided at the time of donation where the donor may be contacted within 8 weeks after donation.

(x) Records of notification of donors deferred or determined not to be eligible for donation, including appropriate followup if the initial attempt at notification fails, performed under § 630.40 of this chapter.

(xi) Records of notification of the referring physician of a deferred autologous donor, including appropriate followup if the initial attempt at notification fails, performed under § 630.40 of this chapter.

(2) Processing records:

(i) Blood processing, including results and interpretation of all tests and retests.

(ii) Component preparation, including all relevant dates and times.

(iii) Separation and pooling of recovered plasma.

(iv) Centrifugation and pooling of source plasma.

(v) Labeling, including initials of the person(s) performing the procedure.

(3) Storage and distribution records:

(i) Distribution and disposition, as appropriate, of blood and blood products.

(ii) Visual inspection of whole blood and red blood cells during storage and immediately before distribution.

(iii) Storage temperature, including initialed temperature recorder charts.

(iv) Reissue, including records of proper temperature maintenance.

(v) Emergency release of blood, including signature of requesting physician obtained before or after release.

(4) Compatibility test records:

(i) Results of all compatibility tests, including crossmatching, testing of patient samples, antibody screening and identification.

(ii) Results of confirmatory testing.

(5) Quality control records:

(i) Calibration and standardization of equipment.

(ii) Performance checks of equipment and reagents.

(iii) Periodic check on sterile technique.

(iv) Periodic tests of capacity of shipping containers to maintain proper temperature in transit.

(v) Proficiency test results.

(6) Transfusion reaction reports and complaints, including records of investigations and followup.

(7) General records:

(i) Sterilization of supplies and reagents prepared within the facility, including date, time interval, temperature and mode.

(ii) Responsible personnel.

(iii) Biological product deviations.

(iv) Maintenance records for equipment and general physical plant.

(v) Supplies and reagents, including name of manufacturer or supplier, lot numbers, expiration date and date of receipt.

(vi) Disposition of rejected supplies and reagents used in the collection, processing and compatibility testing of blood and blood components.

(c) A donor number shall be assigned to each accepted donor, which relates the unit of blood collected to that donor, to his medical record, to any component or blood product from that donor's unit of blood, and to all records describing the history and ultimate disposition of these products.

(d) Records shall be retained for such interval beyond the expiration date for the blood or blood component as necessary to facilitate the reporting of any unfavorable clinical reactions. You must retain individual product records no less than 10 years after the records of processing are completed or 6 months after the latest expiration date for the individual product, whichever is the later date. When there is no expiration date, records shall be retained indefinitely.

(e) *Records of deferred donors.* (1) Establishments must maintain at each location a record of all donors found to be ineligible or deferred at that location so that blood and blood components from an ineligible donor are not collected and/or released while the donor is ineligible or deferred; and

(2) Establishments must maintain at all locations operating under the same license or under common management a cumulative record of donors deferred from donation under § 610.41 of this chapter because their donation tested

reactive under § 610.40(a)(1) of this chapter for evidence of infection due to HIV, HBV, or HCV. In addition, establishments other than Source Plasma establishments must include in this cumulative record donors deferred from donation under § 610.41 of this chapter because their donation tested reactive under § 610.40(a)(2) of this chapter for evidence of infection due to HTLV or Chagas disease.

(3) The cumulative record described in paragraph (e)(2) of this section must be updated at least monthly to add donors newly deferred under § 610.41 of this chapter due to reactive tests for evidence of infection due to HIV, HBV, or HCV, and, if applicable, HTLV or Chagas disease.

(4) Establishments must revise the cumulative record described in paragraph (e)(2) of this section to remove donors who have been requalified under § 610.41(b) of this chapter.

[40 FR 53532, Nov. 18, 1975, as amended at 61 FR 47422, Sept. 9, 1996; 64 FR 45371, Aug. 19, 1999; 65 FR 66635, Nov. 7, 2000; 66 FR 31176, June 11, 2001; 72 FR 48798, Aug. 24, 2007; 80 FR 80651, Dec. 28, 2015; 80 FR 29895, May 22, 2015]

§ 606.165 **Distribution and receipt; procedures and records.**

(a) Distribution and receipt procedures shall include a system by which the distribution or receipt of each unit can be readily determined to facilitate its recall, if necessary.

(b) Distribution records shall contain information to readily facilitate the identification of the name and address of the consignee, the date and quantity delivered, the lot number of the unit(s), the date of expiration or the date of collection, whichever is applicable, or for crossmatched blood and blood components, the name of the recipient.

(c) Receipt records shall contain the name and address of the collecting facility, date received, donor or lot number assigned by the collecting facility and the date of expiration or the date of collection, whichever is applicable.

§ 606.170 **Adverse reaction file.**

(a) Records shall be maintained of any reports of complaints of adverse reactions regarding each unit of blood or blood product arising as a result of

57

blood collection or transfusion. A thorough investigation of each reported adverse reaction shall be made. A written report of the investigation of adverse reactions, including conclusions and followup, shall be prepared and maintained as part of the record for that lot or unit of final product by the collecting or transfusing facility. When it is determined that the product was at fault in causing a transfusion reaction, copies of all such written reports shall be forwarded to and maintained by the manufacturer or collecting facility.

(b) When a complication of blood collection or transfusion is confirmed to be fatal, the Director, Office of Compliance and Biologics Quality, CBER, must be notified by telephone, facsimile, express mail, or electronically transmitted mail as soon as possible. A written report of the investigation must be submitted to the Director, Office of Compliance and Biologics Quality, CBER, by mail, facsimile, or electronically transmitted mail (for mailing address, see § 600.2(a) of this chapter), within 7 days after the fatality by the collecting facility in the event of a donor reaction, or by the facility that performed the compatibility tests in the event of a transfusion reaction.

[40 FR 53532, Nov. 18, 1975, as amended at 49 FR 23833, June 8, 1984; 50 FR 35471, Aug. 30, 1985; 55 FR 11014, Mar. 26, 1990; 64 FR 45371, Aug. 19, 1999; 67 FR 9586, Mar. 4, 2002; 77 FR 18, Jan. 3, 2012; 80 FR 18092, Apr. 3, 2015]

§ 606.171 Reporting of product deviations by licensed manufacturers, unlicensed registered blood establishments, and transfusion services.

(a) *Who must report under this section?* You, a licensed manufacturer of blood and blood components, including Source Plasma; an unlicensed registered blood establishment; or a transfusion service who had control over the product when the deviation occurred, must report under this section. If you arrange for another person to perform a manufacturing, holding, or distribution step, while the product is in your control, that step is performed under your control. You must establish, maintain, and follow a procedure for receiving information from that person on all deviations, complaints, and adverse events concerning the affected product.

(b) *What do I report under this section?* You must report any event, and information relevant to the event, associated with the manufacturing, to include testing, processing, packing, labeling, or storage, or with the holding or distribution, of both licensed and unlicensed blood or blood components, including Source Plasma, if that event meets all the following criteria:

(1) Either:

(i) Represents a deviation from current good manufacturing practice, applicable regulations, applicable standards, or established specifications that may affect the safety, purity, or potency of that product; or

(ii) Represents an unexpected or unforeseeable event that may affect the safety, purity, or potency of that product; and

(2) Occurs in your facility or another facility under contract with you; and

(3) Involves distributed blood or blood components.

(c) *When do I report under this section?* You should report a biological product deviation as soon as possible but you must report at a date not to exceed 45-calendar days from the date you, your agent, or another person who performs a manufacturing, holding, or distribution step under your control, acquire information reasonably suggesting that a reportable event has occurred.

(d) *How do I report under this section?* You must report on Form FDA-3486.

(e) *Where do I report under this section?* You must send the completed Form FDA 3486 to the Center for Biologics Evaluation and Research (CBER), either in paper or electronic format.

(1) If you make a paper filing, send the completed form to the CBER Document Control Center (see mailing address in § 600.2(a) of this chapter), and identify on the envelope that a BPDR (biological product deviation report) is enclosed; or

(2) If you make an electronic filing, send the completed Form FDA3486 electronically using CBER's electronic Web-based application.

(f) *How does this regulation affect other FDA regulations?* This part supplements and does not supersede other provisions of the regulations in this chapter. All biological product deviations, whether or not they are required to be reported under this section, should be investigated in accordance with the applicable provisions of parts 211, 606, and 820 of this chapter.

[65 FR 66635, Nov. 7, 2000, as amended at 70 FR 14984, Mar. 24, 2005; 80 FR 18092, Apr. 3, 2015]

PART 607—ESTABLISHMENT REGISTRATION AND PRODUCT LISTING FOR MANUFACTURERS OF HUMAN BLOOD AND BLOOD PRODUCTS AND LICENSED DEVICES

Subpart A—General Provisions

Sec.
607.1　Scope.
607.3　Definitions.
607.7　Establishment registration and product listing of blood banks and other firms manufacturing human blood and blood products.

Subpart B—Procedures for Domestic Blood Product Establishments

607.20　Who must register and submit a blood product list.
607.21　Times for establishment registration and blood product listing.
607.22　How to register establishments and list blood products.
607.25　Information required for establishment registration and blood product listing.
607.26　Amendments to establishment registration.
607.30　Updating blood product listing information.
607.31　Additional blood product listing information.
607.35　Blood product establishment registration number.
607.37　Public disclosure of establishment registration and blood product listing information.
607.39　Misbranding by reference to establishment registration, validation of registration, or to registration number.

Subpart C—Procedures for Foreign Blood Product Establishments

607.40　Establishment registration and blood product listing requirements for foreign blood product establishments.

Subpart D—Exemptions

607.65　Exemptions for blood product establishments.

Subpart E—Establishment Registration and Product Listing Of Licensed Devices

607.80　Applicability of part 607 to licensed devices.

AUTHORITY: 21 U.S.C. 321, 331, 351, 352, 355, 360, 371, 374, 381, 393; 42 U.S.C. 262, 264, 271.

SOURCE: 40 FR 52788, Nov. 12, 1975, unless otherwise noted.

Subpart A—General Provisions

§ 607.1　Scope.

(a) This part establishes establishment registration and product listing requirements for manufacturers of human blood and blood products.

(b) This part establishes establishment registration and product listing requirements for manufacturers of products that meet the definition of a device under the Federal Food, Drug, and Cosmetic Act and that are licensed under section 351 of the Public Health Service Act, as well as licensed biological products used in the manufacture of a licensed device.

[81 FR 60221, Aug. 31, 2016]

§ 607.3　Definitions.

(a) The term *act* means the Federal Food, Drug, and Cosmetic Act approved June 25, 1938 (52 Stat. 1040 *et seq.*, as amended, 21 U.S.C. 301–392).

(b) *Blood and blood product* means a drug which consists of human whole blood, plasma, or serum or any product derived from human whole blood, plasma, or serum, hereinafter referred to as "blood product." For the purposes of this part only, blood and blood product also means those products that meet the definition of a device under the Federal Food, Drug, and Cosmetic Act and that are licensed under section 351 of the Public Health Service Act, as well as licensed biological products used in the manufacture of a licensed device.

(c) *Establishment* means a place of business under one management at one general physical location. The term includes, among others, human blood and plasma donor centers, blood banks, transfusion services, other blood product manufacturers and independent laboratories that engage in quality control and testing for registered blood product establishments.

(d) *Manufacture* means the collection, preparation, processing or compatibility testing by chemical, physical, biological, or other procedures of any blood product which meets the definition of a drug as defined in section 201(g) of the act, and including manipulation, sampling, testing, or control procedures applied to the final product or to any part of the process. The term includes packaging, labeling, repackaging or otherwise changing the container, wrapper, or labeling of any blood product package in furtherance of the distribution of the blood product from the original place of manufacture to the person who makes final delivery or sale to the ultimate consumer.

(e) *Commercial distribution* means any distribution of a blood product except under the investigational use provisions of part 312 of this chapter, but does not include internal or interplant transfer of a bulk product substance between registered establishments within the same parent, subsidiary, and/or affiliate company. For foreign establishments, the term "commercial distribution" shall have the same meaning except that the term shall not include distribution of any blood or blood product that is neither imported nor offered for import into the United States.

(f) *Any material change* includes but is not limited to any change in the name of the blood product, in the quantity or identity of the active ingredient(s) or in the quantity or identity of the inactive ingredient(s) where quantitative listing of all ingredients is required pursuant to § 607.31(a)(2) and any significant change in the labeling of a blood product. Changes that are not significant include changes in arrangement or printing or changes of an editorial nature.

(g) *Bulk product substance* means any substance that is represented for use in a blood product and when used in the manufacturing of a blood product becomes an active ingredient or a finished dosage form of such product.

(h) *Advertising* and *labeling* include the promotional material described in § 202.1(l) (1) and (2) of this chapter, respectively.

(i) The definitions and interpretations contained in sections 201 and 510 of the act shall be applicable to such terms when used in this part 607.

(j) *United States* agent means a person residing or maintaining a place of business in the United States whom a foreign establishment designates as its agent. This definition excludes mailboxes, answering machines or services, or other places where an individual acting as the foreign establishment's agent is not physically present.

(k) *Importer* means a person in the United States that is an owner, consignee, or recipient, at the time of entry, of a foreign establishment's blood product that is imported into the United States.

(l) *Foreign* for the purpose of registration and listing under this part when used to modify the term "establishment" refers to an establishment that is located in a foreign country and is the site where a blood product that is imported or offered for import into United States was manufactured.

[40 FR 52788, Nov. 12, 1975, as amended at 55 FR 11014, Mar. 26, 1990; 66 FR 59158, Nov. 27, 2001; 81 FR 60222, Aug. 31, 2016]

§ 607.7 Establishment registration and product listing of blood banks and other firms manufacturing human blood and blood products.

All owners or operators of establishments that engage in the manufacturing of blood products are required to register, pursuant to section 510 of the Federal Food, Drug, and Cosmetic Act. Registration and listing of blood products must comply with this part. Registration does not permit any blood bank or similar establishment to ship blood products in interstate commerce.

[81 FR 60222, Aug. 31, 2016]

Subpart B—Procedures for Domestic Blood Product Establishments

§ 607.20 Who must register and submit a blood product list.

(a) Owners or operators of all establishments, not exempt under section 510(g) of the act or subpart D of this part, that engage in the manufacture of blood products shall register and submit a list of every blood product in commercial distribution (except that registration and listing information may be submitted by the parent, subsidiary, and/or affiliate company for all establishments when operations are conducted at more than one establishment and there exists joint ownership and control among all the establishments). Blood products manufactured, prepared, propagated, compounded, or processed in any State as defined in section 201(a)(1) of the act must be listed whether or not the output of such blood product establishment or any particular blood product so listed enters interstate commerce.

(b) Preparatory to engaging in the manufacture of blood products, owners or operators of establishments who are submitting a biologics license application to manufacture blood products are required to register before the biologics license application is approved.

(c) Except in the case of licensed device manufacturers, no registration fee is required. Establishment registration and blood product listing do not constitute an admission or agreement or determination that a blood product is a "drug" within the meaning of section 201(g) of the act.

[40 FR 52788, Nov. 12, 1975, as amended at 64 FR 56452, Oct. 20, 1999; 66 FR 59158, Nov. 27, 2001; 81 FR 60222, Aug. 31, 2016]

§ 607.21 Times for establishment registration and blood product listing.

The owner or operator of an establishment entering into an operation defined in § 607.3(d) shall register such establishment within 5 days after the beginning of such operation and submit a list of every blood product in commercial distribution at the time. If the owner or operator of the establishment has not previously entered into such operation (defined in § 607.3(d) of this chapter) for which a license is required, registration shall follow within 5 days after the submission of a biologics license application in order to manufacture blood products. Owners or operators of all establishments so engaged must register annually between October 1 and December 31 and must update their blood product listing every June and December.

[40 FR 52788, Nov. 12, 1975, as amended at 64 FR 56453, Oct. 20, 1999; 81 FR 60222, Aug. 31, 2016]

§ 607.22 How to register establishments and list blood products.

(a) Initial and subsequent registrations and product listings must be submitted electronically through the Blood Establishment Registration and Product Listing system, or any future superseding electronic system. This information must be submitted in accordance with part 11 of this chapter, except for the requirements in § 11.10(b), (c), and (e), and the corresponding requirements in § 11.30. All information submitted under this part must be transmitted to FDA electronically unless FDA has granted a request for waiver of this requirement prior to the date on which the information is due. Submission of a request for waiver does not excuse timely compliance with the registration and listing requirements. FDA will grant a waiver request if FDA determines that the use of electronic means for submission of registration and listing information is not reasonable for the registrant making the waiver request.

(b) Waiver requests under this section must be submitted in writing and must include the specific reasons why electronic submission is not reasonable for the registrant and a U.S. telephone number and mailing address where FDA can contact the registrant. All waiver requests must be sent to the Director of FDA's Center for Biologics Evaluation and Research through the Document Control Center (see addresses in § 600.2).

(c) If FDA grants the waiver request, FDA may limit its duration and will specify terms of the waiver and provide information on how to submit establishment registration, drug listings, other information, and updates, as applicable.

[81 FR 60222, Aug. 31, 2016]

§ 607.25 Information required for establishment registration and blood product listing.

(a) The Blood Establishment Registration and Product Listing system requires furnishing or confirming registration information required by the Federal Food, Drug, and Cosmetic Act. This information includes the name and street address of the establishment, including post office code; a registration number if previously assigned by FDA and a Unique Facility Identifier in accordance with the system specified under section 510 of the Federal Food, Drug, and Cosmetic Act; all trade names used by the establishment; the kind of ownership or operation (that is, individually owned partnership, or corporation); and the name of the owner or operator of such establishment. The term "name of the owner or operator" must include, in the case of a partnership, the name of each partner and, in the case of a corporation, the name and title of each corporate officer and director and the name of the State of incorporation. The information required must be given separately for each establishment, as defined in § 607.3(c).

(b) The following information must also be provided:

(1) A list of blood products by established name as defined in section 502(e) of the Federal Food, Drug, and Cosmetic Act and by proprietary name, if any, which are being manufactured for commercial distribution at the identified establishment and which have not been included in any list previously submitted to FDA through the Blood Establishment Registration and Product Listing system or any future superseding electronic system.

(2) For each blood product so listed that is subject to section 351 of the Public Health Service Act, the license number of the manufacturer issued by the Center for Biologics Evaluation and Research, Food and Drug Administration.

(3) For each blood product listed, the registration number if previously assigned by FDA and the Unique Facility

Identifier of the parent establishment. An establishment not owned, operated, or controlled by another firm or establishment is its own parent establishment.

[81 FR 60222, Aug. 31, 2016]

§ 607.26 Amendments to establishment registration.

Changes in individual ownership, corporate or partnership structure, location, or blood product handling activity must be made electronically through the Blood Establishment Registration and Product Listing system, or any future superseding electronic system, as an amendment to registration within 5 calendar days of such changes. Changes in the names of officers and directors of the corporations do not require such amendment but must be shown at time of annual registration.

[40 FR 52788, Nov. 12, 1975, as amended at 66 FR 59158, Nov. 27, 2001; 81 FR 60222, Aug. 31, 2016]

§ 607.30 Updating blood product listing information.

(a) After submission of the initial blood product listing information, every person who is required to list blood products under § 607.20 must submit electronically through the Blood Establishment Registration and Product Listing system, or any future superseding electronic system, at a minimum once in June and December of every year, the following information:

(1) A list of each blood product introduced by the registrant for commercial distribution which has not been included in any list previously submitted. All of the information required by § 607.25(b) shall be provided for each such blood product.

(2) A list of each blood product formerly listed pursuant to § 607.25(b) for which commercial distribution has been discontinued, including for each blood product so listed the identity by established name and proprietary name, and date of discontinuance. It is requested but not required that the reason for discontinuance of distribution be included with this information.

(3) A list of each blood product for which a notice of discontinuance was submitted pursuant to paragraph (a)(2)

of this section and for which commercial distribution has been resumed, including for each blood product so listed the identity by established name as defined in section 502(e) of the act and by any proprietary name, the date of resumption, and any other information required by §607.25(b) not previously submitted.

(4) Any material change in any information previously submitted.

(b) When no changes have occurred since the previously submitted list, no listing information is required.

[40 FR 52788, Nov. 12, 1975, as amended at 81 FR 60222, Aug. 31, 2016]

§607.31 Additional blood product listing information.

(a) In addition to the information routinely required by §§607.25 and 607.30, the Director of the Center for Biologics Evaluation and Research may require submission of the following information by letter or by FEDERAL REGISTER notice:

(1) For a particular blood product so listed, upon request made by the Director of the Center for Biologics Evaluation and Research for good cause, a copy of all advertisements.

(2) For a particular blood product so listed, upon a finding by the Director of the Center for Biologics Evaluation and Research that it is necessary to carry out the purposes of the act, a quantitative listing of all ingredients.

(3) For each registrant, upon a finding by the Director of the Center for Biologics Evaluation and Research that it is necessary to carry out the purposes of the act, a list of each listed blood product containing a particular ingredient.

(b) [Reserved]

[66 FR 59158, Nov. 27, 2001]

§607.35 Blood product establishment registration number.

An establishment registration number will be assigned to each blood product establishment registered in accordance with this part.

[81 FR 60223, Aug. 31, 2016]

§607.37 Public disclosure of establishment registration and blood product listing information.

(a) Except as provided in paragraph (b) of this section, all registration and listing information obtained under §§607.25, 607.26, and 607.30 will be made available for public disclosure through the Center for Biologics Evaluation and Research (CBER) Blood Establishment Registration Database Web site by using the CBER electronic Web-based application or by going in person to the Food and Drug Administration, Division of Freedom of Information Public Reading Room (see addresses in §20.120(a) of this chapter).

(b) FDA may find, in limited circumstances and on a case-by-case basis, that it would be consistent with the protection of the public health to exempt from public disclosure specific listing information obtained under §607.25 or §607.30.

(c) Other requests for information regarding blood establishment registrations and blood product listings should be directed to the Food and Drug Administration, Center for Biologics Evaluation and Research Office of Communication, Outreach, and Development, 10903 New Hampshire Ave., Bldg. 71, Rm. 3103, Silver Spring, MD 20993–0002.

[81 FR 60223, Aug. 31, 2016]

§607.39 Misbranding by reference to establishment registration, validation of registration, or to registration number.

Registration of an establishment, validation of registration, or assignment of a registration number does not in any way denote approval of the firm or its products nor does it mean that the products may be legally marketed. Any representation that creates an impression of official approval because of establishment registration, validation of registration, or possession of a registration number is misleading and constitutes misbranding.

[81 FR 60223, Aug. 31, 2016]

Subpart C—Procedures for Foreign Blood Product Establishments

§ 607.40 Establishment registration and blood product listing requirements for foreign blood product establishments.

(a) Every foreign establishment shall comply with the establishment registration and blood product listing requirements contained in subpart B of this part, unless exempt under subpart D of this part or unless the blood product enters a foreign trade zone and is re-exported from that foreign trade zone without having entered U. S. commerce.

(b) No blood product may be imported or offered for import into the United States unless it is the subject of a blood product listing as required under subpart B of this part and is manufactured, prepared, propagated, compounded, or processed at a registered foreign establishment; however, this restriction does not apply to a blood product imported or offered for import under the investigational use provisions of part 312 of this chapter or to a blood product imported under section 801(d)(4) of the act. The establishment registration and blood product listing information shall be in the English language.

(c) Each foreign establishment required to register under paragraph (a) of this section shall, as part of the establishment registration and blood product listing, submit the name and address of the establishment and the name of the individual responsible for submitting establishment registration and blood product listing information. Any changes in this information shall be reported to the Food and Drug Administration at the intervals specified for updating establishment registration information in § 607.26 and blood product listing information in § 607.30(a).

(d) Each foreign establishment required to register under paragraph (a) of this section must submit the name, address, telephone number, and email address of its United States agent as part of its initial and updated registration information in accordance with subpart B of this part. Each foreign establishment must designate only one United States agent.

(1) The United States agent shall reside or maintain a place of business in the United States.

(2) Upon request from FDA, the United States agent shall assist FDA in communications with the foreign establishment, respond to questions concerning the foreign establishment's products that are imported or offered for import into the United States, and assist FDA in scheduling inspections of the foreign establishment. If the agency is unable to contact the foreign establishment directly or expeditiously, FDA may provide information or documents to the United States agent, and such an action shall be considered to be equivalent to providing the same information or documents to the foreign establishment.

(3) The foreign establishment or the United States agent must report changes in the United States agent's name, address, telephone number, or email address to FDA within 30 calendar days of the change.

(e) Each foreign establishment required to register under paragraph (a) of this section must register and list blood products using the Blood Establishment Registration and Product Listing system, or any superseding electronic system, unless FDA waives the electronic submission requirement in accordance with § 607.22.

[66 FR 59159, Nov. 27, 2001, as amended at 81 FR 60223, Aug. 31, 2016]

Subpart D—Exemptions

§ 607.65 Exemptions for blood product establishments.

The following classes of persons are exempt from registration and blood product listing in accordance with this part 607 under the provisions of section 510(g)(1), (g)(2), and (g)(3) of the act, or because the Commissioner of Food and Drugs has found, under section 510(g)(5), that such registration is not necessary for the protection of the public health. The exemptions in paragraphs (a), (b), (f), and (g) of this section are limited to those classes of persons located in any State as defined in section 201(a)(1) of the act.

(a) Pharmacies that are operating under applicable local laws regulating dispensing of prescription drugs and that are not manufacturing blood products for sale other than in the regular course of the practice of the profession of pharmacy including the business of dispensing and selling blood products at retail. The supplying by such pharmacies of blood products to a practitioner licensed to administer such blood products for his use in the course of his professional practice or to other pharmacies to meet temporary inventory shortages are not acts which require such pharmacies to register.

(b) Practitioners who are licensed by law to prescribe or administer drugs and who manufacture blood products solely for use in the course of their professional practice.

(c) Persons who manufacture blood products which are not for sale, rather, are solely for use in research, teaching, or analysis, including laboratory samples.

(d) Carriers, by reason of their receipt, carriage, holding, or delivery of blood products in the usual course of business as carriers.

(e) Persons who engage solely in the manufacture of in vitro diagnostic blood products and reagents not subject to licensing under section 351 of the Public Health Service Act (42 U.S.C. 262). This paragraph does not exempt such persons from registration and listing for medical devices required under part 807 of this chapter.

(f) Transfusion services which are a part of a facility that is certified under the Clinical Laboratory Improvement Amendments of 1988 (42 U.S.C. 263a) and 42 CFR part 493 or has met equivalent requirements as determined by the Centers for Medicare and Medicaid Services and which are engaged in the compatibility testing and transfusion of blood and blood components, but which neither routinely collect nor process blood and blood components. The collection and processing of blood and blood components in an emergency situation as determined by a responsible person and documented in writing, therapeutic collection of blood or plasma, the preparation of recovered human plasma for further manufacturing use, or preparation of red blood cells for transfusion are not acts requiring such transfusion services to register.

(g) Persons who engage solely in the production of any plasma derivative, including, but not limited to, albumin, Immune Globulin, Factor VIII and Factor IX, bulk product substances such as fractionation intermediates or pastes, or recombinant versions of plasma derivatives or animal derived plasma derivatives. These persons must register and list under part 207 of this chapter.

[40 FR 52788, Nov. 12, 1975, as amended at 43 FR 37997, Aug. 25, 1978; 45 FR 85729, Dec. 30, 1980; 49 FR 34449, Aug. 31, 1984; 66 FR 31162, June 11, 2001; 66 FR 59159, Nov. 27, 2001; 72 FR 45886, Aug. 16, 2007; 81 FR 60223, Aug. 31, 2016]

Subpart E—Establishment Registration and Product Listing Of Licensed Devices

§ 607.80 Applicability of part 607 to licensed devices.

Manufacturers of products that meet the definition of a device under the Federal Food, Drug, and Cosmetic Act and that are licensed under section 351 of the Public Health Service Act, as well as licensed biological products used in the manufacture of a licensed device, must register and list following the procedures under this part, with respect to their manufacture of those products, unless otherwise noted in this section.

[81 FR 60223, Aug. 31, 2016]

PART 610—GENERAL BIOLOGICAL PRODUCTS STANDARDS

Subpart A—Release Requirements

AUTHORITY: 21 U.S.C. 321, 331, 351, 352, 353, 355, 360, 360c, 360d, 360h, 360i, 371, 372, 374, 381; 42 U.S.C. 216, 262, 263, 263a, 264.

SOURCE: 38 FR 32056, Nov. 20, 1973, unless otherwise noted.

CROSS REFERENCES: For U.S. Customs Service regulations relating to viruses, serums, and toxins, see 19 CFR 12.21–12.23. For U.S. Postal Service regulations relating to the admissibility to the United States mails see parts 124 and 125 of the Domestic Mail Manual, that is incorporated by reference in 39 CFR part 111.

Subpart A—Release Requirements

§ 610.1   Tests prior to release required for each lot.

No lot of any licensed product shall be released by the manufacturer prior to the completion of tests for conformity with standards applicable to such product. Each applicable test shall be made on each lot after completion of all processes of manufacture which may affect compliance with the standard to which the test applies. The results of all tests performed shall be considered in determining whether or not the test results meet the test objective, except that a test result may be disregarded when it is established that the test is invalid due to causes unrelated to the product.

§ 610.2   Requests for samples and protocols; official release.

(a) *Licensed biological products regulated by CBER.* Samples of any lot of any licensed product together with the protocols showing results of applicable tests, may at any time be required to be sent to the Director, Center for Biologics Evaluation and Research (see mailing addresses in § 600.2(c) of this chapter). Upon notification by the Director, Center for Biologics Evaluation and Research, a manufacturer shall not distribute a lot of a product until the lot is released by the Director, Center for Biologics Evaluation and Research: *Provided,* That the Director, Center for Biologics Evaluation and Research, shall not issue such notification except when deemed necessary for the safety, purity, or potency of the product.

(b) *Licensed biological products regulated by CDER.* Samples of any lot of any licensed product together with the protocols showing results of applicable tests, may at any time be required to be sent to the Director, Center for Drug Evaluation and Research (see mailing addresses in § 600.2(c) of this chapter) for official release. Upon notification by the Director, Center for Drug Evaluation and Research, a manufacturer shall not distribute a lot of a biological product until the lot is released by the Director, Center for Drug Evaluation and Research: *Provided,* That the Director, Center for Drug Evaluation and Research shall not issue such notification except when deemed necessary for the safety, purity, or potency of the product.

[40 FR 31313, July 25, 1975, as amended at 49 FR 23834, June 8, 1984; 50 FR 10941, Mar. 19, 1985; 55 FR 11013, 11014, Mar. 26, 1990; 67 FR 9587, Mar. 4, 2002; 70 FR 14984, Mar. 24, 2005; 80 FR 18093, Apr. 3, 2015]

Subpart B—General Provisions

§610.9 Equivalent methods and processes.

Modification of any particular test method or manufacturing process or the conditions under which it is conducted as required in this part or in the additional standards for specific biological products in parts 620 through 680 of this chapter shall be permitted only under the following conditions:

(a) The applicant presents evidence, in the form of a license application, or a supplement to the application submitted in accordance with §601.12(b) or (c), demonstrating that the modification will provide assurances of the safety, purity, potency, and effectiveness of the biological product equal to or greater than the assurances provided by the method or process specified in the general standards or additional standards for the biological product; and

(b) Approval of the modification is received in writing from the Director, Center for Biologics Evaluation and Research or the Director, Center for Drug Evaluation and Research.

[62 FR 39903, July 24, 1997, as amended at 70 FR 14984, Mar. 24, 2005]

§610.10 Potency.

Tests for potency shall consist of either in vitro or in vivo tests, or both, which have been specifically designed for each product so as to indicate its potency in a manner adequate to satisfy the interpretation of potency given by the definition in §600.3(s) of this chapter.

§610.11–610.11a [Reserved]

§610.12 Sterility.

(a) *The test.* Except as provided in paragraph (h) of this section, manufacturers of biological products must perform sterility testing of each lot of each biological product's final container material or other material, as appropriate and as approved in the biologics license application or supplement for that product.

(b) *Test requirements.* (1) The sterility test must be appropriate to the material being tested such that the material

does not interfere with or otherwise hinder the test.

(2) The sterility test must be validated to demonstrate that the test is capable of reliably and consistently detecting the presence of viable contaminating microorganisms.

(3) The sterility test and test components must be verified to demonstrate that the test method can consistently detect the presence of viable contaminating microorganisms.

(c) *Written procedures.* Manufacturers must establish, implement, and follow written procedures for sterility testing that describe, at a minimum, the following:

(1) The sterility test method to be used;

(i) If culture-based test methods are used, include, at a minimum:

(A) Composition of the culture media;

(B) Growth-promotion test requirements; and

(C) Incubation conditions (time and temperature).

(ii) If non-culture-based test methods are used, include, at a minimum:

(A) Composition of test components;

(B) Test parameters, including acceptance criteria; and

(C) Controls used to verify the method's ability to detect the presence of viable contaminating microorganisms.

(2) The method of sampling, including the number, volume, and size of articles to be tested;

(3) Written specifications for the acceptance or rejection of each lot; and

(4) A statement of any other function critical to the particular sterility test method to ensure consistent and accurate results.

(d) *The sample.* The sample must be appropriate to the material being tested, considering, at a minimum:

(1) The size and volume of the final product lot;

(2) The duration of manufacturing of the drug product;

(3) The final container configuration and size;

(4) The quantity or concentration of inhibitors, neutralizers, and preservatives, if present, in the tested material;

67

(5) For a culture-based test method, the volume of test material that results in a dilution of the product that is not bacteriostatic or fungistatic; and

(6) For a non-culture-based test method, the volume of test material that results in a dilution of the product that does not inhibit or otherwise hinder the detection of viable contaminating microorganisms.

(e) *Verification.* (1) For culture-based test methods, studies must be conducted to demonstrate that the performance of the test organisms and culture media are suitable to consistently detect the presence of viable contaminating microorganisms, including tests for each lot of culture media to verify its growth-promoting properties over the shelf-life of the media.

(2) For non-culture-based test methods, within the test itself, appropriate controls must be used to demonstrate the ability of the test method to continue to consistently detect the presence of viable contaminating microorganisms.

(f) *Repeat test procedures.* (1) If the initial test indicates the presence of microorganisms, the product does not comply with the sterility test requirements unless a thorough investigation by the quality control unit can ascribe definitively the microbial presence to a laboratory error or faulty materials used in conducting the sterility testing.

(2) If the investigation described in paragraph (f)(1) of this section finds that the initial test indicated the presence of microorganisms due to laboratory error or the use of faulty materials, a sterility test may be repeated one time. If no evidence of microorganisms is found in the repeat test, the product examined complies with the sterility test requirements. If evidence of microorganisms is found in the repeat test, the product examined does not comply with the sterility test requirements.

(3) If a repeat test is conducted, the same test method must be used for both the initial and repeat tests, and the repeat test must be conducted with comparable product that is reflective of the initial sample in terms of sample location and the stage in the manufac-

turing process from which it was obtained.

(g) *Records.* The records related to the test requirements of this section must be prepared and maintained as required by §§ 211.167 and 211.194 of this chapter.

(h) *Exceptions.* Sterility testing must be performed on final container material or other appropriate material as defined in the approved biologics license application or supplement and as described in this section, except as follows:

(1) This section does not require sterility testing for Whole Blood, Cryoprecipitated Antihemophilic Factor, Platelets, Red Blood Cells, Plasma, Source Plasma, Smallpox Vaccine, Reagent Red Blood Cells, Anti-Human Globulin, and Blood Grouping Reagents.

(2) A manufacturer is not required to comply with the sterility test requirements if the Director of the Center for Biologics Evaluation and Research or the Director of the Center for Drug Evaluation and Research, as appropriate, determines that data submitted in the biologics license application or supplement adequately establish that the route of administration, the method of preparation, or any other aspect of the product precludes or does not necessitate a sterility test to assure safety, purity, and potency of the product.

[77 FR 26174, May 3, 2012]

§ 610.13   Purity.

Products shall be free of extraneous material except that which is unavoidable in the manufacturing process described in the approved biologics license application. In addition, products shall be tested as provided in paragraphs (a) and (b) of this section.

(a)(1) *Test for residual moisture.* Each lot of dried product shall be tested for residual moisture and shall meet and not exceed established limits as specified by an approved method on file in the biologics license application. The test for residual moisture may be exempted by the Director, Center for Biologics Evaluation and Research or the Director, Center for Drug Evaluation and Research, when deemed not necessary for the continued safety, purity, and potency of the product.

(2) *Records.* Appropriate records for residual moisture under paragraph (a)(1) of this section shall be prepared and maintained as required by the applicable provisions of §§ 211.188 and 211.194 of this chapter.

(b) *Test for pyrogenic substances.* Each lot of final containers of any product intended for use by injection shall be tested for pyrogenic substances by intravenous injection into rabbits as provided in paragraphs (b) (1) and (2) of this section: *Provided,* That notwithstanding any other provision of Subchapter F of this chapter, the test for pyrogenic substances is not required for the following products: Products containing formed blood elements; Cryoprecipitate; Plasma; Source Plasma; Normal Horse Serum; bacterial, viral, and rickettsial vaccines and antigens; toxoids; toxins; allergenic extracts; venoms; diagnostic substances and trivalent organic arsenicals.

(1) *Test dose.* The test dose for each rabbit shall be at least 3 milliliters per kilogram of body weight of the rabbit and also shall be at least equivalent proportionately, on a body weight basis, to the maximum single human dose recommended, but need not exceed 10 milliliters per kilogram of body weight of the rabbit, except that: (i) Regardless of the human dose recommended, the test dose per kilogram of body weight of each rabbit shall be at least 1 milliliter for immune globulins derived from human blood; (ii) for Streptokinase, the test dose shall be at least equivalent proportionately, on a body weight basis, to the maximum single human dose recommended.

(2) *Test procedure, results, and interpretation; standards to be met.* The test for pyrogenic substances shall be performed according to the requirements specified in United States Pharmacopeia XX.

(3) *Retest.* If the lot fails to meet the test requirements prescribed in paragraph (b)(2) of this section, the test may be repeated once using five other rabbits. The temperature rises recorded for all eight rabbits used in testing shall be included in determining

whether the requirements are met. The lot meets the requirements for absence of pyrogens if not more than three of the eight rabbits show individual rises in temperature of 0.6 °C or more, and if the sum of the eight individual maximum temperature rises does not exceed 3.7 °C.

[38 FR 32056, Nov. 20, 1973, as amended at 40 FR 29710, July 15, 1975; 41 FR 10429, Mar. 11, 1976; 41 FR 41424, Sept. 22, 1976; 44 FR 40289, July 10, 1979; 46 FR 62845, Dec. 29, 1981; 49 FR 15187, Apr. 18, 1984; 50 FR 4134, Jan. 29, 1985; 55 FR 28381, July 11, 1990; 64 FR 56453, Oct. 20, 1999; 67 FR 9587, Mar. 4, 2002; 70 FR 14985, Mar. 24, 2005]

§ 610.14   Identity.

The contents of a final container of each filling of each lot shall be tested for identity after all labeling operations shall have been completed. The identity test shall be specific for each product in a manner that will adequately identify it as the product designated on final container and package labels and circulars, and distinguish it from any other product being processed in the same laboratory. Identity may be established either through the physical or chemical characteristics of the product, inspection by macroscopic or microscopic methods, specific cultural tests, or in vitro or in vivo immunological tests.

§ 610.15   Constituent materials.

(a) *Ingredients, preservatives, diluents, adjuvants.* All ingredients used in a licensed product, and any diluent provided as an aid in the administration of the product, shall meet generally accepted standards of purity and quality. Any preservative used shall be sufficiently nontoxic so that the amount present in the recommended dose of the product will not be toxic to the recipient, and in the combination used it shall not denature the specific substances in the product to result in a decrease below the minimum acceptable potency within the dating period when stored at the recommended temperature. Products in multiple-dose containers shall contain a preservative, except that a preservative need not be added to Yellow Fever Vaccine; Poliovirus Vaccine Live Oral; viral vaccines labeled for use with the jet injector;

dried vaccines when the accompanying diluent contains a preservative; or to an Allergenic Product in 50 percent or more volume in volume (v/v) glycerin. An adjuvant shall not be introduced into a product unless there is satisfactory evidence that it does not affect adversely the safety or potency of the product. The amount of aluminum in the recommended individual dose of a biological product shall not exceed:

(1) 0.85 milligrams if determined by assay;

(2) 1.14 milligrams if determined by calculation on the basis of the amount of aluminum compound added; or

(3) 1.25 milligrams determined by assay provided that data demonstrating that the amount of aluminum used is safe and necessary to produce the intended effect are submitted to and approved by the Director, Center for Biologics Evaluation and Research or the Director, Center for Drug Evaluation and Research (see mailing addresses in § 600.2(a) or (b) of this chapter).

(b) *Extraneous protein; cell culture produced vaccines.* Extraneous protein known to be capable of producing allergenic effects in human subjects shall not be added to a final virus medium of cell culture produced vaccines intended for injection. If serum is used at any stage, its calculated concentration in the final medium shall not exceed 1:1,000,000.

(c) *Antibiotics.* A minimum concentration of antibiotics, other than penicillin, may be added to the production substrate of viral vaccines.

(d) The Director of the Center for Biologics Evaluation and Research or the Director of the Center for Drug Evaluation and Research may approve an exception or alternative to any requirement in this section. Requests for such exceptions or alternatives must be in writing.

[38 FR 32056, Nov. 20, 1973, as amended at 46 FR 51903, Oct. 23, 1981; 48 FR 13025, Mar. 29, 1983; 48 FR 37023, Aug. 16, 1983; 49 FR 23834, June 8, 1984; 50 FR 4134, Jan. 29, 1985; 51 FR 15607, Apr. 25, 1986; 55 FR 11013, Mar. 26, 1990; 70 FR 14985, Mar. 24, 2005; 76 FR 20518, Apr. 13, 2011; 80 FR 18093, Apr. 3, 2015]

§ 610.16 Total solids in serums.

Except as otherwise provided by regulation, no liquid serum or antitoxin shall contain more than 20 percent total solids.

§ 610.17 Permissible combinations.

Licensed products may not be combined with other licensed products either therapeutic, prophylactic or diagnostic, except as a license is obtained for the combined product. Licensed products may not be combined with nonlicensable therapeutic, prophylactic, or diagnostic substances except as a license is obtained for such combination.

§ 610.18 Cultures.

(a) *Storage and maintenance.* Cultures used in the manufacture of products shall be stored in a secure and orderly manner, at a temperature and by a method that will retain the initial characteristics of the organisms and insure freedom from contamination and deterioration.

(b) *Identity and verification.* Each culture shall be clearly identified as to source strain. A complete identification of the strain shall be made for each new stock culture preparation. Primary and subsequent seed lots shall be identified by lot number and date of preparation. Periodic tests shall be performed as often as necessary to verify the integrity of the strain characteristics and freedom from extraneous organisms. Results of all periodic tests for verification of cultures and determination of freedom from extraneous organisms shall be recorded and retained.

(c) *Cell lines used for manufacturing biological products*—(1) *General requirements.* Cell lines used for manufacturing biological products shall be:

(i) Identified by history;

(ii) Described with respect to cytogenetic characteristics and tumorigenicity;

(iii) Characterized with respect to in vitro growth characteristics and life potential; and

(iv) Tested for the presence of detectable microbial agents.

(2) *Tests.* Tests that are necessary to assure the safety, purity, and potency of a product may be required by the Director, Center for Biologics Evaluation

and Research or the Director, Center for Drug Evaluation and Research.

(3) *Applicability.* This paragraph applies to diploid and nondiploid cell lines. Primary cell cultures that are not subcultivated and primary cell cultures that are subsequently subcultivated for only a very limited number of population doublings are not subject to the provisions of this paragraph (c).

(d) *Records.* The records appropriate for cultures under this section shall be prepared and maintained as required by the applicable provisions of §§211.188 and 211.194 of this chapter.

[38 FR 32056, Nov. 20, 1973, as amended at 51 FR 44453, Dec. 10, 1986; 55 FR 11013, Mar. 26, 1990; 67 FR 9587, Mar. 4, 2002; 70 FR 14985, Mar. 24, 2005]

Subparts C—D [Reserved]

Subpart E—Testing Requirements for Relevant Transfusion-Transmitted Infections

§610.39 Definitions.

The definitions set out in §630.3 of this chapter apply to this subpart.

[80 FR 29896, May 22, 2015]

§610.40 Test requirements.

(a) *Human blood and blood components.* Except as specified in paragraphs (c) and (d) of this section, you, an establishment that collects blood and blood components for transfusion or for use in manufacturing a product, including donations intended as a component of, or used to manufacture, a medical device, must comply with the following requirements:

(1) Test each donation for evidence of infection due to the relevant transfusion-transmitted infections described in §630.3(h)(1)(i) through (iii) of this chapter (HIV, HBV, and HCV).

(2) Test each donation for evidence of infection due to the relevant transfusion-transmitted infections described in §630.3(h)(1)(iv) through (vii) of this chapter (HTLV, syphilis, West Nile virus, and Chagas disease). The following exceptions apply:

(i) To identify evidence of infection with syphilis in donors of Source Plasma, you must test donors for evidence of such infection in accordance with

§640.65(b) of this chapter, and not under this section.

(ii) You are not required to test donations of Source Plasma for evidence of infection due to the relevant transfusion-transmitted infections described in §630.3(h)(1)(iv), (vi), and (vii) of this chapter (HTLV, West Nile virus, and Chagas disease).

(iii) For each of the relevant transfusion-transmitted infections described in §630.3(h)(1)(iv) through (vii) of this chapter (HTLV, syphilis, West Nile virus, and Chagas disease):

(A) If, based on evidence related to the risk of transmission of that relevant transfusion-transmitted infection, testing each donation is not necessary to reduce adequately and appropriately the risk of transmission of such infection by blood or a blood component, you may adopt an adequate and appropriate alternative testing procedure that has been found acceptable for this purpose by FDA.

(B) If, based on evidence related to the risk of transmission of that relevant transfusion-transmitted infection, testing previously required for that infection is no longer necessary to reduce adequately and appropriately the risk of transmission of such infection by blood or a blood component, you may stop such testing in accordance with procedures found acceptable for this purpose by FDA.

(3) For each of the relevant transfusion-transmitted infections described in §630.3(h)(1)(viii) through (x) of this chapter (CJD, vCJD, malaria) and §630.3(h)(2) of this chapter (other transfusion-transmitted infections):

(i) You must test for evidence of infection when the following conditions are met:

(A) A test(s) for the relevant transfusion-transmitted infection is licensed, approved or cleared by FDA for use as a donor screening test and is available for such use; and

(B) Testing for the relevant transfusion-transmitted infection is necessary to reduce adequately and appropriately the risk of transmission of the relevant transfusion-transmitted infection by blood, or blood component, or blood derivative product manufactured from the collected blood or blood component.

(ii) You must perform this testing on each donation, unless one of the following exceptions applies:

(A) Testing of each donation is not necessary to reduce adequately and appropriately the risk of transmission of such infection by blood, blood component, or blood derivative product manufactured from the collected blood or blood component. When evidence related to the risk of transmission of such infection supports this determination, you may adopt an adequate and appropriate alternative testing procedure that has been found acceptable for this purpose by FDA.

(B) Testing of each donation is not necessary to reduce adequately and appropriately the risk of transmission of such infection by blood, blood component, or blood derivative product manufactured from the collected blood or blood component. When evidence related to the risk of transmission of such infection supports this determination, you may stop such testing in accordance with procedures found acceptable for this purpose by FDA.

(4) Evidence related to the risk of transmission of a relevant transfusion-transmitted infection that would support a determination that testing is not necessary, or that testing of each donation is not necessary, to reduce adequately and appropriately the risk of transmission of such infection by blood or blood component, as described in paragraphs (a)(2)(iii)(A) and (B) of this section, or by blood, blood component, or blood derivative, as described in paragraphs (a)(3)(ii)(A) and (B) of this section, includes epidemiological or other scientific evidence. It may include evidence related to the seasonality or geographic limitation of risk of transmission of such infection by blood or blood component, or other information related to when and how a donation is at risk of transmitting a relevant transfusion-transmitted infection. It may also include evidence related to the effectiveness of manufacturing steps (for example, the use of pathogen reduction technology) that reduce the risk of transmission of the relevant transfusion-transmitted infection by blood, blood components, or blood derivatives, as applicable.

(b) *Testing using one or more licensed, approved, or cleared screening tests.* To perform testing for evidence of infection due to relevant transfusion-transmitted infections as required in paragraph (a) of this section, you must use screening tests that FDA has licensed, approved, or cleared for such use, in accordance with the manufacturer's instructions. You must perform one or more such tests as necessary to reduce adequately and appropriately the risk of transmission of relevant transfusion-transmitted infections.

(c) *Exceptions to testing for dedicated donations, medical devices, and samples.*—(1) *Dedicated donations.* (i) You must test donations of human blood and blood components from a donor whose donations are dedicated to and used solely by a single identified recipient under paragraphs (a), (b), and (e) of this section; except that, if the donor makes multiple donations for a single identified recipient, you may perform such testing only on the first donation in each 30-day period. If an untested dedicated donation is made available for any use other than transfusion to the single, identified recipient, then this exemption from the testing required under this section no longer applies.

(ii) Each donation must be labeled as required under § 606.121 of this chapter and with a label entitled "INTENDED RECIPIENT INFORMATION LABEL" containing the name and identifying information of the recipient. Each donation must also have the following label, as appropriate:

Donor Testing Status	Label
Tests negative Tested negative within the last 30 days	Label as required under § 606.121 "DONOR TESTED WITHIN THE LAST 30 DAYS"

(2) *Medical device.* (i) You are not required to test donations of human blood or blood components intended solely as a component of, or used to prepare, a medical device for evidence of infection due to the relevant transfusion-transmitted infections listed in § 630.3(h)(iv) of this chapter unless the final device contains viable leukocytes.

(ii) Donations of human blood and blood components intended solely as a component of, or used to prepare, a medical device must be labeled "Caution: For Further Manufacturing Use as a Component of, or to Prepare, a Medical Device."

(3) *Samples.* You are not required to test samples of blood, blood components, plasma, or sera if used or distributed for clinical laboratory testing or research purposes and not intended for administration to humans or in the manufacture of a product.

(d) *Autologous donations.* You, an establishment that collects human blood or blood components from autologous donors, or you, an establishment that is a consignee of a collecting establishment, are not required to test donations of human blood or blood components from autologous donors for evidence of infection due to relevant transfusion-transmitted infections listed in paragraph (a) of this section, except:

(1) If you allow any autologous donation to be used for allogeneic transfusion, you must assure that all autologous donations are tested under this section.

(2) If you ship autologous donations to another establishment that allows autologous donations to be used for allogeneic transfusion, you must assure that all autologous donations shipped to that establishment are tested under this section.

(3) If you ship autologous donations to another establishment that does not allow autologous donations to be used for allogeneic transfusion, you must assure that, at a minimum, the first donation in each 30-day period is tested under this section.

(4) Each autologous donation must be labeled as required under §606.121 of this chapter and with the following label, as appropriate:

Donor Testing Status	Label
Untested	"DONOR UNTESTED"
Tests negative	Label as required under §606.121
Reactive on current collection/reactive in the last 30 days	"BIOHAZARD" legend in §610.40(h)(2)(ii)(B)
Tested negative within the last 30 days	"DONOR TESTED WITHIN THE LAST 30 DAYS"

(e) *Further testing.* You must further test each donation, including autologous donations, found to be reactive by a donor screening test performed under paragraphs (a) and (b) of

this section using a licensed, approved, or cleared supplemental test, when available. If no such supplemental test is available, you must perform one or more licensed, approved, or cleared tests as adequate and appropriate to provide additional information concerning the reactive donor's infection status. Except:

(1) For autologous donations:

(i) You must further test under this section, at a minimum, the first reactive donation in each 30 calendar day period; or

(ii) If you have a record for that donor of a positive result on further testing performed under this section, you do not have to further test an autologous donation.

(2) You are not required to perform further testing of a donation found to be reactive by a treponemal donor screening test for syphilis.

(f) *Testing responsibility.* Required testing under this section, must be performed by a laboratory registered in accordance with part 607 of this chapter and either certified to perform such testing on human specimens under the Clinical Laboratory Improvement Amendments of 1988 (42 U.S.C. 263a) under 42 CFR part 493 or has met equivalent requirements as determined by the Centers for Medicare and Medicaid Services in accordance with those provisions.

(g) *Release or shipment prior to testing.* Human blood or blood components that are required to be tested for evidence of infection due to relevant transfusion-transmitted infections designated in paragraph (a) of this section may be released or shipped prior to completion of testing in the following circumstances provided that you label the blood or blood components under §606.121(h) of this chapter, you complete the tests for evidence of infection due to relevant transfusion-transmitted infections as soon as possible after release or shipment, and that you provide the results promptly to the consignee:

(1) Only in appropriately documented medical emergency situations; or

(2) For further manufacturing use as approved in writing by FDA.

(h) *Restrictions on shipment or use*—(1) *Reactive screening test.* You must not ship or use human blood or blood components that have a reactive screening test for evidence of infection due to relevant transfusion-transmitted infection(s) designated in paragraph (a) of this section or that are collected from a donor with a previous record of a reactive screening test for evidence of infection due to relevant transfusion-transmitted infection(s) designated in paragraph (a) of this section; except as provided in paragraphs (h)(2)(i) through (h)(2)(vii) of this section.

(2) *Exceptions.* (i) You may ship or use blood or blood components intended for autologous use, including reactive donations, as described in paragraph (d) of this section.

(ii) You must not ship or use human blood or blood components that have a reactive screening test for evidence of infection due to a relevant transfusion-transmitted infection(s) designated in paragraph (a) of this section or that are collected from a donor deferred under § 610.41(a) unless you meet the following conditions:

(A) Except for autologous donations, you must obtain from FDA written approval for the shipment or use;

(B) You must appropriately label such blood or blood components as required under § 606.121 of this chapter, and with the "BIOHAZARD" legend;

(C) Except for autologous donations, you must label such human blood and blood components as reactive for the appropriate screening test for evidence of infection due to the identified relevant transfusion-transmitted infection(s);

(D) If the blood or blood components are intended for further manufacturing use into injectable products, you must include a statement on the container label indicating the exempted use specifically approved by FDA.

(E) Each blood or blood component with a reactive screening test and intended solely as a component of, or used to prepare a medical device, must be labeled with the following label, as appropriate:

Type of Medical Device	Label
A medical device other than an in vitro diagnostic reagent	"Caution: For Further Manufacturing Use as a Component of a Medical Device For Which There Are No Alternative Sources"

Type of Medical Device	Label
An in vitro diagnostic reagent	"Caution: For Further Manufacturing Into In Vitro Diagnostic Reagents For Which There Are No Alternative Sources"

(iii) The restrictions on shipment or use do not apply to samples of blood, blood components, plasma, or sera if used or distributed for clinical laboratory testing or research purposes, and not intended for administration in humans or in the manufacture of a product.

(iv) You may use human blood or blood components from a donor with a previous record of a reactive screening test(s) for evidence of infection due to a relevant transfusion-transmitted infection(s) designated in paragraph (a) of this section, if:

(A) At the time of donation, the donor is shown or was previously shown to be eligible by a requalification method or process found acceptable for such purposes by FDA under § 610.41(b); and

(B) tests performed under paragraphs (a) and (b) of this section are nonreactive.

(v) Anti-HBc reactive donations, otherwise nonreactive when tested as required under this section, may be used for further manufacturing into plasma derivatives without prior FDA approval or a "BIOHAZARD" legend as required under paragraphs (h)(2)(ii)(A) and (h)(2)(ii)(B) of this section.

(vi) You may use human blood or blood components, excluding Source Plasma, that test reactive by a screening test for syphilis as required under paragraph (a) of this section if, the donation is further tested by an adequate and appropriate test which demonstrates that the reactive screening test is a biological false positive. You must label the blood or blood components with both test results.

(vii) You may use Source Plasma from a donor who tests reactive by a screening test for syphilis as required under § 640.65(b)(1)(i) of this chapter, if the donor meets the requirements of § 640.65(b)(2)(ii) through (iv) of this chapter.

[66 FR 31162, June 11, 2001, as amended at 77 FR 18, Jan. 3, 2012; 80 FR 29896, May 22, 2015; 86 FR 49922, July 9, 2021]

§610.41 Donor deferral.

(a) You, an establishment that collects human blood or blood components, must defer donors testing reactive by a screening test for evidence of infection due to a relevant transfusion-transmitted infection(s) under §610.40(a), from future donations of human blood and blood components, except:

(1) You are not required to defer a donor who tests reactive for anti-HBc or anti-HTLV, types I and II, on only one occasion. However, you must defer the donor if further testing for HBV or HTLV has been performed under §610.40(e) and the donor is found to be positive, or if a second, licensed, cleared, or approved screening test for HBV or HTLV has been performed on the same donation under §610.40(a) and is reactive, or if the donor tests reactive for anti-HBc or anti-HTLV, types I and II, on more than one occasion;

(2) A deferred donor who tests reactive for evidence of infection due to a relevant transfusion-transmitted infection(s) under §610.40(a) may serve as a donor for blood or blood components shipped or used under §610.40(h)(2)(ii);

(3) A deferred donor who showed evidence of infection due to hepatitis B surface antigen (HBsAg) when previously tested under §610.40(a), (b), and (e) subsequently may donate Source Plasma for use in the preparation of Hepatitis B Immune Globulin (Human) provided the current donation tests nonreactive for HBsAg and the donor is otherwise determined to be eligible;

(4) A deferred donor, who otherwise is determined to be eligible for donation and tests reactive for anti-HBc or for evidence of infection due to HTLV, types I and II, may serve as a donor of Source Plasma;

(5) A deferred donor who tests reactive for a relevant transfusion-transmitted infections(s) under §610.40(a), may serve as an autologous donor under §610.40(d).

(b) A deferred donor subsequently may be found to be eligible as a donor of blood or blood components by a requalification method or process found acceptable for such purposes by FDA. Such a donor is considered no longer deferred.

(c) You must comply with the requirements under §§610.46 and 610.47 when a donor tests reactive by a screening test for HIV or HCV required under §610.40(a) and (b), or when you are aware of other reliable test results or information indicating evidence of HIV or HCV infection.

[66 FR 31164, June 11, 2001, as amended at 72 FR 48798, Aug. 24, 2007; 80 FR 29897, May 22, 2015]

§610.42 Restrictions on use for further manufacture of medical devices.

(a) In addition to labeling requirements in subchapter H of this chapter, when a medical device contains human blood or a blood component as a component of the final device, and the human blood or blood component was found to be reactive by a screening test performed under §610.40(a) and (b), then you must include in the device labeling a statement of warning indicating that the product was manufactured from a donation found to be reactive by a screening test for evidence of infection due to the identified relevant transfusion-transmitted infection(s).

(b) FDA may approve an exception or alternative to the statement of warning required in paragraph (a) of this section based on evidence that the reactivity of the human blood or blood component in the medical device presents no significant health risk through use of the medical device.

[66 FR 31164, June 11, 2001, as amended at 80 FR 29897, May 22, 2015]

§610.44 Use of reference panels by manufacturers of test kits.

(a) When available and appropriate to verify acceptable sensitivity and specificity, you, a manufacturer of test kits, must use a reference panel you obtain from FDA or from an FDA designated source to test lots of the following products. You must test each lot of the following products, unless FDA informs you that less frequent testing is appropriate, based on your consistent prior production of products of acceptable sensitivity and specificity:

(1) A test kit approved for use in testing donations of human blood and blood components for evidence of infection due to relevant transfusion-transmitted infections under §610.40(a); and

(2) Human immunodeficiency virus (HIV) test kit approved for use in the diagnosis, prognosis, or monitoring of this relevant transfusion-transmitted infection.

(b) You must not distribute a lot that is found to be not acceptable for sensitivity and specificity under § 610.44(a). FDA may approve an exception or alternative to this requirement. Applicants must submit such requests in writing. However, in limited circumstances, such requests may be made orally and permission may be given orally by FDA. Oral requests and approvals must be promptly followed by written requests and written approvals.

[66 FR 31164, June 11, 2001, as amended at 80 FR 29897, May 22, 2015]

§ 610.46 Human immunodeficiency virus (HIV) "lookback" requirements.

(a) If you are an establishment that collects Whole Blood or blood components, including Source Plasma and Source Leukocytes, you must establish, maintain, and follow an appropriate system for the following actions:

(1) Within 3 calendar days after a donor tests reactive for evidence of human immunodeficiency virus (HIV) infection when tested under § 610.40(a) and (b) or when you are made aware of other reliable test results or information indicating evidence of HIV infection, you must review all records required under § 606.160(d) of this chapter, to identify blood and blood components previously donated by such a donor. For those identified blood and blood components collected:

(i) Twelve months and less before the donor's most recent nonreactive screening tests, or

(ii) Twelve months and less before the donor's reactive direct viral detection test, e.g., nucleic acid test or HIV p24 antigen test, and nonreactive antibody screening test, whichever is the lesser period, you must:

(A) Quarantine all previously collected in-date blood and blood components identified under paragraph (a)(1) of this section if intended for use in another person or for further manufacture into injectable products, except pooled blood components intended sole-

ly for further manufacturing into products that are manufactured using validated viral clearance procedures; and

(B) Notify consignees to quarantine all previously collected in-date blood and blood components identified under paragraph (a)(1) of this section if intended for use in another person or for further manufacture into injectable products, except pooled blood components intended solely for further manufacturing into products that are manufactured using validated viral clearance procedures;

(2) You must perform further testing for HIV as required under § 610.40(e) of this chapter on the reactive donation.

(3) You must notify consignees of the results of further testing for HIV, or the results of the reactive screening test if further testing under paragraph (a)(2) of this section is not available, or if under an investigational new drug application (IND) or investigational device exemption (IDE), is exempted for such use by FDA, within 45 calendar days after the donor tests reactive for evidence of HIV infection under § 610.40(a) and (b) of this chapter. Notification of consignees must include the test results for blood and blood components identified under paragraph (a)(1) of this section that were previously collected from donors who later test reactive for evidence of HIV infection.

(4) You must release from quarantine, destroy, or relabel quarantined in-date blood and blood components, consistent with the results of the further testing performed under paragraph (a)(2) of this section or the results of the reactive screening test if further testing is not available, or if under an IND or IDE, exempted for such use by FDA.

(b) If you are a consignee of Whole Blood or blood components, including Source Plasma and Source Leukocytes, you must establish, maintain, and follow an appropriate system for the following actions:

(1) You must quarantine all previously collected in-date blood and blood components identified under paragraph (a)(1) of this section, except pooled blood components intended solely for further manufacturing into products that are manufactured using validated viral clearance procedures, when

notified by the collecting establishment.

(2) You must release from quarantine, destroy, or relabel quarantined in-date blood and blood components consistent with the results of the further testing performed under paragraph (a)(2) of this section, or the results of the reactive screening test if further testing is not available, or if under an IND or IDE, is exempted for such use by FDA.

(3) When further testing for HIV is positive or when the screening test is reactive and further testing is not available, or if under an IND or IDE is exempted for such use by FDA, you must notify transfusion recipients of previous collections of blood and blood components at increased risk of transmitting HIV infection, or the recipient's physician of record, of the need for recipient HIV testing and counseling. You must notify the recipient's physician of record or a legal representative or relative if the recipient is a minor, deceased, adjudged incompetent by a State court, or, if the recipient is competent but State law permits a legal representative or relative to receive information on behalf of the recipient. You must make reasonable attempts to perform the notification within 12 weeks after receiving the results of further testing for evidence of HIV infection from the collecting establishment, or after receiving the donor's reactive screening test result for HIV if further testing is not available, or if under an IND or IDE is exempted for such use by FDA.

(c) Actions under this section do not constitute a recall as defined in §7.3 of this chapter.

[72 FR 48799, Aug. 24, 2007, as amended at 80 FR 29897, May 22, 2015]

§610.47 **Hepatitis C virus (HCV) "lookback" requirements.**

(a) If you are an establishment that collects Whole Blood or blood components, including Source Plasma and Source Leukocytes, you must establish, maintain, and follow an appropriate system for the following actions:

(1) Within 3 calendar days after a donor tests reactive for evidence of hepatitis C virus (HCV) infection when tested under §610.40(a) and (b) of this

chapter or when you are made aware of other reliable test results or information indicating evidence of HCV infection, you must review all records required under §606.160(d) of this chapter, to identify blood and blood components previously donated by such a donor. For those identified blood and blood components collected:

(i) Twelve months and less before the donor's most recent nonreactive screening tests, or

(ii) Twelve months and less before the donor's reactive direct viral detection test, e.g., nucleic acid test and nonreactive antibody screening test, whichever is the lesser period, you must:

(A) Quarantine all previously collected in-date blood and blood components identified under paragraph (a)(1) of this section if intended for use in another person or for further manufacture into injectable products, except pooled blood components intended solely for further manufacturing into products that are manufactured using validated viral clearance procedures; and

(B) Notify consignees to quarantine all previously collected in-date blood and blood components identified under paragraph (a)(1) of this section if intended for use in another person or for further manufacture into injectable products, except pooled blood components intended solely for further manufacturing into products that are manufactured using validated viral clearance procedures;

(2) You must perform further testing for HCV as required under §610.40(e) on the reactive donation.

(3) You must notify consignees of the results of further testing for HCV, or the results of the reactive screening test if further testing is not available, or if under an investigational new drug application (IND) or investigational device exemption (IDE), is exempted for such use by FDA, within 45 calendar days after the donor tests reactive for evidence of HCV infection under §610.40(a) and (b). Notification of consignees must include the test results for blood and blood components identified under paragraph (a)(1) of this section that were previously collected from donors who later test reactive for evidence of HCV infection.

(4) You must release from quarantine, destroy, or relabel quarantined in-date blood and blood components consistent with the results of the further testing performed under paragraph (a)(2) of this section, or the results of the reactive screening test if further testing is not available, or if under an IND or IDE, exempted for such use by FDA.

(b) If you are a consignee of Whole Blood or blood components, including Source Plasma or Source Leukocytes, you must establish, maintain, and follow an appropriate system for the following actions:

(1) You must quarantine all previously collected in-date blood and blood components identified under paragraph (a)(1) of this section, except pooled blood components intended solely for further manufacturing into products that are manufactured using validated viral clearance procedures, when notified by the collecting establishment.

(2) You must release from quarantine, destroy, or relabel quarantined in-date blood and blood components, consistent with the results of the further testing performed under paragraph (a)(2) of this section, or the results of the reactive screening test if further testing is not available, or if under an IND or IDE, is exempted for such use by FDA.

(3) When the further testing for HCV is positive or when the screening test is reactive and further testing is not available, or if under an IND or IDE, is exempted for such use by FDA, you must notify transfusion recipients of previous collections of blood and blood components at increased risk of transmitting HCV infection, or the recipient's physician of record, of the need for recipient HCV testing and counseling. You must notify the recipient's physician of record or a legal representative or relative if the recipient is a minor, adjudged incompetent by a State court, or if the recipient is competent but State law permits a legal representative or relative to receive information on behalf of the recipient. You must make reasonable attempts to perform the notification within 12 weeks after receiving the results of further testing for evidence of HCV infec-

tion from the collecting establishment, or after receiving the donor's reactive screening test result for HCV if further testing is not available, or if under an IND or IDE, is exempted for such use by FDA.

(c) Actions under this section do not constitute a recall as defined in § 7.3 of this chapter.

[72 FR 48799, Aug. 24, 2007, as amended at 80 FR 29897, May 22, 2015]

§ 610.48 [Reserved]

Subpart F—Dating Period Limitations

§ 610.50 Date of manufacture for biological products.

(a) *When the dating period begins.* The dating period for a product must begin on the date of manufacture as described in paragraphs (b) and (c) of this section. The dating period for a combination of two or more products must be no longer than the dating period of the component with the shortest dating period.

(b) *Determining the date of manufacture for biological products other than Whole Blood and blood components.* The date of manufacture for biological products, other than Whole Blood and blood components, must be identified in the approved biologics license application as one of the following, whichever is applicable: The date of:

(1) Potency test or other specific test as described in a biologics license application or supplement to the application;

(2) Removal from animals or humans;

(3) Extraction;

(4) Solution;

(5) Cessation of growth;

(6) Final sterile filtration of a bulk solution;

(7) Manufacture as described in part 660 of this chapter; or

(8) Other specific manufacturing activity described in a biologics license application or supplement to the biologics license application.

(c) *Determining the date of manufacture for Whole Blood and blood components.* (1) The date of manufacture for Whole Blood and blood components must be one of the following, whichever is applicable:

(i) Collection date and/or time;

(ii) Irradiation date;

(iii) The time the red blood cell product was removed from frozen storage for deglycerolization;

(iv) The time the additive or rejuvenation solution was added;

(v) The time the product was entered for washing or removing plasma (if prepared in an open system);

(vi) As specified in the instructions for use by the blood collection, processing, and storage system approved or cleared for such use by FDA; or

(vii) As approved by the Director, Center for Biologics Evaluation and Research, in a biologics license application or supplement to the application.

(2) For licensed Whole Blood and blood components, the date of manufacture must be identified in the approved biologics license application or supplement to the application.

[81 FR 26691, May 4, 2016]

§610.53 Dating periods for Whole Blood and blood components.

(a) *General.* Dating periods for Whole Blood and blood components are specified in the table in paragraph (b) of this section.

(b) *Table of dating periods.* In using the table in this paragraph, when a product in column A is stored at the storage temperature prescribed in column B, storage of a product must not exceed the dating period specified in column C, unless a different dating period is specified in the instructions for use by the blood collection, processing and storage system approved or cleared for such use by FDA. Container labels for each product must include the recommended storage temperatures.

WHOLE BLOOD AND BLOOD COMPONENTS STORAGE TEMPERATURES AND DATING PERIODS

A	B	C
Product	Storage temperature	Dating period
Whole Blood		
ACD, CPD, CP2D	Between 1 and 6 °C	21 days from date of collection.
CPDA–1	do [1]	35 days from date of collection.
Red Blood Cells		
ACD, CPD, CP2D	Between 1 and 6 °C	21 days from date of collection.
CPDA–1	do	35 days from date of collection.
Additive solutions	do	42 days from date of collection.
Open system	do	24 hours after entering bag.
(e.g., deglycerolized, washed)		
Deglycerolized in closed system with additive solution added.	do	14 days after entering bag.
Irradiated	do	28 days from date of irradiation or original dating, whichever is shorter.
Frozen	−65 °C or colder	10 years from date of collection.
Platelets		
Platelets	Between 20 and 24 °C	5 days from date of collection.
Platelets	Other temperatures according to storage bag instructions.	As specified in the instructions for use by the blood collection, processing and storage system approved or cleared for such use by FDA.
Plasma		
Fresh Frozen Plasma	−18 °C or colder	1 year from date of collection.
Plasma Frozen Within 24 Hours After Phlebotomy.	do	1 year from date of collection.
Plasma Frozen Within 24 Hours After Phlebotomy Held at Room Temperature Up To 24 Hours After Phlebotomy.	do	1 year from date of collection.
Plasma Cryoprecipitate Reduced	do	1 year from date of collection.
Plasma	do	5 years from date of collection.
Liquid Plasma	Between 1 and 6 °C	5 days from end of Whole Blood dating period.
Source Plasma (frozen injectable)	−20 °C or colder	10 years from date of collection.

WHOLE BLOOD AND BLOOD COMPONENTS STORAGE TEMPERATURES AND DATING PERIODS—
Continued

A	B	C
Product	Storage temperature	Dating period
Source Plasma Liquid (injectable)	10 °C or colder	According to approved biologics license application.
Source Plasma (noninjectable)	Temperature appropriate for final product.	10 years from date of collection.
Therapeutic Exchange Plasma	−20 °C or colder	10 years from date of collection.
Cryoprecipitated AHF		
Cryoprecipitated AHF	−18 °C or colder	1 year from date of collection of source blood or from date of collection of oldest source blood in pre-storage pool.
Source Leukocytes		
Source Leukocytes	Temperature appropriate for final product.	In lieu of expiration date, the collection date must appear on the label.

[1] The abbreviation "do." for ditto is used in the table to indicate that the previous line is being repeated.

[81 FR 26691, May 4, 2016]

Subpart G—Labeling Standards

§ 610.60   Container label.

(a) *Full label.* The following items shall appear on the label affixed to each container of a product capable of bearing a full label:

(1) The proper name of the product;

(2) The name, address, and license number of manufacturer;

(3) The lot number or other lot identification;

(4) The expiration date;

(5) The recommended individual dose, for multiple dose containers.

(6) The statement: "'Rx only'" for prescription biologicals.

(7) If a Medication Guide is required under part 208 of this chapter, the statement required under § 208.24(d) of this chapter instructing the authorized dispenser to provide a Medication Guide to each patient to whom the drug is dispensed and stating how the Medication Guide is provided, except where the container label is too small, the required statement may be placed on the package label.

(b) *Package label information.* If the container is not enclosed in a package, all the items required for a package label shall appear on the container label.

(c) *Partial label.* If the container is capable of bearing only a partial label, the container shall show as a minimum the name (expressed either as the proper or common name), the lot number or other lot identification and the name of the manufacturer; in addition, for multiple dose containers, the recommended individual dose. Containers bearing partial labels shall be placed in a package which bears all the items required for a package label.

(d) *No container label.* If the container is incapable of bearing any label, the items required for a container label may be omitted, provided the container is placed in a package which bears all the items required for a package label.

(e) *Visual inspection.* When the label has been affixed to the container a sufficient area of the container shall remain uncovered for its full length or circumference to permit inspection of the contents.

[38 FR 32056, Nov. 20, 1973, as amended at 47 FR 22518, May 25, 1982; 63 FR 66400, Dec. 1, 1998; 67 FR 4907, Feb. 1, 2002]

§ 610.61   Package label.

The following items shall appear on the label affixed to each package containing a product:

(a) The proper name of the product;

(b) The name, address, and license number of manufacturer;

(c) The lot number or other lot identification;

(d) The expiration date;

(e) The preservative used and its concentration, or if no preservative is used and the absence of a preservative is a safety factor, the words "no preservative";

(f) The number of containers, if more than one;

(g) The amount of product in the container expressed as (1) the number of doses, (2) volume, (3) units of potency, (4) weight, (5) equivalent volume (for dried product to be reconstituted), or (6) such combination of the foregoing as needed for an accurate description of the contents, whichever is applicable;

(h) The recommended storage temperature;

(i) The words "Shake Well", "Do not Freeze" or the equivalent, as well as other instructions, when indicated by the character of the product;

(j) The recommended individual dose if the enclosed container(s) is a multiple-dose container;

(k) The route of administration recommended, or reference to such directions in an enclosed circular;

(l) Known sensitizing substances, or reference to an enclosed circular containing appropriate information;

(m) The type and calculated amount of antibiotics added during manufacture;

(n) The inactive ingredients when a safety factor, or reference to an enclosed circular containing appropriate information;

(o) The adjuvant, if present;

(p) The source of the product when a factor in safe administration;

(q) The identity of each microorganism used in manufacture, and, where applicable, the production medium and the method of inactivation, or reference to an enclosed circular containing appropriate information;

(r) Minimum potency of product expressed in terms of official standard of potency or, if potency is a factor and no U.S. standard of potency has been prescribed, the words "No U.S. standard of potency."

(s) The statement: "'Rx only'" for prescription biologicals.

[38 FR 32056, Nov. 20, 1973, as amended at 47 FR 22518, May 25, 1982; 55 FR 10423, Mar. 21, 1990; 67 FR 4907, Feb. 1, 2002]

§610.62 Proper name; package label; legible type.

(a) *Position.* The proper name of the product on the package label shall be placed above any trademark or trade name identifying the product and symmetrically arranged with respect to other printing on the label.

(b) *Prominence.* The point size and typeface of the proper name shall be at least as prominent as the point size and typeface used in designating the trademark and trade name. The contrast in color value between the proper name and the background shall be at least as great as the color value between the trademark and trade name and the background. Typography, layout, contrast, and other printing features shall not be used in a manner that will affect adversely the prominence of the proper name.

(c) *Legible type.* All items required to be on the container label and package label shall be in legible type. "Legible type" is type of a size and character which can be read with ease when held in a good light and with normal vision.

§610.63 Divided manufacturing responsibility to be shown.

If two or more licensed manufacturers participate in the manufacture of a biological product, the name, address, and license number of each must appear on the package label, and on the label of the container if capable of bearing a full label.

[64 FR 56453, Oct. 20, 1999]

§610.64 Name and address of distributor.

The name and address of the distributor of a product may appear on the label provided that the name, address, and license number of the manufacturer also appears on the label and the name of the distributor is qualified by one of the following phrases: "Manufactured for ____", "Distributed by ____", "Manufactured by ____ for ____", "Manufactured for ____ by ____", "Distributor: ____", or "Marketed by ____". The qualifying phrases may be abbreviated.

[61 FR 57330, Nov. 6, 1996]

§610.65 Products for export.

Labels on packages or containers of products for export may be adapted to meet specific requirements of the regulations of the country to which the product is to be exported provided that in all such cases the minimum label requirements prescribed in § 610.60 are observed.

§ 610.67 Bar code label requirements.

Biological products must comply with the bar code requirements at § 201.25 of this chapter. However, the bar code requirements do not apply to devices regulated by the Center for Biologics Evaluation and Research or to blood and blood components intended for transfusion. For blood and blood components intended for transfusion, the requirements at § 606.121(c)(13) of this chapter apply instead.

[69 FR 9171, Feb. 26, 2004]

§ 610.68 Exceptions or alternatives to labeling requirements for biological products held by the Strategic National Stockpile.

(a) The appropriate FDA Center Director may grant an exception or alternative to any provision listed in paragraph (f) of this section and not explicitly required by statute, for specified lots, batches, or other units of a biological product, if the Center Director determines that compliance with such labeling requirement could adversely affect the safety, effectiveness, or availability of such product that is or will be included in the Strategic National Stockpile.

(b)(1)(i) A Strategic National Stockpile official or any entity that manufactures (including labeling, packing, relabeling, or repackaging), distributes, or stores a biological product that is or will be included in the Strategic National Stockpile may submit, with written concurrence from a Strategic National Stockpile official, a written request for an exception or alternative described in paragraph (a) of this section to the Center Director.

(ii) The Center Director may grant an exception or alternative described in paragraph (a) of this section on his or her own initiative.

(2) A written request for an exception or alternative described in paragraph (a) of this section must:

(i) Identify the specified lots, batches, or other units of the biological

product that would be subject to the exception or alternative;

(ii) Identify the labeling provision(s) listed in paragraph (f) of this section that are the subject of the exception or alternative request;

(iii) Explain why compliance with such labeling provision(s) could adversely affect the safety, effectiveness, or availability of the specified lots, batches, or other units of the biological product that are or will be included in the Strategic National Stockpile;

(iv) Describe any proposed safeguards or conditions that will be implemented so that the labeling of the product includes appropriate information necessary for the safe and effective use of the product, given the anticipated circumstances of use of the product;

(v) Provide a draft of the proposed labeling of the specified lots, batches, or other units of the biological product subject to the exception or alternative; and

(vi) Provide any other information requested by the Center Director in support of the request.

(c) The Center Director must respond in writing to all requests under this section.

(d) A grant of an exception or alternative under this section will include any safeguards or conditions deemed appropriate by the Center Director so that the labeling of product subject to the exception or alternative includes the information necessary for the safe and effective use of the product, given the anticipated circumstances of use.

(e) If you are a sponsor receiving a grant of a request for an exception or alternative to the labeling requirements under this section:

(1) You need not submit a supplement under § 601.12(f)(1) through (f)(2) of this chapter; however,

(2) You must report any grant of a request for an exception or alternative under this section as part of your annual report under § 601.12(f)(3) of this chapter.

(f) The Center Director may grant an exception or alternative under this section to the following provisions of this chapter, to the extent that the requirements in these provisions are not explicitly required by statute:

(1) § 610.60;

(2) §610.61(c) and (e) through (r);
(3) §610.62;
(4) §610.63;
(5) §610.64;
(6) §610.65; and
(7) §312.6.

[72 FR 73600, Dec. 28, 2007]

PART 630—REQUIREMENTS FOR BLOOD AND BLOOD COMPONENTS INTENDED FOR TRANSFUSION OR FOR FURTHER MANUFACTURING USE

Subpart A—General Provisions

AUTHORITY: 21 U.S.C. 321, 331, 351, 352, 355, 360, 371; 42 U.S.C. 216, 262, 264.

SOURCE: 66 FR 31176, June 11, 2001, unless otherwise noted.

Subpart A—General Provisions

SOURCE: 80 FR 29898, May 22, 2015, unless otherwise noted.

§630.1 Purpose and scope.

(a) *What is the purpose of subparts A, B, and C of this part?* The purpose of these subparts, together with §§610.40 and 610.41 of this chapter, is to provide certain minimum criteria for each donation of blood and blood components, for:

(1) Determining the eligibility of a donor of blood and blood components;

(2) Determining the suitability of the donation of blood and blood components; and

(3) Notifying a donor who is deferred from donation.

(b) *Who must comply with subparts A, B, and C of this part?* Blood establishments that manufacture blood and blood components, as defined in §630.3(a) and (b), must comply with subparts A, B, and C of this part.

§630.3 Definitions.

As used in this part and in part 610, subpart E, and part 640 of this chapter:

(a) *Blood* means a product that is a fluid containing dissolved and suspended elements which was collected from the vascular system of a human.

(b) *Blood component* means a product containing a part of blood separated by physical or mechanical means.

(c) *Donor* means a person who: (1) Donates blood or blood components for transfusion or for further manufacturing use; or

(2) Presents as a potential candidate for such donation.

(d) *Eligibility of a donor* means the determination that the donor is qualified to donate blood and blood components.

(e) *Infrequent plasma donor* means a donor who has:

(1) Not donated plasma by plasmapheresis or a co-collection of plasma with another blood component in the preceding 4 weeks; and

(2) Not donated more than 12.0 liters of plasma (14.4 liters of plasma for donors weighing more than 175 pounds) in the past year.

(f) *Intimate contact with risk for a relevant transfusion-transmitted infection* means having engaged in an activity that could result in the transfer of potentially infectious body fluids from one person to another.

(g) *Physician substitute* means a trained and qualified person(s) who is:

(1) A graduate of an education program for health care workers that includes clinical training;

(2) Currently licensed or certified as a health care worker in the jurisdiction where the collection establishment is located;

(3) Currently certified in cardiopulmonary resuscitation; and

(4) Trained and authorized under State law, and/or local law when applicable, to perform the specified functions under the direction of the responsible physician.

(h) *Relevant transfusion-transmitted infection* means:

(1) Any of the following transfusion-transmitted infections:

(i) Human immunodeficiency virus, types 1 and 2 (referred to, collectively, as HIV);

(ii) Hepatitis B virus (referred to as HBV);

(iii) Hepatitis C virus (referred to as HCV);

(iv) Human T-lymphotropic virus, types I and II (referred to, collectively, as HTLV);

(v) *Treponema pallidum* (referred to as syphilis);

(vi) West Nile virus;

(vii) *Trypanosoma cruzi* (referred to as Chagas disease);

(viii) Creutzfeldt-Jakob disease (referred to as CJD);

(ix) Variant Creutzfeldt-Jakob disease (referred to as vCJD); and

(x) *Plasmodium* species (referred to as malaria).

(2) A transfusion-transmitted infection not listed in paragraph (h)(1) of this section when the following conditions are met:

(i) Appropriate screening measures for the transfusion-transmitted infection have been developed and/or an appropriate screening test has been licensed, approved, or cleared for such use by FDA and is available; and

(ii) The disease or disease agent:

(A) May have sufficient incidence and/or prevalence to affect the potential donor population; or

(B) May have been released accidentally or intentionally in a manner that could place potential donors at risk of infection.

(i) *Responsible physician* means an individual who is:

(1) Licensed to practice medicine in the jurisdiction where the collection establishment is located;

(2) Adequately trained and qualified to direct and control personnel and relevant procedures concerning the determination of donor eligibility; collection of blood and blood components; the immunization of a donor; and the

return of red blood cells or other blood components to the donor during collection of blood component(s) by apheresis; and

(3) Designated by the collection establishment to perform the activities described in paragraph (i)(2) of this section.

(j) *Suitability of the donation* means a determination of whether the donation is acceptable for transfusion or for further manufacturing use.

(k) *Trained person* means an individual, including a physician substitute, who is authorized under State law, and/or local law when applicable, and adequately instructed and qualified to perform the specified functions under the direction of the responsible physician.

(l) *Transfusion-transmitted infection* means a disease or disease agent:

(1) That could be fatal or life-threatening, could result in permanent impairment of a body function or permanent damage to a body structure, or could necessitate medical or surgical intervention to preclude permanent impairment of body function or permanent damage to a body structure; and

(2) For which there may be a risk of transmission by blood or blood components, or by a blood derivative product manufactured from blood or blood components, because the disease or disease agent is potentially transmissible by that blood, blood component, or blood derivative product.

Subpart B—Donor Eligibility Requirements

SOURCE: 80 FR 29898, May 22, 2015, unless otherwise noted.

§ 630.5 Medical supervision.

(a) *Who must determine the eligibility of a donor?* The responsible physician must determine the eligibility of a donor of blood or blood components in accordance with this subchapter.

(b) *Which activities related to the collection of blood and blood components, other than Source Plasma and plasma collected by plasmapheresis, may the responsible physician delegate?*

(1) The responsible physician may delegate the following activities to a

physician substitute or other trained person:

(i) Determining the eligibility of a donor and documenting assessments related to that determination, except the responsible physician must not delegate:

(A) The examination and determination of the donor's health required in § 630.10(f)(2) for donors with blood pressure measurements outside specified limits, or for certain more frequent donations under § 630.15(a)(1)(ii);

(B) The determination of the health of the donor required in §§ 630.10(f)(4), 630.20(a), and 640.21(e)(4) of this chapter. The responsible physician may make this determination by telephonic or other offsite consultation; or

(C) The determination of the health of the donor and the determination that the blood or blood component collected would present no undue medical risk to the transfusion recipient, as required in § 630.20(c). The responsible physician may make these determinations by telephonic or other offsite consultation.

(ii) Collecting blood or blood components;

(iii) Returning red blood cells to the donor during apheresis;

(iv) Obtaining the informed consent of a plateletpheresis donor as described in § 640.21(g) of this chapter; or

(v) Other activities provided that the Director, Center for Biologics Evaluation and Research, determines that delegating the activities would present no undue medical risk to the donor or to the transfusion recipient, and authorizes the delegation of such activities.

(2) The responsible physician need not be present at the collection site when activities delegated under paragraph (b)(1) of this section are performed, provided that the responsible physician has delegated oversight of these activities to a trained person who is adequately trained and experienced in the performance of these activities and is also adequately trained and experienced in the recognition of and response to the known adverse responses associated with blood collection procedures.

(c) *Which activities related to the collection of Source Plasma and plasma col-* *lected by plasmapheresis may the responsible physician delegate?*

(1) *Donor eligibility and blood component collection activities.* (i) The responsible physician may delegate to a physician substitute or other trained person any of the activities described in paragraph (c)(1)(i)(A) of this section, provided that the responsible physician or a physician substitute is on the premises at the collection site:

(A) The activities listed in paragraphs (b)(1)(i) through (iii) and (b)(1)(v) of this section, with respect to Source Plasma and plasma collected by plasmapheresis. However, the responsible physician must not delegate:

(1) The examination and determination of the donor's health required in § 630.10(f)(2) for donors with blood pressure measurements outside specified limits, or in § 630.15(b)(7) for certain donors who have experienced red blood cell loss;

(2) The determination of the health of the donor required in §§ 630.10(f)(4) and 630.20(a) and (b). The responsible physician may make this determination by telephonic or other offsite consultation;

(3) The determination of the health of the donor and the determination that the blood component would present no undue medical risk to the transfusion recipient, as required in § 630.20(c). The responsible physician may make this determination by telephonic or other offsite consultation.

(4) The determination related to a donor's false-positive reaction to a serologic test for syphilis in accordance with § 640.65(b)(2)(iii) of this chapter; and

(5) The determination to permit plasmapheresis of a donor with a reactive serological test for syphilis in accordance with § 640.65(b)(2)(iv) of this chapter.

(B) The collection of Source Plasma in an approved collection program from a donor who is otherwise determined to be ineligible.

(C) The collection of a blood sample in accordance with § 640.65(b)(1)(i) of this chapter.

(ii) The responsible physician, who may or may not be present when these activities are performed, may delegate to a physician substitute the following activities:

(A) Approval and signature for a plasmapheresis procedure as provided in § 640.65(b)(1)(ii) of this chapter; and

(B) Review and signature for accumulated laboratory data, the calculated values of each component, and the collection records in accordance with § 640.65(b)(2)(i) of this chapter. However, the responsible physician must not delegate the decision to reinstate the deferred donor in accordance with that provision.

(2) *Donor immunization.* The responsible physician must not delegate activities performed in accordance with § 640.66 of this chapter, except that:

(i) The responsible physician may delegate to a physician substitute or other trained person the administration of an immunization other than red blood cells to a donor in an approved collection program, provided that the responsible physician or a physician substitute is on the premises at the collection site when the immunization is administered.

(ii) The responsible physician may delegate to a physician substitute the administration of red blood cells to a donor in an approved collection program, provided that the responsible physician has approved the procedure and is on the premises at the collection site when the red blood cells are administered.

(3) *Medical history, physical examination, informed consent, and examination before immunization.* Provided that such activities are performed under the supervision of the responsible physician, the responsible physician may delegate to a physician substitute the activities described in § 630.15(b)(1), (2), and (5). The responsible physician is not required to be present at the collection site when the physician substitute performs these activities under supervision.

(4) *Infrequent plasma donors.* (i) For infrequent plasma donors other than those described in paragraph (c)(4)(ii) of this section, the responsible physician may delegate to a trained person the activities listed in paragraphs (b)(1)(i) through (iii) and (b)(1)(v) of this section and the informed consent requirements described in § 630.15(b)(2).

The responsible physician or a physician substitute need not be present at the collection site when any of these activities are performed, provided that the responsible physician has delegated oversight of these activities to a trained person who is not only adequately trained and experienced in the performance of these activities but also adequately trained and experienced in the recognition of and response to the known adverse responses associated with blood collection procedures. However, the responsible physician must not delegate:

(A) The examination and determination of the donor's health required in § 630.10(f)(2) for donors with blood pressure measurements outside specified limits, or in § 630.15(b)(7) for certain donors who have experienced red blood cell loss; or

(B) The determination of the health of the donor required in § 630.10(f)(4).

(ii) For infrequent plasma donors who are otherwise ineligible or are participating in an approved immunization program, the responsible physician may delegate only in accordance with paragraphs (c)(1) through (3) of this section.

(d) *Must rapid emergency medical services be available?* Establishments that collect blood or blood components must establish, maintain, and follow standard operating procedures for obtaining rapid emergency medical services for donors when medically necessary. In addition, establishments must assure that an individual (responsible physician, physician substitute, or trained person) who is currently certified in cardiopulmonary resuscitation is located on the premises whenever collections of blood or blood components are performed.

§ 630.10 General donor eligibility requirements.

(a) *What factors determine the eligibility of a donor?* You, an establishment that collects blood or blood components, must not collect blood or blood components before determining that the donor is eligible to donate or before determining that an exception to this provision applies. To be eligible, the donor must be in good health and free from transfusion-transmitted infections as can be determined by the processes in this subchapter. A donor is not eligible if the donor is not in good health or if you identify any factor(s) that may cause the donation to adversely affect:

(1) The health of the donor; or

(2) The safety, purity, or potency of the blood or blood component.

(b) *What educational material must you provide to the donor before determining eligibility?* You must provide educational material concerning relevant transfusion-transmitted infections to donors before donation when donor education about that relevant transfusion-transmitted infection, such as HIV, is necessary to assure the safety, purity, and potency of blood and blood components. The educational material must include an explanation of the readily identifiable risk factors closely associated with exposure to the relevant transfusion-transmitted infection. You must present educational material in an appropriate form, such as oral, written or multimedia, and in a manner designed to be understood by the donor. The educational material must instruct the donor not to donate blood and blood components when a risk factor is present. When providing educational material to donors under this section, you may include in those materials the information required to be provided to donors under paragraph (g)(2)(ii)(E) of this section.

(c) *When must you determine the eligibility of a donor?* You must determine donor eligibility on the day of donation, and before collection. Except:

(1) When a donor is donating blood components that cannot be stored for more than 24 hours, you may determine the donor's eligibility and collect a sample for testing required under §610.40 of this chapter, no earlier than 2 calendar days before the day of donation, provided that your standard operating procedures address these activities.

(2) In the event that, upon review, you find that a donor's responses to the donor questions before collection were incomplete, within 24 hours of the time of collection, you may clarify a donor's response or obtain omitted information required under paragraph (e) of this section, provided that your standard operating procedures address these activities.

(d) *How must you determine the eligibility of a donor?* You must determine the donor's eligibility before collection of blood or blood components, by the following procedures:

(1) You must consult the records of deferred donors maintained under §606.160(e)(1) and (2) of this chapter. Exception: If pre-collection review of the record described in §606.160(e)(2) of this chapter is not feasible because you cannot consult the cumulative record at the collection site, you must consult the cumulative record prior to release of any blood or blood component prepared from the collection.

(2) Assure that the interval since the donor's last donation is appropriate;

(3) Assess the donor's medical history; and

(4) Perform a physical assessment of the donor.

(e) *How do you assess the donor's medical history?* Before collection you must conduct a medical history interview as described in this section to determine if the donor is in good health; to identify risk factors closely associated with exposure to, or clinical evidence of a relevant transfusion-transmitted infection; and to determine if there are other conditions that may adversely affect the health of the donor or the safety, purity, or potency of the blood or blood components or any product manufactured from the blood or blood components. Your assessment must include each of the following factors:

(1) Factors that make the donor ineligible to donate because of an increased risk for, or evidence of, a relevant transfusion-transmitted infection. A donor is ineligible to donate when information provided by the donor or other reliable evidence indicates possible exposure to a relevant transfusion-transmitted infection if that risk of exposure is still applicable at the time of donation. Information and evidence indicating possible exposure to a relevant transfusion-transmitted infection include:

(i) Behaviors associated with a relevant transfusion-transmitted infection;

(ii) Receipt of blood or blood components or other medical treatments and procedures associated with possible exposure to a relevant transfusion-transmitted infection;

(iii) Signs and/or symptoms of a relevant transfusion-transmitted infection;

(iv) Institutionalization for 72 hours or more consecutively in the past 12 months in a correctional institution;

(v) Intimate contact with risk for a relevant transfusion-transmitted infection; and

(vi) Nonsterile percutaneous inoculation.

(2) Other factors that make the donor ineligible to donate. A donor is ineligible to donate when donating could adversely affect the health of the donor, or when the safety, purity, or potency of the blood or blood component could be affected adversely. Your assessment of the donor must include each of the following factors:

(i) Symptoms of a recent or current illness;

(ii) Certain medical treatments or medications;

(iii) Travel to, or residence in, an area endemic for a transfusion-transmitted infection, when such screening is necessary to assure the safety, purity, and potency of blood and blood components due to the risks presented by donor travel and the risk of transmission of that transfusion-transmitted infection by such donors;

(iv) Exposure or possible exposure to an accidentally or intentionally released disease or disease agent relating to a transfusion-transmitted infection, if you know or suspect that such a release has occurred;

(v) Pregnancy at the time of, or within 6 weeks prior to, donation;

(vi) Whether, in the opinion of the interviewer, the donor appears to be under the influence of any drug, alcohol or for any reason does not appear to be providing reliable answers to medical history questions, or if the donor says that the purpose of donating is to obtain test results for a relevant transfusion-transmitted infection; and

(vii) The donor is a xenotransplantation product recipient.

(f) *How do you perform a physical assessment of the donor?* You must determine on the day of donation, and before collection that the donor is in good health based on the following, at a minimum:

(1) *Temperature.* The donor's oral body temperature must not exceed 37.5 °C (99.5 °F), or the equivalent if measured at another body site;

(2) *Blood pressure.* The donor's systolic blood pressure must not measure above 180 mm of mercury, or below 90 mm of mercury, and the diastolic blood pressure must not measure above 100 mm of mercury or below 50 mms of mercury. A donor with measurements outside these limits may be permitted to donate only when the responsible physician examines the donor and determines and documents that the health of the donor would not be adversely affected by donating.

(3) *Hemoglobin or hematocrit determination.* You must determine the donor's hemoglobin level or hematocrit value by using a sample of blood obtained by fingerstick, venipuncture, or by a method that provides equivalent results. Blood obtained from the earlobe is not acceptable.

(i) Allogeneic donors must have a hemoglobin level or hematocrit value that is adequate to assure donor safety and product potency. The following minimum standards apply.

(A) Female allogeneic donors must have a hemoglobin level that is equal to or greater than 12.5 grams of hemoglobin per deciliter of blood, or a hematocrit value that is equal to or greater than 38 percent. Recognizing that lower levels are also within normal limits for female donors, you may collect blood from female allogeneic donors who have a hemoglobin level between 12.0 and 12.5 grams per deciliter of blood, or a hematocrit value between 36 and 38 percent, provided that you have taken additional steps to assure that this alternative standard is adequate to ensure that the health of the donor will not be adversely affected due to the donation, in accordance with a procedure that has been found acceptable for this purpose by FDA.

(B) Male allogeneic donors must have a hemoglobin level that is equal to or greater than 13.0 grams of hemoglobin

§630.15

per deciliter of blood, or a hematocrit value that is equal to or greater than 39 percent.

(ii) An autologous donor must have a hemoglobin level no less than 11.0 grams of hemoglobin per deciliter of blood, or a hematocrit value no less than 33 percent.

(4) *Pulse.* The donor's pulse must be regular and between 50 and 100 beats per minute. A donor with an irregular pulse or measurements outside these limits may be permitted to donate only when the responsible physician determines and documents that the health of the donor would not be adversely affected by donating.

(5) *Weight.* The donor must weigh a minimum of 50 kilograms (110 pounds).

(6) *Skin examination.* (i) The donor's phlebotomy site must be free of infection, inflammation, and lesions; and

(ii) The donor's arms and forearms must be free of punctures and scars indicative of injected drugs of abuse.

(g) *Are there additional requirements for determining the eligibility of the donor?* You must obtain the following from the donor on the day of donation:

(1) *Proof of identity and postal address.* You must obtain proof of identity of the donor and a postal address where the donor may be contacted for 8 weeks after donation; and

(2) *Donor's acknowledgement.* (i) Prior to each donation, you must provide information to the donor addressing the elements specified in paragraphs (g)(2)(ii)(A) through (E) of this section and obtain the donor's acknowledgement that the donor has reviewed the information. You must establish procedures in accordance with §606.100 of this chapter to assure that the donor has reviewed this material, and provide for a signature or other documented acknowledgement.

(ii) The donor acknowledgement must not include any exculpatory language through which the donor is made to waive or appear to waive any of the donor's legal rights. It must, at a minimum clearly address the following:

(A) The donor has reviewed the educational material provided under paragraph (b) of this section regarding relevant transfusion-transmitted infections;

(B) The donor agrees not to donate if the donation could result in a potential risk to recipients as described in the educational material;

(C) A sample of the donor's blood will be tested for specified relevant transfusion-transmitted infections;

(D) If the donation is determined to be not suitable under §630.30(a) or if the donor is deferred from donation under §610.41 of this chapter, the donor's record will identify the donor as ineligible to donate and the donor will be notified under §630.40 of the basis for the deferral and the period of deferral;

(E) The donor has been provided and reviewed information regarding the risks and hazards of the specific donation procedure; and

(F) The donor has the opportunity to ask questions and withdraw from the donation procedure.

(h) *What must you do when a donor is not eligible?* You must not collect blood or blood components from a donor found to be ineligible prior to collection based on criteria in §§630.10 or 630.15, or deferred under §610.41 of this chapter or §630.30(b)(2), unless this subchapter provides an exception. You must defer donors found to be ineligible and you must notify the donor of their deferral under §630.40.

§630.15 Donor eligibility requirements specific to Whole Blood, Red Blood Cells and Plasma collected by apheresis.

(a) *What additional donor eligibility requirements apply when you, an establishment that collects blood or blood components, collect Whole Blood or Red Blood Cells by apheresis?*

(1) *Donation frequency must be consistent with protecting the health of the donor.*

(i) For a collection resulting in a single unit of Whole Blood or Red Blood Cells collected by apheresis, donation frequency must be no more than once in 8 weeks, and for apheresis collections resulting in two units of Red Blood Cells, the donor must not donate more than once in 16 weeks.

(ii) The limitations in paragraph (a)(1)(i) of this section apply unless the responsible physician examines the donor at the time of donation and one of the following conditions exists:

89

(A) The donation is for autologous use as prescribed by the donor's physician and the responsible physician determines and documents that the donation may proceed; or

(B) The donation is a dedicated donation based on the intended recipient's documented exceptional medical need and the responsible physician determines and documents that the health of the donor would not be adversely affected by donating.

(2) *Therapeutic phlebotomy.* When a donor who is determined to be eligible under § 630.10 undergoes a therapeutic phlebotomy under a prescription to promote the donor's health, you may collect from the donor more frequently than once in 8 weeks for collections resulting in a single unit of Whole Blood or Red Blood Cells, or once in 16 weeks for apheresis collections resulting in two units of Red Blood Cells, provided that the container label conspicuously states the disease or condition of the donor that necessitated phlebotomy. However, no labeling for the disease or condition is required under this section if:

(i) The donor meets all eligibility criteria;

(ii) The donor undergoes a therapeutic phlebotomy as prescribed by a licensed health care provider treating the donor for:

(A) Hereditary hemochromatosis; or

(B) Another disease or condition, when the health of a donor with that disease or condition will not be adversely affected by donating, and the donor's disease or condition will not adversely affect the safety, purity, and potency of the blood and blood components, or any products manufactured from them, and the collection is in accordance with a procedure that has been found acceptable for this purpose by FDA; and

(iii) You perform without charge therapeutic phlebotomies for all individuals with that disease or condition.

(b) *What additional donor eligibility requirements apply when you, an establishment that collects blood or blood components, collect Source Plasma or plasma by plasmapheresis?*

(1) *Medical history and physical examination.* Except as provided in § 630.25:

(i) The responsible physician must conduct an appropriate medical history and physical examination of the donor on the day of the first donation or no more than 1 week before the first donation and at subsequent intervals of no longer than 1 year.

(ii) The responsible physician must examine the donor for medical conditions that would place the donor at risk from plasmapheresis. If the donor is determined to be at risk, you must defer the donor from donating.

(iii) The responsible physician must conduct a new medical history and physical examination of a donor who does not return for 6 months.

(2) *What requirements apply to obtaining informed consent?*

(i) The responsible physician must obtain the informed consent of a plasma donor on the first day of donation or no more than 1 week before the first donation, and at subsequent intervals of no longer than 1 year.

(ii) The responsible physician must obtain the informed consent of a plasma donor who does not return within 6 months of the last donation.

(iii) The responsible physician must explain the risks and hazards of the procedure to the donor. The explanation must include the risks of a hemolytic transfusion reaction if the donor is given the cells of another donor and the risks involved if the donor is immunized. The explanation must be made in such a manner that the donor may give their consent and has a clear opportunity to refuse the procedure.

(iv) If a donor is enrolled in a new program, such as an immunization or special collection program, the responsible physician must again obtain an informed consent specific for that program.

(3) *Weight.* You must weigh a donor at each donation.

(4) *Total protein level.* You must determine the donor's total plasma protein level before each plasmapheresis procedure. The donor must have a total plasma protein level of no less than 6.0 grams per deciliter and no more than 9.0 grams per deciliter in a plasma sample or a serum sample.

(5) *Examination before immunization.* (i) No more than 1 week before the first

immunization injection for the production of high-titer antibody plasma, the responsible physician must conduct an appropriate medical history and physical examination, as described in paragraph (b)(1) of this section, in addition to assessing the general donor eligibility requirements under § 630.10. It is not necessary to repeat the medical history and physical examination requirement in paragraph (b)(1) of this section, if the immunized donor's plasma is collected within 3 weeks of the first immunization injection.

(ii) You are not required to repeat the medical history and physical examination required under paragraph (b)(1) of this section for a donor currently participating in a plasmapheresis collection program and determined to be eligible under § 630.10 unless the medical history and physical examination are due under paragraph (b)(1)(i) or (b)(1)(iii) of this section.

(6) *Deferral of donors due to red blood cell loss.* (i) You must defer a donor from donating plasma by plasmapheresis for 8 weeks if the donor has donated a unit of Whole Blood, or a single unit of Red Blood Cells by apheresis. However, you may collect plasma by plasmapheresis after a donation of Whole Blood or a single unit of Red Blood Cells by apheresis after at least 2 calendar days have passed, provided that the extracorporeal volume of the apheresis device is less than 100 milliliters.

(ii) You must defer a donor from donating plasma by plasmapheresis for a period of 16 weeks if the donor donates two units of Red Blood Cells during a single apheresis procedure;

(iii) You must defer a donor for 8 weeks or more if the cumulative red blood cell loss in any 8 week period could adversely affect donor health.

(7) *Exceptions to deferral due to red blood cell loss.* You are not required to defer a Source Plasma donor from donating plasma by plasmapheresis due to red blood cell loss if the following conditions are met:

(i) The responsible physician examines the donor at the time of the current donation and determines and documents that the donor is in good health and the donor's health permits the plasmapheresis;

(ii) The donor's plasma possesses a property, such as an antibody, antigen, or protein deficiency that is transitory, of a highly unusual or infrequent specificity, or of an unusually high titer;

(iii) The special characteristics of the donor's plasma and the need for plasmapheresis of the donor under § 630.20(b) are documented at your establishment; and

(iv) The extracorporeal volume of the apheresis device is less than 100 milliliters.

(8) *Malaria.* Freedom from risk of malaria is not required for a donor of Source Plasma.

(9) You must comply with other requirements for collection of plasma in part 640 of this chapter and this part including restrictions on frequency of collection as specified in §§ 640.32 and 640.65 of this chapter.

§ 630.20 **Exceptions for certain ineligible donors.**

After assessing donor eligibility under §§ 630.10 and 630.15, an establishment may collect blood and blood components from a donor who is determined to be not eligible to donate under any provision of § 630.10(e) and (f) or § 630.15(a) if one of the following sets of conditions are met:

(a) The donation is for autologous use only as prescribed by the donor's physician, the donor has a hemoglobin level no less than 11.0 grams of hemoglobin per deciliter of blood or a hematocrit value no less than 33 percent, and the responsible physician determines and documents that the donor's health permits the collection procedure; or

(b) The donation is collected under a Source Plasma collection program which has received prior written approval from the Director, Center for Biologics Evaluation and Research, to collect plasma for further manufacturing use into in vitro products for which there are no alternative sources, the donor meets the criteria in § 630.10(f)(1) through (6), and the responsible physician determines and documents for each donation that the donor's health permits the collection procedure, and the collection takes place under the medical oversight specified in the approved plasmapheresis program.

(c) The donation is restricted for use solely by a specific transfusion recipient based on documented exceptional medical need, and the responsible physician determines and documents that the donor's health permits the collection procedure, and that the donation presents no undue medical risk to the transfusion recipient.

§ 630.25 Exceptions from certain donor eligibility requirements for infrequent plasma donors.

For an infrequent plasma donor who is not participating in an immunization program, establishments are not required to:

(a) Perform a medical history and physical examination of the donor under § 630.15(b)(1);

(b) Perform a test for total protein under § 630.15(b)(4);

(c) Determine the total plasma or serum protein and immunoglobulin composition under § 640.65(b)(1)(i) of this chapter; or

(d) Review the data and records as required in § 640.65(b)(2)(i) of this chapter.

§ 630.30 Donation suitability requirements.

(a) *When is a donation suitable?* A donation is suitable when:

(1) The donor is not currently deferred from donation as determined by review of the records of deferred donors required under § 606.160(e) of this chapter;

(2) The results in accordance with §§ 630.10 through 630.25 indicate that the donor is in good health and procedures were followed to ensure that the donation would not adversely affect the health of the donor;

(3) The results in accordance with § 630.10(e) indicate that the donor is free from risk factors for, or evidence of, relevant transfusion-transmitted infections and other factors that make the donor ineligible to donate;

(4) The donor's blood is tested in accordance with § 610.40 of this chapter, and is negative or nonreactive, unless an exception applies under § 610.40(h) of this chapter; and

(5) The donation meets other requirements in this subchapter.

(b) *What must you do when the donation is not suitable?* (1) You must not release the donation for transfusion or further manufacturing use unless it is an autologous donation, or an exception is provided in this chapter.

(2) You must defer the donor when a donation is determined to be unsuitable based on the criteria in paragraphs (a)(1) through (4) of this section.

(3) You must defer the donor of bacterially contaminated platelets when the contaminating organism is identified in accordance with § 606.145(d) of this chapter as likely to be associated with a bacterial infection that is endogenous to the bloodstream of the donor.

(4) You must notify the deferred donor in accordance with the notification requirements in § 630.40.

§ 630.35 Requalification of previously deferred donors.

Establishments may determine a deferred donor to be eligible as a donor of blood and blood components if, at the time of the current collection, the donor meets the eligibility criteria in this part, except for the record of the previous deferral, and you determine that the criteria that were the basis for the previous deferral are no longer applicable. Criteria for the previous deferral are no longer applicable if the following conditions are met:

(a) The previous deferral was for a defined period of time and that time period has passed, or the deferral was otherwise temporary, such as a deferral based on eligibility criteria described in §§ 630.10(f)(1) through (5) or 630.15(b)(4); or

(b) For a donor deferred for reasons other than under § 610.41(a) of this chapter, you determine that the donor has met criteria for requalification by a method or process found acceptable for such purpose by FDA.

Subpart C—Donor Notification

SOURCE: 80 FR 29898, May 22, 2015, unless otherwise noted.

§ 630.40 Requirements for notifying deferred donors.

(a) *Notification of donors.* You, an establishment that collects blood or blood components, must make reasonable attempts to notify any donor, including an autologous donor, who has been deferred based on the results of tests for evidence of infection with a relevant transfusion-transmitted infection(s) as required by § 610.41(a) of this chapter; any donor who has been deferred as required under § 630.30(b)(3) because their donated platelets have been determined under § 606.145(d) of this chapter to be contaminated with an organism that is identified as likely to be associated with a bacterial infection that is endogenous to the bloodstream of the donor; and any donor who has been determined not to be eligible as a donor based on eligibility criteria under §§ 630.10 and 630.15. You must attempt to obtain the results of further testing required under § 610.40(e) of this chapter prior to notifying a donor of the deferral. If notification occurs prior to receipt of such results, you must also notify a deferred donor of the results of the further testing. You must notify a donor as described in paragraph (b) of this section.

(b) *Content of notification.* You must provide the following information to a donor deferred or determined not to be eligible as a donor as described in paragraph (a) of this section:

(1) That the donor is deferred or determined not to be eligible for donation and the reason for that decision;

(2) Where appropriate, the types of donation of blood or blood components that the donor should not donate in the future;

(3) Where applicable, the results of tests for evidence of infection due to relevant transfusion-transmitted infection(s) that were a basis for deferral under § 610.41 of this chapter, including results of further testing as required in § 610.40(e) of this chapter; and,

(4) Where appropriate, information concerning medical followup and counseling.

(c) *Time period for notification.* You must make reasonable attempts to notify the donor within 8 weeks after determining that the donor is deferred or determined not to be eligible for donation as described in paragraph (a) of this section. You must document that you have successfully notified the donor or when you are unsuccessful

that you have made reasonable attempts to notify the donor.

(d) *Autologous donors.* (1) You also must provide the following information to the referring physician of an autologous donor who is deferred based on the results of tests for evidence of infection with a relevant transfusion-transmitted infection(s) or whose platelets indicate evidence of a bacterial infection that is endogenous to the bloodstream of the donor as described in paragraph (a) of this section:

(i) Information that the autologous donor is deferred based on the results of tests for evidence of infection due to relevant transfusion-transmitted infection(s), as required under § 610.41 of this chapter, and the reason for that decision;

(ii) Where appropriate, the types of donation of blood or blood components that the autologous donor should not donate in the future; and

(iii) The results of tests for evidence of infection due to relevant transfusion-transmitted infection(s), that were a basis for deferral under § 610.41 of this chapter, including results of further testing as required in § 610.40(e) of this chapter.

(2) You must make reasonable attempts to notify the autologous donor's referring physician within 8 weeks after determining that the autologous donor is deferred as described in paragraph (a) of this section. You must document that you have successfully notified the autologous donor's referring physician or when you are unsuccessful that you have made reasonable attempts to notify the physician.

[66 FR 31176, June 11, 2001. Redesignated and amended at 80 FR 29898, May 22, 2015]

PART 640—ADDITIONAL STANDARDS FOR HUMAN BLOOD AND BLOOD PRODUCTS

Subpart A—Whole Blood

AUTHORITY: 21 U.S.C. 321, 351, 352, 353, 355, 360, 371; 42 U.S.C. 216, 262, 263, 263a, 264.

SOURCE: 38 FR 32089, Nov. 20, 1973, unless otherwise noted.

CROSS REFERENCES: For U.S. Customs Service regulations relating to viruses, serums, and toxins, see 19 CFR 12.21–12.23. For U.S. Postal Service regulations relating to the admissibility to the United States mails see parts 124 and 125 of the Domestic Mail Manual, that is incorporated by reference in 39 CFR part 111.

Subpart A—Whole Blood

§ 640.1 Whole Blood.

The proper name of this product shall be Whole Blood. Whole Blood is defined as blood collected from human donors for transfusion to human recipients.

[38 FR 32089, Nov. 20, 1973, as amended at 50 FR 4138, Jan. 29, 1985]

§ 640.2 General requirements.

(a) *Manufacturing responsibility.* All manufacturing of Whole Blood, including donor examination, blood collection, laboratory tests, labeling, storage and issue, shall be done under the supervision and control of the same licensed establishment except that the Director, Center for Biologics Evaluation and Research, may approve arrangements, upon joint request of two or more licensed establishments, which he finds are of such a nature as to assure compliance otherwise with the provisions of this subchapter.

(b) *Blood container.* The blood container shall not be entered prior to issue for any purpose except for blood collection or when the method of processing requires use of a different container. The container shall be uncolored and transparent to permit visual inspection of the contents and any closure shall be such as will maintain a hermetic seal and prevent contamination of the contents. The container material shall not interact with the contents under the customary conditions of storage and use, in such a manner as to have an adverse effect upon the safety, purity, or potency of the blood.

(c) *Reissue of blood.* Blood that has been removed from storage controlled by a licensed establishment shall not be reissued by a licensed establishment unless the following conditions are observed:

(1) The container has a tamper-proof seal when originally issued and this seal remains unbroken;

(2) A segment is properly attached and has not been removed, except that blood lacking a properly attached segment may be reissued in an emergency provided it is accompanied by instructions for sampling and for use within 6 hours after entering the container for sampling;

(3) The blood has been stored continuously at 1 to 6 °C and shipped between 1 and 10 °C;

(4) The blood is held for observation until a significant inspection consistent with the requirements of §640.5(e) can be made.

[38 FR 32089, Nov. 20, 1973, as amended at 41 FR 4015, Jan. 28, 1976; 42 FR 59878, Nov. 22, 1977; 43 FR 34460, Aug. 4, 1978; 49 FR 15187, Apr. 18, 1984; 49 FR 23834, June 8, 1984; 50 FR 4138, Jan. 29, 1985; 53 FR 116, Jan. 5, 1988; 55 FR 11013, Mar. 26, 1990; 63 FR 16685, Apr. 6, 1998; 64 FR 45371, Aug. 19, 1999; 66 FR 1836, Jan. 10, 2001; 66 FR 31165, June 11, 2001; 66 FR 40889, Aug. 6, 2001; 67 FR 9587, Mar. 4, 2002]

§640.4 **Collection of the blood.**

(a) [Reserved]

(b) *The donor center.* The pertinent requirements of §§600.10 and 600.11 of this chapter shall apply at both the blood establishment and at any other place where the bleeding is performed.

(c) *Blood containers.* Blood containers and donor sets shall be pyrogen-free, sterile and identified by lot number. The amount of anticoagulant required for the quantity of blood to be collected shall be in the blood container when it is sterilized. In addition, all container and donor set surfaces that come in contact with blood used in the processing of Heparin Whole Blood shall be water repellent.

(d) *The anticoagulant solution.* The anticoagulant solution shall be sterile and pyrogen-free. Anticoagulant solutions shall be compounded and used according to a formula approved by the Director, Center for Biologics Evaluation and Research.

(e) *Donor identification.* Each unit of blood shall be so marked or identified by number or other symbol as to relate it to the individual donor whose identity shall be established to the extent necessary for compliance with §630.10 of this chapter.

(f) *Prevention of contamination of the blood.* The skin of the donor at the site of phlebotomy shall be prepared thoroughly and carefully by a method that gives maximum assurance of a sterile container of blood. The blood shall be collected by aseptic methods in a sterile system which may be closed or may be vented if the vent protects the blood against contamination.

(g) *Samples and segments for laboratory tests.* Samples and segments for laboratory tests shall meet the following standards:

(1) One or more segments shall be provided with each unit of blood when issued or reissued except as provided in §640.2(c)(2) and all segments shall be from the donor who is the source of the unit of blood.

(2) All samples for laboratory tests performed by the manufacturer and all segments accompanying a unit of blood shall be collected at the time of filling the original blood container.

(3) All containers for all samples shall bear the donor's identification before collecting the samples.

(4) All segments accompanying a unit of blood shall be attached to the whole blood container before blood collection,

in a tamperproof manner that will conspicuously indicate removal and reattachment.

(5) Segments for compatibility testing shall contain blood mixed with the appropriate anticoagulant.

(h) *Storage.* Whole Blood must be placed in storage at a temperature between 1 and 6 °C immediately after collection unless the blood is to be further processed into another component or the blood must be transported from the donor center to the processing laboratory. If transported, the blood must be placed in temporary storage having sufficient refrigeration capacity to cool the blood continuously toward a temperature range between 1 and 10 °C until arrival at the processing laboratory. At the processing laboratory, blood must be stored at a temperature between 1 and 6 °C. Blood from which a component is to be prepared must be held in an environment maintained at a temperature range specified for that component in the directions for use for the blood collecting, processing, and storage system approved for such use by the Director, CBER.

[38 FR 32089, Nov. 20, 1973, as amended at 42 FR 59878, Nov. 22, 1977; 43 FR 34460, Aug. 4, 1978; 49 FR 23834, June 8, 1984; 50 FR 4138, Jan. 29, 1985; 55 FR 11013, Mar. 26, 1990; 64 FR 45372, Aug. 19, 1999; 66 FR 1836, Jan. 10, 2001; 66 FR 40889, Aug. 6, 2001; 72 FR 45887, Aug. 16, 2007; 73 FR 7464, Feb. 8, 2008; 80 FR 29904, May 22, 2015]

§ 640.5 Testing the blood.

All laboratory tests shall be made on a specimen of blood taken from the donor, and these tests shall include the following:

(a) [Reserved]

(b) *Determination of blood group.* Each container of Whole Blood shall be classified as to ABO blood group. At least two blood group tests shall be made and the unit shall not be issued until grouping tests by different methods or with different lots of antiserums are in agreement. Only those Anti-A and Anti-B Blood Grouping Reagents licensed under, or that otherwise meet the requirements of, the regulations of this subchapter shall be used, and the technique used shall be that for which the serum is specifically designed to be effective.

(c) *Determination of the Rh factors.* Each container of Whole Blood shall be classified as to Rh type on the basis of tests done on the sample. The label shall indicate the extent of typing and the results of all tests performed. If the test, using Anti-D Blood Grouping Reagent, is positive, the container may be labeled "Rh Positive." If the test is negative, the results shall be confirmed by further testing which shall include tests for the "weak D (formerly D^u)." Blood may be labeled "Rh Negative" if further testing is negative. Units testing positive after additional more specific testing shall be labeled as "Rh Positive." Only Anti-Rh Blood Grouping Reagents licensed under, or that otherwise meet the requirements of, this subchapter shall be used, and the technique used shall be that for which the reagent is specifically designed to be effective.

(d) *Sterility test.* Whole Blood intended for transfusion shall not be tested for sterility by a method that entails entering the final container before the blood is used for transfusion.

(e) *Inspection.* Whole Blood shall be inspected visually during storage and immediately prior to issue. If the color or physical appearance is abnormal or there is any indication or suspicion of microbial contamination the unit of Whole Blood shall not be issued for transfusion.

(f) *Test for relevant transfusion-transmitted infections.* Whole Blood shall be tested for evidence of infection due to relevant transfusion-transmitted infections as required under § 610.40 of this chapter.

[38 FR 32089, Nov. 20, 1973, as amended at 50 FR 4138, Jan. 29, 1985; 53 FR 117, Jan. 5, 1988; 53 FR 12764, Apr. 19, 1988; 64 FR 45372, Aug. 19, 1999; 66 FR 1836, Jan. 10, 2001; 66 FR 31165, June 11, 2001; 66 FR 40889, Aug. 6, 2001; 80 FR 29904, May 22, 2015]

§ 640.6 Modifications of Whole Blood.

Upon approval by the Director, Center for Biologics Evaluation and Research, of a supplement to the biologics license application for Whole Blood a manufacturer may prepare Whole Blood from which the antihemophilic factor has been removed, provided the

Whole Blood meets the applicable requirements of this subchapter and the following conditions are met:

(a) The antihemophilic factor shall be removed in accordance with paragraphs (a), (b), and (c) of §640.52.

(b) Although the closed system between the red blood cells and plasma shall be maintained, the red blood cells shall be maintained between 1 and 6 °C at all times, including that time when the plasma is being frozen for removal of the antihemophilic factor.

[38 FR 32089, Nov. 20, 1973, as amended at 49 FR 23834, June 8, 1984; 50 FR 4138, Jan. 29, 1985; 55 FR 11013, Mar. 26, 1990; 59 FR 49351, Sept. 28, 1994; 64 FR 45372, Aug. 19, 1999; 64 FR 56453, Oct. 20, 1999]

Subpart B—Red Blood Cells

§640.10 Red Blood Cells.

The proper name of this product shall be Red Blood Cells. The product is defined as red blood cells remaining after separating plasma from human blood.

[38 FR 32089, Nov. 20, 1973, as amended at 50 FR 4138, Jan. 29, 1985]

§640.11 General requirements.

(a) *Storage.* Immediately after processing, the Red Blood Cells shall be placed in storage and maintained at a temperature between 1 and 6 °C.

(b) *Inspection.* The product shall be inspected immediately after separation of the plasma, periodically during storage, and at the time of issue. The product shall not be issued if there is any abnormality in color or physical appearance or if there is any indication of microbial contamination.

[38 FR 32089, Nov. 20, 1973, as amended at 41 FR 18292, May 3, 1976; 42 FR 59878, Nov. 11, 1977; 50 FR 4139, Jan. 29, 1985]

§640.12 Eligibility of donor.

Establishments must determine the eligibility of donors of the source blood for Red Blood Cells in accordance with §§630.10 and 630.15 of this chapter.

[80 FR 29904, May 22, 2015]

§640.13 Collection of the blood.

(a) The source blood shall be collected as prescribed in §640.4.

(b) Source blood may also be derived from Whole Blood manufactured in accordance with applicable provisions of this subchapter.

[38 FR 32089, Nov. 20, 1973, as amended at 50 FR 4139, Jan. 29, 1985; 64 FR 45372, Aug. 19, 1999]

§640.14 Testing the blood.

Blood from which Red Blood Cells are prepared shall be tested as prescribed in §610.40 of this chapter and §640.5 (b) and (c).

[53 FR 117, Jan. 5, 1988, as amended at 66 FR 31165, June 11, 2001; 80 FR 29904, May 22, 2015]

§640.15 Segments for testing.

Segments collected in integral tubing shall meet the following standards:

(a) One or more segments shall be provided with each unit of Whole Blood or Red Blood Cells when issued or reissued.

(b) Before they are filled, all segments shall be marked or identified so as to relate them to the donor of that unit of red cells.

(c) All segments accompanying a unit of Red Blood Cells shall be filled at the time the blood is collected or at the time the final product is prepared.

[66 FR 40890, Aug. 6, 2001]

§640.16 Processing.

(a) *Separation.* Within the timeframe specified in the directions for use for the blood collecting, processing, and storage system used, Red Blood Cells may be prepared either by centrifugation, done in a manner that will not tend to increase the temperature of the blood, or by normal undisturbed sedimentation. A portion of the plasma sufficient to insure optimal cell preservation shall be left with the red cells except when a cryoprotective substance or additive solution is added for prolonged storage.

(b) *Sterile system.* All surfaces that come in contact with the red cells shall be sterile and pyrogen-free.

(c) *Final containers.* Final containers used for Red Blood Cells shall be the original blood containers unless the method of processing requires a different container. The final container shall meet the requirements for blood containers prescribed in §640.2(c). At the time of filing, if a different container is used, it shall be marked or identified by number or other symbol so as to relate it to the donor of that unit of red cells.

[38 FR 32089, Nov. 20, 1973, as amended at 43 FR 34460, Aug. 4, 1978; 50 FR 4139, Jan. 29, 1985; 64 FR 45372, Aug. 19, 1999; 66 FR 1836, Jan. 10, 2001; 66 FR 40890, Aug. 6, 2001]

§ 640.17   Modifications   for   specific products.

Red   Blood   Cells   Frozen: A cryophylactic substance may be added to the Red Blood Cells for extended manufacturers' storage at −65 °C or colder, provided the manufacturer submits data considered by the Director, Center for Biologics Evaluation and Research, as adequately demonstrating through in vivo cell survival and other appropriate tests that the addition of the substance, the materials used and the processing methods results in a final product that meets the required standards of safety, purity, and potency for Red Blood Cells, and that the frozen product will maintain those properties for the prescribed dating period. Section 640.11 (a) and (b) do not apply while a cryophylactic substance is present.

[38 FR 32089, Nov. 20, 1973, as amended at 41 FR 18292, May 3, 1976; 49 FR 23834, June 8, 1984; 50 FR 4139, Jan. 29, 1985; 55 FR 11013, Mar. 26, 1990; 63 FR 16685, Apr. 6, 1998]

Subpart C—Platelets

§ 640.20   Platelets.

(a) *Proper name and definition.* The proper name of this product shall be Platelets. The product is defined as platelets collected from one unit of blood and resuspended in an appropriate volume of original plasma, as prescribed in § 640.24(d).

(b) *Source.* The source material for Platelets is plasma which may be obtained by whole blood collection or by plateletpheresis.

[40 FR 4304, Jan. 29, 1975, as amended at 47 FR 49021, Oct. 29, 1982; 50 FR 4139, Jan. 29, 1985; 72 FR 45887, Aug. 16, 2007]

§ 640.21   Eligibility of donors.

(a) Establishments must determine the eligibility of donors of platelets derived from Whole Blood and donors of platelets collected by plateletpheresis

in accordance with §§ 630.10 and 630.15 of this chapter, except as provided in this section.

(b) A plateletpheresis donor must not serve as the source of platelets for transfusion if the donor has recently ingested a drug that adversely affects platelet function.

(c) A Whole Blood donor must not serve as the source of platelets for transfusion if the donor has recently ingested a drug that adversely affects platelet function unless the unit is labeled to identify the ingested drug that adversely affects platelet function.

(d) If you are collecting platelets by plateletpheresis, you must assess and monitor the donor's platelet count.

(1) You must take adequate and appropriate steps to assure that the donor's platelet count is at least 150,000 platelets per microliter (μL) before plateletpheresis begins. Exception: If you do not have records of a donor's platelet count from prior donations and you are not able to assess the donor's platelet count either prior to or immediately following the initiation of the collection procedure, you may collect platelets by plateletpheresis, but you must not collect 9.0×10^{11} or more platelets from that donor.

(2) You must defer from platelet donation a donor whose pre-donation platelet count is less than 150,000 platelets/μL until a subsequent pre-donation platelet count indicates that the donor's platelet count is at least 150,000 platelets/μL; and

(3) You must take appropriate steps to assure that the donor's intended post-donation platelet count will be no less than 100,000 platelets/μL.

(e) *Frequency of plateletpheresis collection.* (1) The donor may donate no more than a total of 24 plateletpheresis collections during a 12-month rolling period.

(2) When you collect fewer than 6×10^{11} platelets, you must wait at least 2 calendar days before any subsequent plateletpheresis collection. You must not attempt to collect more than 2 collections within a 7 calendar day period.

(3) When you collect 6×10^{11} or more platelets, you must wait at least 7 calendar days before any subsequent plateletpheresis collection.

(4) *Exception.* For a period not to exceed 30 calendar days, a donor may serve as a dedicated plateletpheresis donor for a single recipient, in accordance with §610.40(c)(1) of this chapter, as often as is medically necessary, provided that the donor is in good health, as determined and documented by the responsible physician, and the donor's platelet count is at least 150,000 platelets/μL, measured at the conclusion of the previous donation or before initiating plateletpheresis for the current donation.

(f) *Deferral of plateletpheresis donors due to red blood cell loss.* (1) You must defer a donor from donating platelets by plateletpheresis or a co-collection of platelets and plasma by apheresis for 8 weeks if the donor has donated a unit of Whole Blood, or a single unit of Red Blood Cells by apheresis unless at least 2 calendar days have passed and the extracorporeal volume of the apheresis device is less than 100 milliliters.

(2) You must defer a donor from donating platelets for a period of 16 weeks if the donor donates two units of Red Blood Cells during a single apheresis procedure.

(3) You must defer a donor for 8 weeks or more if the cumulative red blood cell loss in any 8 week period could adversely affect donor health.

(g) The responsible physician must obtain the informed consent of a plateletpheresis donor on the first day of donation, and at subsequent intervals no longer than 1 year.

(1) The responsible physician must explain the risks and hazards of the procedure to the donor; and

(2) The explanation must be made in such a manner that the donor may give consent, and has a clear opportunity to refuse the procedure.

[80 FR 29904, May 22, 2015]

§640.22 Collection of source material.

(a) Whole blood used as the source of Platelets shall be collected as prescribed in §640.4.

(b) [Reserved]

(c) If plateletpheresis is used, the procedure for collection must be as prescribed in §§640.21, 640.64 (except paragraph (c)), and 640.65, or as described in an approved biologics license

application (BLA) or an approved supplement to a BLA.

(d) The phlebotomy shall be performed by a single uninterrupted venipuncture with minimal damage to, and minimal manipulation of, the donor's tissue.

[40 FR 4304, Jan. 29, 1975, as amended at 45 FR 27927, Apr. 25, 1980; 49 FR 23834, June 8, 1984; 50 FR 4139, Jan. 29, 1985; 55 FR 11013, Mar. 26, 1990; 59 FR 49351, Sept. 28, 1994; 64 FR 45372, Aug. 19, 1999; 64 FR 56453, Oct. 20, 1999; 72 FR 45887, Aug. 16, 2007; 80 FR 29904, May 22, 2015]

§640.23 Testing the blood.

(a) Blood from which plasma is separated for the preparation of Platelets shall be tested as prescribed in §610.40 of this chapter and §640.5 (b) and (c).

(b) The tests shall be performed on a sample of blood collected at the time of collecting the source blood, and such sample container shall be labeled with the donor's number before the container is filled.

[40 FR 4304, Jan. 29, 1975, as amended at 50 FR 4139, Jan. 29, 1985; 53 FR 117, Jan. 5, 1988; 64 FR 45372, Aug. 19, 1999; 66 FR 1836, Jan. 10, 2001; 66 FR 31165, June 11, 2001; 80 FR 29904, May 22, 2015]

§640.24 Processing.

(a) Separation of plasma and platelets and resuspension of the platelets must be in a closed system. Platelets must not be pooled during processing unless the platelets are pooled as specified in the directions for use for the blood collecting, processing, and storage system approved for such use by the Director, Center for Biologics Evaluation and Research.

(b) Immediately after collection, the whole blood or plasma shall be held in storage between 20 and 24 °C unless it must be transported from the collection center to the processing laboratory. During such transport, all reasonable methods shall be used to maintain the temperature as close as possible to a range between 20 and 24 °C until it arrives at the processing laboratory where it shall be held between 20 and 24 °C until the platelets are separated. The platelet concentrate shall be separated within 4 hours or within the timeframe specified in the directions for use for the blood collecting, processing, and storage system.

(c) The time and speed of centrifugation must have been demonstrated to produce an unclumped product, without visible hemolysis, that yields a count of not less than 5.5×10^{10} platelets per unit in at least 75 percent of the units tested.

(d) The volume of original plasma used for resuspension of the platelets shall be determined by the maintenance of a pH of not less than 6.2 during the storage period. The pH shall be measured on a sample of platelets which has been stored for the maximum dating period at the selected storage temperature. One of the following storage temperatures shall be used continuously:

(1) 20 to 24 °C.

(2) 1 to 6 °C.

(e) Final containers used for Platelets shall be colorless and transparent to permit visual inspection of the contents; any closure shall maintain a hermetic seal and prevent contamination of the contents. The container material shall not interact with the contents, under the customary conditions of storage and use, in such a manner as to have an adverse effect upon the safety, purity, potency, or efficacy of the product. At the time of filling, the final container shall be marked or identified by number so as to relate it to the donor.

[40 FR 4304, Jan. 29, 1975, as amended at 42 FR 10983, Feb. 25, 1977; 47 FR 49021, Oct. 29, 1982; 50 FR 4139, Jan. 29, 1985; 63 FR 16685, Apr. 6, 1998; 64 FR 45372, Aug. 19, 1999; 66 FR 1836, Jan. 10, 2001; 66 FR 40890, Aug. 6, 2001; 72 FR 45887, Aug. 16, 2007; 73 FR 7464, Feb. 8, 2008]

§ 640.25 General requirements.

(a) *Storage.* Immediately after resuspension, Platelets shall be placed in storage at the selected temperature range. If stored at 20 to 24 °C, a continuous gentle agitation of the platelet concentrate shall be maintained throughout the storage period. Agitation is optional if stored at a temperature between 1 and 6 °C.

(b) *Quality control testing.* Each month four units prepared from different donors shall be tested at the end of the storage period as follows:

(1) Platelet count.

(2) pH of not less than 6.2 measured at the storage temperature of the unit.

(3) Measurement of actual plasma volume.

(4) If the results of the quality control testing indicate that the product does not meet the prescribed requirements, immediate corrective action shall be taken and a record maintained of such action.

(c) *Manufacturing responsibility.* All manufacturing of Platelets shall be performed at the same licensed establishment, except that the quality control testing under paragraph (b) of this section may be performed by a clinical laboratory which meets the standards of the Clinical Laboratories Improvement Amendments of 1988 (CLIA) (42 U.S.C. 263a) and is qualified to perform platelet counts. Such arrangements must be approved by the Director, Center for Biologics Evaluation and Research, Food and Drug Administration. Such testing shall not be considered as divided manufacturing, as described in § 610.63 of this chapter, provided the following conditions are met:

(1) The results of each test are received within 10 days of the preparation of the platelet concentrate, and are maintained by the establishment licensed for Platelets so that they may be reviewed by an authorized representative of the Food and Drug Administration.

(2) The licensed Platelets manufacturer has obtained a written agreement that the testing laboratory will permit an authorized representative of the Food and Drug Administration to inspect its testing procedures and facilities during reasonable business hours.

(3) The testing laboratory will participate in any proficiency testing programs undertaken by the Center for Biologics Evaluation and Research, Food and Drug Administration.

[40 FR 4304, Jan. 29, 1975, as amended at 47 FR 49021, Oct. 29, 1982; 49 FR 23834, June 8, 1984; 50 FR 4139, Jan. 29, 1985; 55 FR 11013, Mar. 26, 1990; 66 FR 1836, Jan. 10, 2001; 72 FR 45888, Aug. 16, 2007]

Subpart D—Plasma

§640.30 Plasma.

(a) *Proper name and definition.* The proper name of this component is Plasma. The component is defined as:

(1) The fluid portion of one unit of human blood intended for intravenous use which is collected in a closed system, stabilized against clotting, and separated from the red cells; or

(2) The fluid portion of human blood intended for intravenous use which is prepared by apheresis methods as specified in the directions for use for the blood collecting, processing, and storage system including closed and open systems.

(b) *Source.* (1) Plasma shall be obtained by separating plasma from blood collected from blood donors or by plasmapheresis.

(2) Plasma may be obtained from a unit of Whole Blood collected by another licensed establishment.

[42 FR 59878, Nov. 22, 1977; 48 FR 13026, Mar. 29, 1983, as amended at 50 FR 4139, Jan. 29, 1985; 72 FR 45888, Aug. 16, 2007]

§640.31 Eligibility of donors.

(a) Whole Blood donors must meet the criteria for donor eligibility prescribed in §§630.10 and 630.15 of this chapter.

(b) Collection establishments must determine the eligibility of plasmapheresis donors in accordance with §§630.10 and 630.15 of this chapter.

[80 FR 29904, May 22, 2015]

§640.32 Collection of source material.

(a) Whole Blood must be collected, transported, and stored as prescribed in §640.4. When whole blood is intended for Plasma, Fresh Frozen Plasma, and Liquid Plasma, until the plasma is removed, the whole blood must be maintained at a temperature between 1 and 6 °C or as specified in the directions for use for the blood collecting, processing, and storage system approved for such use by the Director, Center for Biologics Evaluations and Research. Whole blood intended for Platelet Rich Plasma must be maintained as prescribed in §640.24 until the plasma is removed. The red blood cells must be placed in storage at a temperature between 1 and 6 °C immediately after the plasma is separated.

(b) Plasma obtained by plasmapheresis shall be collected as prescribed in §640.64 (except that paragraph (c)(3) of §640.64 shall not apply), and §640.65.

[42 FR 59878, Nov. 22, 1977, as amended at 45 FR 27927, Apr. 25, 1980; 50 FR 4139, Jan. 29, 1985; 64 FR 45372, Aug. 19, 1999; 72 FR 45888, Aug. 16, 2007; 80 FR 29905, May 22, 2015]

§640.33 Testing the blood.

(a) Blood from which plasma is separated shall be tested as prescribed in §610.40 of this chapter and §640.5 (b) and (c).

(b) Manufacturers of Plasma collected by plasmapheresis shall have testing and recordkeeping responsibilities equivalent to those prescribed in §§640.71 and 640.72.

[42 FR 59878, Nov. 22, 1977, as amended at 44 FR 17658, Mar. 23, 1979; 50 FR 4139, Jan. 29, 1985; 53 FR 117, Jan. 5, 1988; 66 FR 31165, June 11, 2001; 80 FR 29905, May 22, 2015]

§640.34 Processing.

(a) *Plasma.* Plasma shall be separated from the red blood cells and shall be stored at −18 °C or colder within 6 hours after transfer to the final container or within the timeframe specified in the directions for use for the blood collecting, processing, and storage system unless the product is to be stored as Liquid Plasma.

(b) *Fresh Frozen Plasma.* Fresh frozen plasma shall be prepared from blood collected by a single uninterrupted venipuncture with minimal damage to and minimal manipulation of the donor's tissue. The plasma must be separated from the red blood cells or collected by an apheresis procedure, and placed in a freezer within 8 hours or within the timeframe specified in the directions for use for the blood collecting, processing, and storage system, and stored at −18 °C or colder.

(c) *Liquid Plasma.* Liquid Plasma shall be separated from the red blood cells and shall be stored at a temperature of 1 to 6 °C within 4 hours after filling the final container or within the timeframe specified in the directions for use for the blood collecting, processing, and storage system.

(d) *Platelet Rich Plasma.* Platelet rich plasma shall be prepared from blood collected by a single uninterrupted venipuncture with minimal damage to and manipulation of the donor's tissue. The plasma shall be separated from the red blood cells by centrifugation within 4 hours after completion of the phlebotomy or within the timeframe specified in the directions for use for the blood collecting, processing, and storage system. The time and speed of the centrifugation shall have been shown to produce a product with at least 250,000 platelets per microliter. The plasma shall be stored at a temperature between 20 and 24 °C immediately after filling the final container. A gentle and continuous agitation of the product shall be maintained throughout the storage period, if stored at a temperature of 20 to 24 °C.

(e) *Modifications of Plasma.* It is possible to separate Platelets and/or Cryoprecipitated AHF from Plasma. When these components are to be separated, the plasma shall be collected as described in § 640.32 for Plasma.

(1) Platelets shall be separated as prescribed in subpart C of part 640, prior to freezing the plasma. The remaining plasma may be labeled "Fresh Frozen Plasma," if frozen within 6 hours after filling the final container or within the timeframe specified in the directions for use for the blood collecting, processing, and storage system.

(2) Cryoprecipitated AHF shall be removed as prescribed in subpart F of part 640. The remaining plasma shall be labeled "Plasma, Cryoprecipitate Reduced."

(3) Plasma remaining after both Platelets and Cryoprecipitated AHF have been removed may be labeled "Plasma, Cryoprecipitate Reduced."

(f) *The final container.* (1) The final container shall have no color added to the plastic and shall be transparent to permit visual inspection of the contents; any closure shall maintain a hermetic seal and prevent contamination of the contents.

(2) The final container material shall not interact with the contents, under the customary conditions of storage and use, in such a manner as to have an adverse effect upon the safety, purity,

potency, and effectiveness of the product.

(3) Prior to filling, the final container shall be identified by number so as to relate it to the donor.

(g) *The final product.* (1) The final product shall be inspected immediately after separation of the plasma and shall not be issued for transfusion if there is (i) any abnormality in color or physical appearance, or (ii) any indication of contamination.

(2) With the exception of Platelet Rich Plasma and Liquid Plasma the final product shall be inspected for evidence of thawing or breakage at the time of issuance, however, the containers need not be stored in a manner that shows evidence of thawing if records of continuous monitoring of the storage temperature establish that the temperature remained at −18 °C or colder. If continuous monitoring of the product is not available, the final product shall be stored in a manner that will show evidence of thawing and shall not be issued if there is any evidence of thawing.

(3) No preservative shall be added to the final product.

[42 FR 59878, Nov. 22, 1977, as amended at 43 FR 34460, Aug. 4, 1978; 48 FR 13026, Mar. 29, 1983; 50 FR 4139, Jan. 29, 1985; 64 FR 45373, Aug. 19, 1999; 66 FR 1836, Jan. 10, 2001; 66 FR 40890, Aug. 6, 2001; 72 FR 45888, Aug. 16, 2007]

Subpart E [Reserved]

Subpart F—Cryoprecipitate

§ 640.50 Cryoprecipitated AHF.

(a) *Proper name and definition.* The proper name of this product shall be Cryoprecipitated AHF. The product is defined as a preparation of antihemophilic factor, which is obtained from a single unit of plasma collected and processed in a closed system.

(b) *Source.* The source material for Cryoprecipitated AHF shall be plasma which may be obtained by whole blood collection or by plasmapheresis.

[42 FR 21774, Apr. 29, 1977; 48 FR 13026, Mar. 29, 1983, as amended at 50 FR 4139, Jan. 29, 1985]

§ 640.51 Eligibility of donors.

(a) Whole blood donors must meet the criteria for eligibility prescribed in §§ 630.10 and 630.15 of this chapter.

(b) Collection establishments must determine the eligibility of plasmapheresis donors in accordance with §§ 630.10 and 630.15 of this chapter.

[80 FR 29905, May 22, 2015]

§ 640.52 Collection of source material.

(a) Whole blood used as a source of Cryoprecipitated AHF shall be collected as prescribed in § 640.4. Whole blood from which both Platelets and Cryoprecipitated AHF is derived shall be maintained as required under § 640.24 until the platelets are removed.

(b) If plasmapheresis is used, the procedure for collection shall be as prescribed in § 640.64 (except that paragraph (c)(3) of that section shall not apply), and 640.65.

[42 FR 21774, Apr. 29, 1977, as amended at 50 FR 4139, Jan. 29, 1985; 64 FR 45373, Aug. 19, 1999; 80 FR 29905, May 22, 2015]

§ 640.53 Testing the blood.

(a) Blood from which plasma is separated for the preparation of Cryoprecipitated AHF shall be tested as prescribed in § 610.40 of this chapter and § 640.5 (b) and (c).

(b) The tests shall be performed on a sample of blood collected at the time of collecting the source blood, and such sample container shall be labeled with the donor's number before the container is filled.

(c) Manufacturers of Cryoprecipitated AHF obtained from plasma collected by plasmapheresis shall have testing and record-keeping responsibilities equivalent to those prescribed in §§ 640.71 and 640.72.

[42 FR 21774, Apr. 29, 1977, as amended at 42 FR 37546, July 22, 1977; 42 FR 43063, Aug. 26, 1977; 50 FR 4139, Jan. 29, 1985; 53 FR 117, Jan. 5, 1988; 66 FR 31165, June 11, 2001; 80 FR 29905, May 22, 2015]

§ 640.54 Processing.

(a) *Processing the plasma.* (1) The plasma shall be separated from the red blood cells by centrifugation to obtain essentially cell-free plasma.

(2) The plasma shall be placed in a freezer within 8 hours after blood col-

lection or within the timeframe specified in the directions for use for the blood collecting, processing, and storage system. A combination of dry ice and organic solvent may be used for freezing: *Provided,* That the procedure has been shown not to cause the solvent to penetrate the container or leach plasticizer from the container into the plasma.

(3) Immediately after separation and freezing of the plasma, the plasma shall be stored and maintained at −18 °C or colder until thawing of the plasma for further processing to remove the Cryoprecipitated AHF.

(b) *Processing the final product.* (1) The Cryoprecipitated AHF shall be separated from the plasma by a procedure that has been shown to produce an average of no less than 80 units of antihemophilic factor per final container.

(2) No diluent shall be added to the product by the manufacturer prior to freezing.

(3) The final container used for Cryoprecipitated AHF shall be colorless and transparent to permit visual inspection of the contents; any closure shall maintain a hermetic seal and prevent contamination of the contents. The container material shall not interact with the contents under customary conditions of storage and use in such a manner as to have an adverse effect upon the safety, purity, potency and effectiveness of the product. At the time of filling, the final container shall be identified by a number so as to relate it to the donor.

[42 FR 21774, Apr. 29, 1977, as amended at 47 FR 15330, Apr. 9, 1982; 50 FR 4139, Jan. 29, 1985; 64 FR 45373, Aug. 19, 1999; 66 FR 1837, Jan. 10, 2001; 66 FR 40890, Aug. 6, 2001]

§ 640.55 U.S. Standard preparation.

A U.S. Standard Antihemophilic Factor (Factor VIII) preparation may be obtained from the Center for Biologics Evaluation and Research, (HFM–407) (see mailing addresses in § 600.2 of this chapter) for use in the preparation of a working reference to be employed in a quality control potency test of Cryoprecipitated AHF.

[42 FR 21774, Apr. 29, 1977, as amended at 49 FR 23834, June 8, 1984; 50 FR 4140, Jan. 29, 1985; 55 FR 11013, Mar. 26, 1990; 70 FR 14985, Mar. 24, 2005]

§ 640.56 Quality control test for potency.

(a) Quality control tests for potency of antihemophilic factor shall be conducted each month on at least four representative containers of Cryoprecipitated AHF.

(b) The results of each test are received by the establishment licensed for Cryoprecipitated AHF within 30 days of the preparation of the cryoprecipitated antihemophilic factor and are maintained at that establishment so that they may be reviewed by an authorized representative of the Food and Drug Administration.

(c) The quality control test for potency may be performed by a clinical laboratory which meets the standards of the Clinical Laboratories Improvement Amendments of 1988 (CLIA) (42 U.S.C. 263a) and is qualified to perform potency tests for antihemophilic factor. Such arrangements must be approved by the Director, Center for Biologics Evaluation and Research, Food and Drug Administration. Such testing shall not be considered as divided manufacturing, as described in § 610.63 of this chapter, provided the following conditions are met:

(1) The establishment licensed for Cryoprecipitated AHF has obtained a written agreement that the testing laboratory will permit an authorized representative of the Food and Drug Administration to inspect its testing procedures and facilities during reasonable business hours.

(2) The testing laboratory will participate in any proficiency testing programs undertaken by the Center for Biologics Evaluation and Research, Food and Drug Administration.

(d) If the average potency level of antihemophilic factor in the containers tested is less than 80 units of antihemophilic factor per container, immediate corrective actions shall be taken and a record maintained of such action.

[42 FR 21774, Apr. 29, 1977, as amended at 49 FR 23834, June 8, 1984; 50 FR 4140, Jan. 29, 1985; 55 FR 11013, Mar. 26, 1990; 64 FR 45373, Aug. 19, 1999; 66 FR 1837, Jan. 10, 2001]

Subpart G—Source Plasma

§ 640.60 Source Plasma.

The proper name of the product shall be Source Plasma. The product is defined as the fluid portion of human blood collected by plasmapheresis and intended as source material for further manufacturing use. The definition excludes single donor plasma products intended for intravenous use.

[41 FR 10768, Mar. 12, 1976, as amended at 50 FR 4140, Jan. 29, 1985]

§ 640.64 Collection of blood for Source Plasma.

(a) [Reserved]

(b) *Blood containers.* Blood containers and donor sets must be pyrogen-free, sterile, and identified by lot number.

(c) *The anticoagulant solution.* The anticoagulant solution must be sterile and pyrogen-free. Anticoagulant solutions must be compounded and used according to a formula that has been approved for the applicant by the Director, Center for Biologics Evaluation and Research.

(d) *Donor identification.* Each unit of blood and plasma shall be so marked or identified by number or other symbol so as to relate it directly to the donor.

(e) *Prevention of contamination of the blood and plasma.* The skin of the donor at the site of phlebotomy shall be prepared thoroughly and carefully by a method that gives maximum assurance of a sterile container of blood. The blood shall be collected, the plasma separated, and the cells returned to the donor by aseptic methods in a sterile system which may be closed, or may be vented if the vent protects the blood cells and plasma against contamination.

[38 FR 32089, Nov. 20, 1973; 39 FR 13632, Apr. 16, 1974, as amended at 41 FR 10768, Mar. 12, 1976; 49 FR 23834, June 8, 1984; 50 FR 4140, Jan. 29, 1985; 55 FR 11013, Mar. 26, 1990; 59 FR 49351, Sept. 28, 1994; 63 FR 16685, Apr. 6, 1998; 64 FR 56453, Oct. 20, 1999; 72 FR 45888, Aug. 16, 2007; 80 FR 29905, May 22, 2015]

§ 640.65 Plasmapheresis.

(a) *Procedure-general.* The plasmapheresis procedure is a procedure in which, during a single visit to the establishment, blood is removed from a donor, the plasma separated from the formed elements, and at least the red blood cells returned to the donor. This procedure shall be described in detail in the biologics license application.

(b) *Procedures-specific requirements.* The plasmapheresis procedure shall meet the following requirements:

(1)(i) Except as provided under § 630.25 of this chapter, the responsible physician must draw a sample of blood from each donor on the day of the initial physical examination or plasmapheresis, whichever comes first, and at least every 4 months thereafter. A serologic test for syphilis, a total plasma or serum protein determination, and a plasma or serum protein electrophoresis or quantitative immuno-diffusion test or an equivalent test to determine immunoglobulin composition of the plasma or serum shall be performed on the sample.

(ii) A repeat donor who does not return for plasmapheresis at the time the 4-month sample is due to be collected may be plasmapheresed on the day he appears: *Provided,* That no longer than 6 months has elapsed since the last sample was collected, and the responsible physician approves the plasmapheresis procedure and so indicates by signing the donor's record before such procedure is performed. The sample for the 4-month tests shall be collected on the day of the donor's return.

(iii) A repeat donor from whom the plasmapheresis center is unable to obtain a sample for testing as prescribed in paragraph (b)(1)(i) of this section for a total period exceeding 6 months shall be processed as a new donor.

(2)(i) Except as provided under § 630.25 of this chapter, the responsible physician must review the accumulated laboratory data, including any tracings of the plasma or serum protein electrophoresis pattern, the calculated values of the protein composition of each component, and the collection records within 14 calendar days after the sample is drawn to determine whether or not the donor should be deferred from further donation. If a determination is not made within 14 calendar days, the donor must be deferred pending such a determination. The responsible physician must sign the review. If the protein composition is not within normal limits established by the testing laboratory, or if the total protein level is less than 6.0 grams per deciliter or more than 9.0 grams per deciliter in a plasma sample or serum sample, the donor must be deferred from donation until the protein composition returns to acceptable levels. Reinstatement of the donor into the plasmapheresis program when the donor's protein composition values have returned to an acceptable level must first be approved by the responsible physician.

(ii) A donor with a reactive serologic test for syphilis shall not be plasmapheresed again until the donor's serum is tested and found to be nonreactive to a serologic test for syphilis, except as provided in paragraph (b)(2) (iii) and (iv) of this section.

(iii) A donor whose serum is determined to have a biologic false-positive reaction to a serologic test for syphilis may be plasmapheresed: *Provided,* That the donor's file identifies the serologic test for syphilis and results used to confirm the biologic false-positive reaction and indicates that the responsible physician has determined the false-positive reaction is not the result of an underlying disorder that would disqualify the donor from participation in the plasmapheresis program. If the serologic test for syphilis is performed at a facility other than the plasmapheresis center, all applicable provisions of § 640.71 shall be met.

(iv) A donor with a reactive serologic test for syphilis may be plasmapheresed only to obtain plasma to be used for further manufacturing into control serum for the serologic test for syphilis: *Provided,* That the responsible physician approves the donation, the donor's file contains a signed statement from a physician or clinic establishing that treatment for syphilis has been initiated and that continuance in the plasmapheresis program will not interfere with or jeopardize the treatment of the syphilitic donor.

(3) A donor identification system shall be established that positively identifies each donor and relates such

105

donor directly to his blood and its components as well as to his accumulated records and laboratory data. Such system shall include either a photograph of each donor which shall be used on each visit to confirm the donor's identity, or some other method that provides equal or greater assurance of positively identifying the donor.

(4) The amount of whole blood, not including anticoagulant, removed from a donor during a manual plasmapheresis procedure or in any 2-day period shall not exceed 1,000 milliliters unless the donor's weight is 175 pounds or greater, in which case the amount of whole blood, not including anticoagulant, removed from the donor during a manual plasmapheresis procedure or in any 2-day period shall not exceed 1,200 milliliters.

(5) The amount of whole blood, not including anticoagulant, removed from a donor during a manual plasmapheresis procedure within a 7-day period shall not exceed 2,000 milliliters unless the donor's weight is 175 pounds or greater, in which case the amount of whole blood, not including anticoagulant, removed from a donor during a manual plasmapheresis procedure within a 7-day period shall not exceed 2,400 milliliters.

(6) No more than 500 milliliters of whole blood shall be removed from a donor at one time, unless the donor's weight is 175 pounds or greater, in which case no more than 600 milliliters of whole blood shall be removed from the donor at one time.

(7) The plasma shall be separated from the red blood cells immediately after blood collection. The maximum feasible volume of red blood cells shall be returned to the donor before another unit is collected.

(8) The volume of plasma collected during an automated plasmapheresis collection procedure shall be consistent with the volumes specifically approved by the Director, Center for Biologics Evaluation and Research, and collection shall not occur less than 2 days apart or more frequently than twice in a 7-day period.

[38 FR 32089, Nov. 20, 1973, as amended at 41 FR 10769, Mar. 12, 1976; 64 FR 45373, Aug. 19, 1999; 64 FR 56453, Oct. 20, 1999; 80 FR 29905, May 22, 2015]

§ 640.66 Immunization of donors.

If specific immunization of a donor is to be performed, the selection, scheduling and administration of the antigen, and the evaluation of each donor's clinical response, shall be by the responsible physician. Any material used for immunization shall be either a product licensed under section 351 of the Public Health Service Act for such purpose or one specifically approved by the Director, Center for Biologics Evaluation and Research, Food and Drug Administration. Immunization procedures shall be on file at each plasmapheresis center where immunizations are performed.

[38 FR 32089, Nov. 20, 1973, as amended at 49 FR 23834, June 8, 1984; 55 FR 11013, Mar. 26, 1990; 80 FR 29905, May 22, 2015]

§ 640.67 Laboratory tests.

Each unit of Source Plasma shall be tested for evidence of infection due to relevant transfusion-transmitted infections as required under § 610.40 of this chapter.

[66 FR 31165, June 11, 2001, as amended at 80 FR 29905, May 22, 2015]

§ 640.68 Processing.

(a) *Sterile system.* All administration and transfer sets inserted into blood containers used for processing Source Plasma intended for manufacturing into injectable or noninjectable products and all interior surfaces of plasma containers used for processing Source Plasma intended for manufacturing into injectable products shall be sterile, pyrogen-free, nontoxic, and compatible with the contents under normal conditions of use. Only Sodium Chloride Injection USP shall be used as a red blood cell diluent. If the method of separation of the plasma intended for injectable products involves a system in which an airway must be inserted into the plasma container, the airway shall be sterile and constructed so as to exclude microorganisms and maintain a sterile system.

(b) *Final containers.* Final containers used for Source Plasma, whether integrally attached or separated from the original blood container, shall not be entered prior to issuance for any purpose except for filling with the plasma.

Such containers shall be uncolored and hermetically sealed, and shall permit clear visibility of the contents. Final containers and their components shall not interact with the plasma contents under conditions of storage and use so as to alter the safety, quality, purity, or potency of the plasma and shall provide adequate protection against external factors that may cause deterioration or contamination. Prior to filling, the final container shall be marked or identified by number or other symbol which will relate it directly to the donor.

(c) *Preservative.* Source Plasma shall not contain a preservative.

[38 FR 32089, Nov. 20, 1973, as amended at 41 FR 10769, Mar. 12, 1976; 50 FR 4140, Jan. 29, 1985]

§640.69 General requirements.

(a) *Pooling.* Two units of Source Plasma from the same donor may be pooled if such units are collected during one plasmapheresis procedure: *Provided,* That the pooling is done by a procedure that does not introduce a risk of contamination of the red blood cells and, for plasma intended for injectable products, gives maximum assurance of a sterile container of plasma.

(1) The pooling of plasma from two or more donors is not permitted in the manufacture of Source Plasma intended for manufacturing into injectable products.

(2) The pooling of plasma from two or more donors by the manufacturer of Source Plasma intended for manufacturing into noninjectable products is permitted: *Provided,* That the plasma from two or more donors is pooled after the plasma has been removed from the red blood cells, and after the red blood cell containers are sealed.

(b) *Storage.* Immediately after filling, plasma intended for manufacturing into injectable products shall be stored at a temperature not warmer than −20 °C, except for plasma collected as provided in §640.74. Plasma intended for manufacturing into noninjectable products may be stored at temperatures appropriate for the intended use of the final product, provided these temperatures are included in the Source Plasma license application.

(c) *Inspection.* Source Plasma intended for manufacturing into injectable products shall be inspected for evidence of thawing at the time of issuance, except that inspection of individual plasma containers need not be made if the records of continuous monitoring of the storage temperature establish that the temperature remained at −20 °C or colder. If there is evidence that the storage temperature has not been maintained at −20 °C or colder, the plasma may be relabeled and issued as provided in §640.76(a).

(d) *Samples.* If samples are provided, they shall meet the following standards:

(1) Prior to filling, all samples shall be marked or identified so as to relate them directly to the donor of that unit of plasma.

(2) All samples shall be filled at the time the final product is prepared by the person who prepares the final product.

(3) All samples shall be representative of the contents of the final product or be collected from the donor at the time of filling the collection container.

(4) All samples shall be collected in a manner that does not contaminate the contents of the final container.

(e) *Restrictions on distribution.* Establishments must ensure that Source Plasma donated by paid donors not be used for further manufacturing into injectable products until the donor has a record of being found eligible to donate in accordance with §630.10 of this chapter and a record of negative test results on all tests required under §610.40(a) of this chapter on two occasions in the past 6 months.

(f) *Hold.* Source Plasma donated by paid donors determined to be suitable for further manufacturing into injectable products must be held in quarantine for a minimum of 60 calendar days before it is released for further manufacturing. If, after placing a donation in quarantine under this section, the donor is subsequently deferred under §610.41 of this chapter, or you subsequently determine a donor to be ineligible under §630.10 of this chapter due to risk factors closely associated with exposure to, or clinical evidence of, infection due to a relevant transfusion-transmitted infection, you

107

must not distribute quarantined donations from that donor for further manufacturing use to make an injectable product.

[38 FR 32089, Nov. 20, 1973, as amended at 41 FR 10769, Mar. 12, 1976; 41 FR 14367, Apr. 5, 1976; 50 FR 4140, Jan. 29, 1985; 63 FR 16685, Apr. 6, 1998; 64 FR 45374, Aug. 19, 1999; 80 FR 29905, May 22, 2015]

§ 640.71 Manufacturing responsibility.

(a) All steps in the manufacturing of Source Plasma, including donor examination, blood collection, plasmapheresis, laboratory testing, labeling, storage, and issuing shall be performed by personnel of the establishment licensed to manufacture Source Plasma, except that testing performed in accordance with § 610.40 of this chapter and § 640.65(b) may be performed by personnel of an establishment licensed for blood and blood derivatives under section 351(a) of the Public Health Service Act, or by a clinical laboratory that meets the standards of the Clinical Laboratories Improvement Amendments of 1988 (CLIA) (42 U.S.C. 263a): *Provided*, The establishment or clinical laboratory is qualified to perform the assigned test(s).

(b) Such testing shall not be considered divided manufacturing, which requires two biologics licenses for Source Plasma: *Provided*, That

(1) The results of such tests are maintained by the licensed manufacturer of the Source Plasma whereby such results may be reviewed by a responsible physician as required in § 640.65(b)(2) of this chapter and by an authorized representative of the Food and Drug Administration.

(2) The Source Plasma manufacturer has obtained a written agreement that the testing laboratory will permit authorized representatives of the Food and Drug Administration to inspect its testing procedures and facilities during reasonable business hours.

(3) The testing laboratory will participate in any proficiency testing programs undertaken by the Center for Biologics Evaluation and Research, Food and Drug Administration.

[41 FR 10770, Mar. 12, 1976, as amended at 49 FR 23834, June 8, 1984; 50 FR 4140, Jan. 29, 1985; 53 FR 117, Jan. 5, 1988; 55 FR 11013, Mar. 26, 1990; 64 FR 45374, Aug. 19, 1999; 64 FR 56453, Oct. 20, 1999; 66 FR 1837, Jan. 10, 2001; 80 FR 29905, May 22, 2015]

§ 640.72 Records.

(a) In addition to the recordkeeping requirements of this subchapter, the following records shall be maintained:

(1) Documentation shall be available to ensure that the shipping temperature requirements of § 600.15 of this title and of § 640.74(b)(2) are being met for Source Plasma intended for manufacture into injectable products.

(2)(i) For each donor, establishments must maintain records including a separate and complete record of initial and periodic examinations, tests, laboratory data, and interviews, etc., as required in §§ 630.10 and 630.15 of this chapter and §§ 640.65, 640.66, and 640.67, except as provided in paragraph (a)(2)(ii) of this section.

(ii) Negative results for testing for evidence of infection due to relevant transfusion-transmitted infections required in § 610.40 of this chapter, and the volume or weight of plasma withdrawn from a donor need not be recorded on the individual donor record if such information is maintained on the premises of the plasmapheresis center where the donor's plasma has been collected.

(3) The original or a clear copy or other durable record which may be electronic of the donor's consent for participation in the plasmapheresis program or for immunization.

(4) Records of the medical history and physical examination of the donor conducted in accordance with § 630.15(b)(1) of this chapter and, where applicable, § 630.15(b)(5) of this chapter must document the eligibility of the donor as a plasmapheresis donor and, when applicable, as an immunized donor.

(5) If plasma that is reactive to a serologic test for syphilis is issued as prescribed in § 640.65(b)(2)(iv), the distribution records shall indicate by number those units that are reactive.

(b) Each donor record must be directly cross-referenced to the unit(s) of Source Plasma associated with the donor.

(c) If a repeat donor is rejected or a donor's plasma is found unsuitable, the donor's record shall contain a full explanation for the rejection.

(d) If a donor has a reaction while on the plasmapheresis premises, or a donor reaction is reported to the center after the donor has left the premises, the donor's record shall contain a full explanation of the reaction, including the measures taken to assist the donor and the outcome of the incident.

[41 FR 10770, Mar. 12, 1976, as amended at 50 FR 4140, Jan. 29, 1985; 53 FR 117, Jan. 5, 1988; 64 FR 45374, Aug. 19, 1999; 67 FR 9587, Mar. 4, 2002; 80 FR 29905, May 22, 2015]

§ 640.73 **Reporting of fatal donor reactions.**

If a donor has a fatal reaction which, in any way, may be associated with plasmapheresis the Director of the Center for Biologics Evaluation and Research shall be notified by telephone as soon as possible. If the facility is located outside of the continental United States, notification by cable or telegram shall be acceptable.

[41 FR 10770, Mar. 12, 1976, as amended at 49 FR 23834, June 8, 1984; 55 FR 11013, Mar. 26, 1990]

§ 640.74 **Modification of Source Plasma.**

(a) Upon approval by the Director, Center for Biologics Evaluation and Research, Food and Drug Administration, of a supplement to the biologics license application for Source Plasma, a manufacturer may prepare Source Plasma as a liquid product for a licensed blood derivative manufacturer who has indicated a need for a liquid product.

(b) Source Plasma Liquid shall meet all standards of the frozen Source Plasma except:

(1) Source Plasma Liquid shall be stored in nonleachable containers so that the containers and their components will not interact with the plasma contents under conditions of storage and use so as to alter the safety, quality, purity, or potency of the plasma and shall provide adequate protection

against external factors that may cause deterioration or contamination.

(2) Source Plasma Liquid shall be shipped, stored and labeled for storage at a temperature of 10 °C or colder. An exception to the shipping or storage temperature shall be approved by the Director, Center for Biologics Evaluation and Research, Food and Drug Administration, based upon his receipt of substantial evidence to support another temperature. Such evidence may be submitted by either the licensed manufacturer of the Source Plasma Liquid or the manufacturer of the final blood derivative product who has requested the Source Plasma Liquid.

(3) The label for the Source Plasma Liquid shall be easily distinguished from that of the frozen product. Color coding shall not be used for this purpose.

(4) The label affixed to each container of Source Plasma Liquid shall contain, in addition to the information required by § 606.121 of this chapter, but excluding § 606.121(e)(5)(ii) of this chapter, the name the manufacturer of the final blood derivative product for whom it was prepared.

(5) Source Plasma Liquid shall be inspected immediately prior to issuance. If the color or physical appearance is abnormal, or there is any indication or suspicion of microbial contamination, the unit of Source Plasma Liquid shall not be issued.

[38 FR 32089, Nov. 20, 1973. Redesignated and amended at 41 FR 10770, Mar. 12, 1976; 49 FR 23834, June 8, 1984; 50 FR 4140, Jan. 29, 1985; 55 FR 11013, Mar. 26, 1990; 59 FR 49351, Sept. 28, 1994; 63 FR 16685, Apr. 6, 1998; 64 FR 56454, Oct. 20, 1999; 77 FR 18, Jan. 3, 2012]

§ 640.76 **Products stored or shipped at unacceptable temperatures.**

(a) *Storage temperature.* (1) Except as provided in paragraph (a)(2) of this section, Source Plasma intended for manufacture into injectable products that is inadvertently exposed (i.e., an unforeseen occurrence in spite of compliance with good manufacturing practice) to a storage temperature warmer than −20 °C and colder than + 10 °C may be issued only if labeled as "Source Plasma Salvaged." The label shall be revised before issuance, and appropriate records shall be maintained identifying the units involved, describing their disposition, and explaining fully the conditions that caused the inadvertent temperature exposure.

(2) Source Plasma intended for manufacture into injectable products that is exposed inadvertently (i.e., an unforeseen occurrence in spite of compliance with good manufacturing practice) to one episode of storage temperature fluctuation that is warmer than −20 °C and colder than −5 °C for not more than 72 hours is exempt from the labeling requirements of paragraph (a)(1) of this section, provided that the plasma has been and remains frozen solid. Appropriate records shall be maintained identifying the units involved, describing their disposition, explaining fully the conditions that caused the inadvertent temperature exposure, and documenting that the episode of temperature elevation did not exceed 72 hours, that the temperature did not rise to warmer than −5 °C in storage, and that the plasma remained frozen solid throughout the period of elevated temperature. When requested, copies of the records shall be provided to the plasma derivative manufacturer.

(b) *Shipping temperature.* If Source Plasma for manufacture into injectable products is exposed inadvertently (i.e., an unforeseen occurrence in spite of compliance with good manufacturing practice) to a shipping temperature warmer than −5 °C and colder than + 10 °C, the plasma derivative manufacturer shall label it "Source Plasma Salvaged." Appropriate records shall be maintained identifying the units involved, describing their disposition, and explaining fully the conditions that caused the inadvertent temperature exposure.

(c) *Relabeling.* If Source Plasma is required to be relabeled as "Source Plasma Salvaged" under paragraph (a)(1) or (b) of this section, the person responsible for the relabeling shall cover the original label with either (1) a complete new label containing the appropriate information or (2) a partial label affixed to the original label and containing the appropriate new information, which covers the incorrect information regarding storage temperature.

[45 FR 80501, Dec. 5, 1980, as amended at 50 FR 4140, Jan. 29, 1985]

Subpart H—Albumin (Human)

§ 640.80 Albumin (Human).

(a) *Proper name and definition.* The proper name of the product shall be Albumin (Human). The product is defined as a sterile solution of the albumin derived from human plasma.

(b) *Source material.* The source material of Albumin (Human) shall be plasma recovered from Whole Blood prepared as prescribed in §§ 640.1 through 640.5, or Source Plasma prepared as prescribed in §§ 640.60 through 640.76.

(c) *Additives in source material.* Source material shall not contain an additive unless it is shown that the processing method yields a final product free of the additive to such extent that the continued safety, purity, potency, and effectiveness of the final product will not be adversely affected.

[42 FR 27582, May 31, 1977, as amended at 50 FR 4140, Jan. 29, 1985; 64 FR 26286, May 14, 1999]

§ 640.81 Processing.

(a) *Date of manufacture.* The date of manufacture shall be the date of final sterile filtration of a uniform pool of bulk solution.

(b) *Processing method.* The processing method shall not affect the integrity of the product, and shall have been shown to yield consistently a product which is safe for intravenous injection.

(c) *Microbial contamination.* All processing steps shall be conducted in a manner to minimize the risk of contamination from microorganisms, pyrogens, or other impurities. Preservatives to inhibit growth of microorganisms shall not be used during processing.

(d) *Storage of bulk fraction.* Bulk concentrate to be held more than 1 week prior to further processing shall be stored in clearly identified closed vessels at a temperature of −5 °C or colder. Any other bulk form of the product, exclusive of the sterile bulk solution, to be held more than 1 week prior to further processing shall be stored in clearly identified closed vessels at a temperature of 5 °C or colder. Any bulk fraction to be held one week or less prior to further processing shall be stored in clearly identified closed vessels at a temperature of 5 °C or colder.

(e) *Heat treatment.* Heating of the final containers of Albumin (Human) shall begin within 24 hours after completion of filling. Heat treatment shall be conducted so that the solution is heated continuously for not less than 10, or more than 11 hours, at an attained temperature of 60±0.5 °C.

(f) *Stabilizer.* Either 0.08±0.016 millimole sodium caprylate, or 0.08±0.016 millimole sodium acetyltryptophanate and 0.08±0.016 millimole sodium caprylate per gram of protein shall be present as a stabilizer(s). Calculations of the stabilizer concentration may employ the labeled value for the protein concentration of the product as referred to in § 640.84(d).

(g) *Incubation.* All final containers of Albumin (Human) shall be incubated at 20 to 35 °C for at least 14 days following the heat treatment prescribed in paragraph (e) of this section. At the end of this incubation period, each final container shall be examined and all containers showing any indication of turbidity or microbial contamination shall not be issued. The contents of turbid final containers shall be examined microscopically and tested for sterility. If growth occurs, organisms shall be identified as to genus, and the material from such containers shall not be used for further manufacturing.

[42 FR 27582, May 31, 1977, as amended at 50 FR 4140, Jan. 29, 1985; 64 FR 26286, May 14, 1999; 65 FR 13679, Mar. 14, 2000; 65 FR 52018, Aug. 28, 2000]

§ 640.82 Tests on final product.

Tests shall be performed on the final product to determine that it meets the following standards:

(a) *Protein concentration.* Final product shall conform to one of the following concentrations: 4.0 ±0.25 percent; 5.0 ±0.30 percent; 20.0 ±1.2 percent; and 25.0 ±1.5 percent solution of protein.

(b) *Protein composition.* At least 96 percent of the total protein in the final product shall be albumin, as determined by a method that has been ap-

proved for each manufacturer by the Director, Center for Biologics Evaluation and Research, Food and Drug Administration.

(c) *pH.* The pH shall be 6.9 ±0.5 when measured in a solution of the final product diluted to a concentration of 1 percent protein with 0.15 molar sodium chloride.

(d) *Sodium concentration.* The sodium concentration of the final product shall be 130 to 160 milliequivalents per liter.

(e) *Potassium concentration.* The potassium concentration of the final product shall not exceed 2 milliequivalents per liter.

(f) *Heat stability.* A final container sample of Albumin (Human) shall remain unchanged, as determined by visual inspection, after heating at 57 °C for 50 hours, when compared to its control consisting of a sample, from the same lot, which has not undergone this heating.

[42 FR 27582, May 31, 1977, as amended at 49 FR 23834, June 8, 1984; 50 FR 4140, Jan. 29, 1985; 55 FR 11013, Mar. 26, 1990; 64 FR 26286, May 14, 1999]

§ 640.83 General requirements.

(a) *Preservative.* The final product shall not contain a preservative.

(b) *Storage of bulk solution.* After all processing steps have been completed, the sterile bulk solution shall be stored in a manner that will ensure the continued sterility of the product, and at a temperature that shall not exceed the recommended storage temperature of the final product prescribed in § 610.53 of this chapter.

[42 FR 27582, May 31, 1977]

§ 640.84 Labeling.

In addition to the labeling requirements of §§ 610.60, 610.61, and 610.62 of this chapter, the container and package labels shall contain the following information:

(a) The osmotic equivalent in terms of plasma, and the sodium concentration in terms of a value or a range in milliequivalents per liter;

(b) The cautionary statement placed in a prominent position on the label, "Do Not Use if Turbid. Do Not Begin Administration More Than 4 Hours

After the Container Has Been Entered.'';

(c) The need for additional fluids when 20 percent or 25 percent albumin is administered to a patient with marked dehydration;

(d) The protein concentration, expressed as a 4 percent, 5 percent, 20 percent, or 25 percent solution.

[42 FR 27582, May 31, 1977, as amended at 49 FR 2244, Jan. 19, 1984; 64 FR 26286, May 14, 1999]

Subpart I—Plasma Protein Fraction (Human)

SOURCE: 42 FR 27583, May 31, 1977, unless otherwise noted.

§ 640.90 Plasma Protein Fraction (Human).

(a) *Proper name and definition.* The proper name of the product shall be Plasma Protein Fraction (Human). The product is defined as a sterile solution of protein composed of albumin and globulin, derived from human plasma.

(b) *Source material.* The source material of Plasma Protein Fraction (Human) shall be plasma recovered from Whole Blood prepared as prescribed in §§ 640.1 through 640.5, or Source Plasma prepared as prescribed in §§ 640.60 through 640.76.

(c) *Additives in source material.* Source material shall not contain an additive unless it is shown that the processing method yields a final product free of the additive to such extent that the continued safety, purity, potency, and effectiveness of the final product will not be adversely affected.

[42 FR 27583, May 31, 1977, as amended at 64 FR 26286, May 14, 1999]

§ 640.91 Processing.

(a) *Date of manufacture.* The date of manufacture shall be the date of final sterile filtration of a uniform pool of bulk solution.

(b) *Processing method.* The processing method shall not affect the integrity of the product, and shall have been shown to yield consistently a product which:

(1) After the heating prescribed in paragraph (e) of this section does not show an increase in the components with electrophoretic mobility similar to that of alpha globulin that amounts to more than 5 percent of the total protein.

(2) Contains less than 5 percent protein with a sedimentation coefficient greater than 7.0 S.

(3) Is safe for intravenous injection.

(c) *Microbial contamination.* All processing steps shall be conducted in a manner to minimize the risk of contamination from microorganisms, pyrogens, or other impurities. Preservatives to inhibit growth of microorganisms shall not be used during processing.

(d) *Storage of bulk fraction.* Bulk concentrate to be held more than 1 week prior to further processing shall be stored in clearly identified closed vessels at a temperature of −5 °C or colder. Any other bulk form of the product (exclusive of the sterile bulk solution) to be held more than 1 week prior to further processing, shall be stored in clearly identified closed vessels at a temperature of 5 °C or colder. Any bulk fraction to be held one week or less prior to further processing shall be stored in clearly identified closed vessels at a temperature of 5 °C or colder.

(e) *Heat treatment.* Heating of the final containers of Plasma Protein Fraction (Human) shall begin within 24 hours after completion of filling. Heat treatment shall be conducted so that the solution is heated continuously for not less than 10 or more than 11 hours at an attained temperature of 60±0.5 °C.

(f) *Stabilizer.* Either 0.08±0.016 millimole sodium caprylate, or 0.08±0.016 millimole sodium acetyltryptophanate and 0.08±0.016 millimole sodium caprylate per gram of protein shall be present as a stabilizer(s). Calculations of the stabilizer concentration may employ the labeled value 5 percent for the protein concentration of the product.

(g) *Incubation.* All final containers of Plasma Protein Fraction (Human) shall be incubated at 20 to 35 °C for at least 14 days following the heat treatment prescribed in paragraph (e) of this section. At the end of this incubation period, each final container shall be examined and all containers showing any indication of turbidity or microbial contamination shall not be issued. The contents of turbid final containers shall be examined microscopically and tested for sterility. If growth occurs, the types of organisms shall be identified as to genus and the material from such containers shall not be used for further manufacturing.

[42 FR 27583, May 31, 1977, as amended at 64 FR 26286, May 14, 1999]

§ 640.92 Tests on final product.

Tests shall be performed on the final product to determine that it meets the following standards:

(a) *Protein concentration.* The final product shall be a 5.0 ±0.30 percent solution of protein.

(b) *Protein composition.* The total protein in the final product shall consist of at least 83 percent albumin, and no more than 17 percent globulins. No more than 1 percent of the total protein shall be gamma globulin. The protein composition shall be determined by a method that has been approved for each manufacturer by the Director, Center for Biologics Evaluation and Research, Food and Drug Administration.

(c) *pH.* The pH shall be 7.0 ±0.3 when measured in a solution of the final product diluted to a concentration of 1 percent protein with 0.15 molar sodium chloride.

(d) *Sodium concentration.* The sodium concentration of the final product shall be 130 to 160 milliequivalents per liter.

(e) *Potassium concentration.* The potassium concentration of the final product shall not exceed 2 milliequivalents per liter.

(f) *Heat stability.* A final container sample of Plasma Protein Fraction (Human) shall remain unchanged, as determined by visual inspection, after heating at 57 °C for 50 hours, when compared to its control consisting of a sample, from the same lot, which has not undergone this heating.

[42 FR 27583, May 31, 1977, as amended at 49 FR 23834, June 8, 1984; 55 FR 11013, Mar. 26, 1990; 64 FR 26286, May 14, 1999; 65 FR 13679, Mar. 14, 2000]

§ 640.93 General requirements.

(a) *Preservative.* The final product shall not contain a preservative.

(b) *Storage of bulk solution.* After all processing steps have been completed, the sterile bulk solution shall be stored in a manner that will ensure the continued sterility of the product, and at a temperature that shall not exceed the recommended storage temperature of the final product prescribed in § 610.53 of this chapter.

§ 640.94 Labeling.

In addition to the labeling requirements of §§ 610.60, 610.61, and 610.62 of this chapter, the container and package labels shall contain the following information:

(a) The osmotic equivalent in terms of plasma, and the sodium concentration in terms of a value or a range in milliequivalents per liter.

(b) The cautionary statement placed in a prominent position on the label, "Do Not Use if Turbid. Do Not Begin Administration More than 4 Hours After the Container Has Been Entered."

[42 FR 27583, May 31, 1977, as amended at 49 FR 2244, Jan. 19, 1984; 64 FR 26286, May 14, 1999]

Subpart J—Immune Globulin (Human)

§ 640.100 Immune Globulin (Human).

(a) *Proper name and definition.* The proper name of this product shall be Immune Globulin (Human). The product is defined as a sterile solution containing antibodies derived from human plasma.

(b) *Source material.* The source material of Immune Globulin (Human) shall be plasma recovered from Whole Blood prepared as prescribed in §§ 640.1 through 640.5, or Source Plasma prepared as prescribed in §§ 640.60 through 640.76.

(c) *Additives in source material.* The source material shall contain no additives other than citrate or acid citrate dextrose anticoagulant solution, unless it is shown that the processing method yields a product free of the additive to such an extent that the safety, purity, and potency of the product will not be affected adversely.

[38 FR 32089, Nov. 20, 1973, as amended at 50 FR 4140, Jan. 29, 1985; 64 FR 26287, May 14, 1999]

§ 640.101 General requirements.

(a) *Heat stability test.* Approximately 2 ml. of completely processed material of each lot shall not show any visible sign of gelation after heating in a 12 × 75 mm. stoppered glass tube at 57 °C for 4 hours.

(b) *pH.* The pH of final container material shall be 6.8 ±0.4 when measured in a solution diluted to 1 percent protein with 0.15 molar sodium chloride.

(c) *Turbidity.* The product shall be free of turbidity as determined by visual inspection of final containers.

(d) *Date of manufacture.* The date of manufacture is the date of initiating the last valid measles or poliomyelitis antibody test (§ 640.104(b) (2) and (3)) whichever date is earlier.

(e) *Labeling.* In addition to complying with all applicable labeling required in this subchapter, labeling shall indicate that:

(1) There is no prescribed potency for viral hepatitis antibodies.

(2) The product is not recommended for intravenous administration.

[38 FR 32089, Nov. 20, 1973; 48 FR 13026, Mar. 29, 1983, as amended at 49 FR 23834, June 8, 1984; 50 FR 4140, Jan. 29, 1985; 51 FR 15611, Apr. 25, 1986; 55 FR 11013, Mar. 26, 1990; 63 FR 16685, Apr. 6, 1998; 64 FR 26287, May 14, 1999]

§ 640.102 Manufacture of Immune Globulin (Human).

(a) *Processing method.* The processing method shall be one that has been shown: (1) To be capable of concentrating tenfold from source material at least two different antibodies; (2) not to affect the integrity of the globulins; (3) to consistently yield a product which is safe for subcutaneous and intramuscular injection and (4) not to transmit viral hepatitis.

(b) *Microbial contamination.* Low temperatures or aseptic techniques shall be used to minimize contamination by microorganisms. Preservatives to inhibit growth of microorganisms shall not be used during processing.

(c) *Bulk storage.* The globulin fraction may be stored in bulk prior to further processing provided it is stored in clearly identified hermetically closed vessels. Globulin as either a liquid concentrate or a solid and containing alcohol or more than 5 percent moisture shall be stored at a temperature of −10

°C or lower. Globulin as a solid free from alcohol and containing less than 5 percent moisture, shall be stored at a temperature of 0 °C or lower.

(d) *Determination of the lot.* Each lot of Immune Globulin (Human) shall represent a pooling of approximately equal amounts of material from not less than 1,000 donors.

(e) *Sterilization and heating.* The final product shall be sterilized promptly after solution. At no time during processing shall the product be exposed to temperatures above 45 °C, and after sterilization the product shall not be exposed to temperatures above 32 °C for more than 72 hours.

[38 FR 32089, Nov. 20, 1973, as amended at 50 FR 4140, Jan. 29, 1985; 63 FR 16685, Apr. 6, 1998; 64 FR 26287, May 14, 1999; 65 FR 13679, Mar. 14, 2000; 65 FR 52018, Aug. 28, 2000]

§ 640.103 The final product.

(a) *Final solution.* The final product shall be a 16.5 ±1.5 percent solution of globulin containing 0.3 molar glycine and a preservative.

(b) *Protein composition.* At least 96 percent of the total protein shall be immunoglobulin G (IgG), as determined by a method that has been approved for each manufacturer by the Director, Center for Biologics Evaluation and Research, Food and Drug Administration.

[38 FR 32089, Nov. 20, 1973, as amended at 64 FR 26287, May 14, 1999]

§ 640.104 Potency.

(a) *Antibody levels and tests.* Each lot of final product shall contain at least the minimum levels of antibodies for diphtheria, measles, and for at least one type of poliomyelitis. In the event the final bulk solution is stored at a temperature above 5 °C the antibody level tests shall be performed after such storage with a sample of the stored material.

(b) *Minimum levels.* The minimum antibody levels are as follows:

(1) No less than 2 units of diphtheria antitoxin per ml.

(2) A measles neutralizing antibody level that, when compared with that of a reference material designated by the Center for Biologics Evaluation and Research (CBER), Food and Drug Administration, as indicated in paragraph

(c) of this section, demonstrates adequate potency. The Director, CBER, shall notify manufacturers when a new reference material will be used and will advise manufacturers of an appropriate antibody level taking into account a comparison of the new reference material to the previous reference material.

(3) A poliomyelitis Type 1, Type 2, or Type 3 neutralizing antibody level that, when compared with that of a reference material designated by the Center for Biologics Evaluation and Research, Food and Drug Administration, as indicated in paragraph (c) of this section, demonstrates adequate potency. The Director, CBER, shall notify manufacturers when a new reference material will be used and will advise manufacturers of an appropriate antibody level taking into account a comparison of the new reference material to the previous reference material.

(c) *Reference materials.* The following reference materials shall be obtained from the Center for Biologics Evaluation and Research:

(1) Reference Immune Globulin for correlation of measles antibody titers.

(2) Reference Immune Globulin for correlation of poliomyelitis antibody titers, Types 1, 2, and 3.

[38 FR 32089, Nov. 20, 1973, as amended at 39 FR 9661, Mar. 13, 1974; 49 FR 23834, June 8, 1984; 50 FR 4140, Jan. 29, 1985; 55 FR 11013, Mar. 26, 1990; 63 FR 16685, Apr. 6, 1998; 64 FR 26287, May 14, 1999]

Subpart K [Reserved]

Subpart L—Alternative Procedures

§640.120 Alternative procedures.

(a) The Director, Center for Biologics Evaluation and Research, may issue an exception or alternative to any requirement in subchapter F of chapter I of title 21 of the Code of Federal Regulations regarding blood, blood components, or blood products. The Director may issue such an exception or alternative in response to:

(1) A written request from an establishment. Licensed establishments must submit such requests in accordance with §601.12 of this chapter;

(2) An oral request from an establishment, if there are difficult circumstances and submission of a written request is not feasible. Establishments must follow up such oral request by submitting written requests under paragraph (a)(1) of this section within 5 working days.

(b) To respond to a . public health need, the Director may issue a notice of exception or alternative to any requirement in subchapter F of chapter I of title 21 of the Code of Federal Regulations regarding blood, blood components, or blood products, if a variance under this section is necessary to assure that blood, blood components, or blood products will be available in a specified location or locations to address an urgent and immediate need for blood, blood components, or blood products or to provide for appropriate donor screening and testing.

(c) If the Director issues such an exception or alternative orally, the Director will follow up by issuing a written notice of the exception or alternative. Periodically, FDA will provide a list of approved exceptions and alternative procedures on the FDA Center for Biologics Evaluation and Research Web site.

[80 FR 29906, May 22, 2015]

Subpart M—Definitions and Medical Supervision

Source: 80 FR 29906, May 22, 2015, unless otherwise noted.

§640.125 Definitions.

The definitions set out in §630.3 of this chapter apply to the use of those defined terms in this part.

§640.130 Medical supervision.

The requirements for medical supervision established in §630.5 of this chapter supplement the regulations in this part.

PART 660—ADDITIONAL STANDARDS FOR DIAGNOSTIC SUBSTANCES FOR LABORATORY TESTS

AUTHORITY: 21 U.S.C. 321, 331, 351, 352, 353, 355, 360, 360c, 360d, 360h, 360i, 371, 372; 42 U.S.C. 216, 262, 263, 263a, 264.

CROSS REFERENCES: For U.S. Customs Service regulations relating to viruses, serums, and toxins, see 19 CFR 12.21–12.23. For U.S. Postal Service regulations relating to the admissibility to the United States mails see parts 124 and 125 of the Domestic Mail Manual, that is incorporated by reference in 39 CFR part 111.

Subpart A—Antibody to Hepatitis B Surface Antigen

§ 660.1 Antibody to Hepatitis B Surface Antigen.

(a) *Proper name and definition.* The proper name of this product shall be Antibody to Hepatitis B Surface Antigen. The product is defined as a preparation of serum containing antibody to hepatitis B surface antigen.

(b) *Source.* The source of this product shall be plasma or blood, obtained aseptically from animals immunized with hepatitis B surface antigen, which have met the applicable requirements of § 600.11 of this chapter, or from human donor whose blood is positive for hepatitis B surface antigen.

[40 FR 29711, July 15, 1975]

§ 660.2 General requirements.

(a) *Processing.* The processing method shall be one that has been shown to consistently yield a specific and potent final product free of properties which would adversely affect the test results when the product is tested by the methods recommended by the manufacturer in the package enclosure.

(b) *Ancillary reagents and materials.* All ancillary reagents and materials supplied in the package with the product shall meet generally accepted standards of purity and quality and shall be effectively segregated and otherwise manufactured in a manner (such as heating at 60 °C. for 10 hours) that will reduce the risk of contaminating the product and other biological products. Ancillary reagents and materials accompanying the product which are used in the performance of the test as described by the manufacturer's recommended test procedures shall have been shown not to adversely affect the product within the prescribed dating period.

(c) *Labeling.* (1) In addition to the items required by other applicable labeling provisions of this subchapter, the following shall also be included:

(i) Indication of the source of the product immediately following the proper name on both the final container and package label, *e.g.*, human, guinea pig.

(ii) Name of the test method(s) recommended for the product on the package label and on the final container label when capable of bearing a full label (see §610.60(a) of this chapter).

(iii) A warning on the package label and on the final container label if capable of bearing a full label (see §610.60(a) of this chapter) indicating that the product and antigen if supplied, shall be handled as if capable of transmitting hepatitis.

(iv) If the product is dried, the final container label shall indicate "Reconstitution date: ___" and a statement indicating the period within which the product may be used after reconstitution.

(v) The package shall include a package enclosure providing:

(A) Adequate instructions for use;

(B) A description of all recommended test methods; and

(C) Warnings as to possible hazards, including hepatitis, in handling the product and any ancillary reagents and materials accompanying the product.

(2) The applicant may provide the labeling information referenced in paragraph (c)(1) of this section in the form of:

(i) A symbol accompanied by explanatory text adjacent to the symbol;

(ii) A symbol not accompanied by adjacent explanatory text that:

(A) Is contained in a standard that FDA recognizes under its authority in section 514(c) of the Federal Food, Drug, and Cosmetic Act;

(B) Is used according to the specifications for use of the symbol set forth in FDA's section 514(c) recognition; and

(C) Is explained in a paper or electronic symbols glossary that is included in the labeling for the device and the labeling on or within the package containing the device bears a prominent and conspicuous statement identifying the location of the symbols glossary that is written in English or, in the case of articles distributed solely in Puerto Rico or in a Territory where the predominant language is one other than English, the predominant language may be used; or

(iii) A symbol not accompanied by adjacent explanatory text that:

(A) Is established in a standard developed by a standards development organization (SDO);

(B) Is not contained in a standard that is recognized by FDA under its authority in section 514(c) of the Federal Food, Drug, and Cosmetic Act or is contained in a standard that is recognized by FDA but is not used according to the specifications for use of the symbol set forth in FDA's section 514(c) recognition;

(C) Is determined by the manufacturer to be likely to be read and understood by the ordinary individual under customary conditions of purchase and use in compliance with section 502(c) of the Federal Food, Drug, and Cosmetic Act;

(D) Is used according to the specifications for use of the symbol set forth in the SDO-developed standard; and

(E) Is explained in a paper or electronic symbols glossary that is included in the labeling for the device and the labeling on or within the package containing the device bears a prominent and conspicuous statement identifying the location of the symbols glossary that is written in English or, in the case of articles distributed solely in Puerto Rico or in a Territory where the predominant language is one other than English, the predominant language may be used.

(3) The use of symbols to provide the labeling information referenced in paragraph (c)(1) of this section which do not meet the requirements of paragraph (c)(2) of this section renders a device misbranded under section 502(c) of the Federal Food, Drug, and Cosmetic Act.

(4) For purposes of paragraph (c)(2) of this section:

(i) An SDO is an organization that is nationally or internationally recognized and that follows a process for standard development that is transparent, (*i.e.*, open to public scrutiny), where the participation is balanced, where an appeals process is included, where the standard is not in conflict with any statute, regulation, or policy under which FDA operates, and where the standard is national or international in scope.

(ii) The term "symbols glossary" means a compiled listing of:

(A) Each SDO-established symbol used in the labeling for the device;

(B) The title and designation number of the SDO-developed standard containing the symbol; .

(C) The title of the symbol and its reference number, if any, in the standard; and

(D) The meaning or explanatory text for the symbol as provided in the FDA recognition or, if FDA has not recognized the standard or portion of the standard in which the symbol is located or the symbol is not used according to the specifications for use of the symbol set forth in FDA's section 514(c) recognition, the explanatory text as provided in the standard.

(d) *Final container.* A final container shall be sufficiently transparent to permit visual inspection of the contents for presence of particulate matter and increased turbidity. The effectiveness of the contents of a final container shall be maintained throughout its dating period.

(e) *Date of manufacture.* The date of manufacture of Antibody to Hepatitis B surface Antigen that has been iodinated with radioactive iodine (^{125}I) shall be the day of labeling the antibody with the radionuclide.

(f) *Retention samples.* Each manufacturer shall retain representative samples of the product in accordance with § 600.13 of this chapter except for that which has been iodinated with radioactive iodine. Retention samples of Antibody to Hepatitis B Surface Antigen iodinated with ^{125}I shall consist of a minimum of two complete finished packages of each lot of the diagnostic test kit and shall be retained for a period of at least 90 days from the date of manufacture.

[38 FR 32098, Nov. 20, 1973, as amended at 40 FR 29711, July 15, 1975; 46 FR 36134, July 14, 1981; 49 FR 1684, Jan. 13, 1984; 81 FR 38924, June 15, 2016]

§ 660.3 Reference panel.

A Reference Hepatitis B Surface Antigen Panel shall be obtained from the Food and Drug Administration, Center for Biologics Evaluation and Research, Reagents and Standards Shipping, 10903 New Hampshire Ave.,

Bldg. 75, Rm. G704, Silver Spring, MD 20993–0002 and shall be used for determining the potency and specificity of Antibody to Hepatitis B Surface Antigen.

[40 FR 29711, July 15, 1975, as amended at 49 FR 23834, June 8, 1984; 55 FR 11013, Mar. 26, 1990; 70 FR 14985, Mar. 24, 2005; 80 FR 18093, Apr. 3, 2015]

§ 660.4 Potency test.

To be satisfactory for release, each filling of Antibody to Hepatitis B Surface Antigen shall be tested against the Reference Hepatitis B Surface Antigen Panel and shall be sufficiently potent to detect the antigen in the appropriate sera of the reference panel by all test methods recommended by the manufacturer in the package insert.

[40 FR 29711, July 15, 1975]

§ 660.5 Specificity.

Each filling of the product shall be specific for antibody to hepatitis B surface antigen, as determined by specificity tests found acceptable by the Director, Center for Biologics Evaluation and Research.

[40 FR 29712, July 15, 1975, as amended at 49 FR 23834, June 8, 1984; 55 FR 11013, Mar. 26, 1990]

§ 660.6 Samples; protocols; official release.

(a) *Samples.* (1) For the purposes of this section, a sample of product not iodinated with ^{125}I means a sample from each filling of each lot packaged as for distribution, including all ancillary reagents and materials; and a sample of product iodinated with ^{125}I means a sample from each lot of diagnostic test kits in a finished package, including all ancillary reagents and materials.

(2) Unless the Director, Center for Biologics Evaluation and Research, determines that the reliability and consistency of the finished product can be assured with a smaller quantity of sample or no sample and specifically reduces or eliminates the required quantity of sample, each manufacturer shall submit the following samples to the Director, Center for Biologics Evaluation and Research (see mailing addresses in § 600.2(c) of this chapter),

within 5 working days after the manufacturer has satisfactorily completed all tests on the samples:

(i) One sample until written notification of official release is no longer required under paragraph (c)(2) of this section.

(ii) One sample at periodic intervals of 90 days, beginning after written notification of official release is no longer required under paragraph (c)(2) of this section. The sample submitted at the 90-day interval shall be from the first lot or filling, as applicable, released by manufacturer, under the requirements of §610.1 of this chapter, after the end of the previous 90-day interval. The sample shall be identified as "surveillance sample" and shall include the date of manufacture.

(iii) Samples may at any time be required to be submitted to the Director, Center for Biologics Evaluation and Research, if the Director finds that continued evaluation is necessary to ensure the potency, quality, and reliability of the product.

(b) *Protocols.* For each sample submitted as required in paragraph (a)(1) of this section, the manufacturer shall send a protocol that consists of a summary of the history of manufacture of the product, including all results of each test for which test results are requested by the Director, Center for Biologics Evaluation and Research. The protocols submitted with the samples at periodic intervals as provided in paragraph (a)(2)(ii) of this section shall be identified by the manufacturer as "surveillance test results."

(c) *Official release.* (1) The manufacturer shall not distribute the product until written notification of official release is received from the Director, Center for Biologics Evaluation and Research, except as provided in paragraph (c)(2) of this section. Official release is required for samples from at least five consecutive lots or fillings, as applicable, manufactured after licensure of the product.

(2) After written notification of official release is received from the Director, Center for Biologics Evaluation and Research, for at least five consecutive lots or fillings, as applicable, manufactured after licensure of the product, and after the manufacturer receives from the Director, Center for Biologics Evaluation and Research, written notification that official release is no longer required, subsequent lots or fillings may be released by the manufacturer under the requirements of §610.1 of this chapter.

(3) The manufacturer shall not distribute lots or fillings, as applicable, of products that required sample submission under paragraph (a)(2)(iii) of this section until written notification of official release or notification that official release is no longer required is received from the Director, Center for Biologics Evaluation and Research.

[48 FR 20407, May 6, 1983, as amended at 49 FR 23834, June 8, 1984; 51 FR 15611, Apr. 25, 1986; 55 FR 11013, 11014, Mar. 26, 1990; 70 FR 14985, Mar. 24, 2005; 80 FR 18093, Apr. 3, 2015]

Subpart B [Reserved]

Subpart C—Blood Grouping Reagent

SOURCE: 53 FR 12764, Apr. 19, 1988, unless otherwise noted.

§660.20 Blood Grouping Reagent.

(a) *Proper name and definition.* The proper name of this product shall be Blood Grouping Reagent and it shall consist of an antibody-containing fluid containing one or more of the blood grouping antibodies listed in §660.28(a)(4).

(b) *Source.* The source of this product shall be blood, plasma, serum, or protein-rich fluids, such as those derived from stable immunoglobulin-secreting cell lines maintained either in tissue cultures or in secondary hosts.

[53 FR 12764, Apr. 19, 1988, as amended at 65 FR 77499, Dec. 12, 2000; 81 FR 38925, June 15, 2016]

§660.21 Processing.

(a) *Processing method.* (1) The processing method shall be one that has been shown to yield consistently a specific, potent final product, free of properties that would affect adversely the intended use of the product throughout its dating period. Stability testing shall be performed on an adequate number of representative samples of each group of products manufactured in the same fashion.

(2) Only that material that has been fully processed, thoroughly mixed in a single vessel, and filtered shall constitute a lot.

(3) A lot may be subdivided into sublots. If lots are to be subdivided, the manufacturer shall include this information in the biologics license application. The manufacturer shall describe the test specifications to verify that each sublot is identical to other sublots of the lot.

(4) Each lot of Blood Grouping Reagent shall be identified by a lot number. Each sublot shall be identified by that lot number to which a distinctive prefix or suffix shall be added. Final container and package labels shall bear the lot number and all distinctive prefixes and suffixes that have been applied to identify the sublot from which filling was accomplished.

(b) *Color coding of reagents.* Blood Grouping Reagents may be colored provided the added colorant does not adversely affect the safety, purity, or potency of the product and the colorant is approved by the Director, Center for Biologics Evaluation and Research.

(c) *Final containers and dropper assemblies.* Final containers and dropper pipettes shall be colorless and sufficiently transparent to permit observation of the contents to detect particulate matter or increased turbidity during use.

(d) *Volume of final product.* Each manufacturer shall identify the possible final container volumes in the biologics license application.

(e) *Date of manufacture.* The date of manufacture shall be the date the manufacturer begins the last entire group of potency tests.

[53 FR 12764, Apr. 19, 1988, as amended at 64 FR 56454, Oct. 20, 1999; 65 FR 77499, Dec. 12, 2000; 67 FR 9587, Mar. 4, 2002; 70 FR 14985, Mar. 24, 2005]

§ 660.22 Potency requirements with reference preparations.

(a) *Potency requirements.* Products for which reference Blood Grouping Reagents are available shall have a potency titer value at least equal to that of the reference preparation.

(b) *Reference preparations.* Reference Blood Grouping Reagents shall be obtained from the Food and Drug Administration, Center for Biologics Evaluation and Research, Reagents and Standards Shipping, 10903 New Hampshire Ave., Bldg. 75, Rm. G704, Silver Spring, MD 20993–0002, and shall be used as described in the accompanying package insert for determining the potency of Blood Grouping Reagents.

[53 FR 12764, Apr. 19, 1988, as amended at 67 FR 9587, Mar. 4, 2002; 70 FR 14985, Mar. 24, 2005; 80 FR 18093, Apr. 3, 2015]

§ 660.25 Potency tests without reference preparations.

Products for which Reference Blood Grouping Reagents are not available shall be tested for potency by a method approved by the Director, Center for Biologics Evaluation and Research.

(a) *Potency requirements.* Blood Grouping Reagents recommended for the test tube methods, including the indirect antiglobulin tests, shall have the following potency titer values, unless other values are approved by the Director, Center for Biologics Evaluation and Research.

(1) For Anti-K, Anti-k̄, Anti-Jk^a, Anti-Fy^a, Anti-C^w, at least 1 + reaction with a 1:8 dilution of the reagent.

(2) For Anti-S, Anti-s̄, Anti-P$_1$, Anti-M, Anti-I, Anti-e (saline), Anti-c̄ (saline), and Anti-A$_1$, at least 1 + reaction with a 1:4 dilution of the reagent.

(3) For Anti-U, Anti-Kp^a, Anti-Kp^b, Anti-Js^a, Anti-Js^b, Anti-Fy^b, Anti-N, Anti-Le^a, Anti-Le^b, Anti-Lu^a, Anti-Lu^b, Anti-Di^a, Anti-M^g, Anti-Jk^b, Anti-Co^b, Anti-Wr^a, and Anti-Xg^a, at least 2 + reaction with undiluted reagent.

(b) *Products recommended for slide tests or microplate techniques.* Blood Grouping Reagent recommended for slide test methods or microplate techniques shall produce clearly positive macroscopic results when both undiluted reagent and reagent diluted with an equal volume of diluent are tested by all methods recommended in the manufacturer's package insert using red blood cells showing heterozygous or diminished expression of the corresponding antigen. The dilution shall be made with an equal volume of compatible serum or approved diluent.

(c) *Products recomended for use in an automated system.* The manufacturer of Blood Grouping Reagent that is recommended for use in an automated system shall demonstrate that its product when used both undiluted and diluted with an equal volume of diluent satisfactorily performs when tested with cells representing heterozygous or diminished expression of the corresponding antigen.

[53 FR 12764, Apr. 19, 1988, as amended at 67 FR 9587, Mar. 4, 2002; 70 FR 14985, Mar. 24, 2005]

§ 660.26 Specificity tests and avidity tests.

Specificity and avidity tests shall be performed using test procedures approved by the Director, Center for Biologics Evaluation and Research.

[53 FR 12764, Apr. 19, 1988, as amended at 67 FR 9587, Mar. 4, 2002; 70 FR 14985, Mar. 24, 2005]

§ 660.28 Labeling.

(a) In addition to the applicable labeling requirements of §§ 610.62 through 610.65 and § 809.10 of this chapter, and in lieu of the requirements in §§ 610.60 and 610.61 of this chapter, the following requirements shall be met:

(1) *Final container label*—(i) *Color coding.* The final container label of all Blood Grouping Reagents shall be completely white, except that all or a portion of the final container label of the following Blood Grouping Reagents may be color coded with the specified color which shall be a visual match to a specific color sample designated by the Director, Center for Biologics Evaluation and Research. Printing on all final container labels shall be in solid black. A logo or company name may be placed on the final container label; however, the logo or company name shall be located along the bottom or end of the label, outside the main panel.

Blood grouping reagent	Color of label paper
Anti-A	Blue.
Anti-B	Yellow.
Slide and rapid tube test blood grouping reagents only:	
Anti-C	Pink.
Anti-D	Gray.
Anti-E	Brown.
Anti-CDE	Orange.

Blood grouping reagent	Color of label paper
Anti-c̄	Lavender.
Anti-e	Green.

(ii) *Required information.* The proper name "Blood Grouping Reagent" need not appear on the final container label provided the final container is distributed in a package and the package label bears the proper name. The final container label shall bear the following information:

(A) Name of the antibody or antibodies present as set forth in paragraph (a)(4) of this section.

(B) Name, address (including ZIP code), and license number of the manufacturer.

(C) Lot number, including sublot designations.

(D) Expiration date.

(E) Source of product if other than human plasma or serum.

(F) Test method(s) recommended.

(G) Recommended storage temperature in degrees Celsius.

(H) Volume of product if a liquid, or equivalent volume for a dried product if it is to be reconstituted.

(I) If a dried product, to remind users to record the reconstitution date on the label, the statement "RECONSTITUTION DATE ___. EXPIRES 1 YEAR AFTER RECONSTITUTION DATE."

(iii) *Lettering size.* The type size for the specificity of the antibody designation on the labels of a final container with a capacity of less than 5 milliliters shall be not less than 12 point. The type size for the specificity of the antibody designations on the label of a container with a capacity of 5 milliliters or more shall be not less than 18 point.

(iv) *Visual inspection.* When the label has been affixed to the final container, a sufficient area of the container shall remain uncovered for its full length or no less than 5 millimeters of the lower circumference to permit inspection of the contents. The label on a final product container for antibodies Anti-c, Anti-k, or Anti-s shall display a bar immediately over the specificity letter used in the name, *i.e.*, Anti-c̄, Anti-k̄, or Anti-s̄.

121

(2) *Package label.* The following information shall appear either on the package label or on the final container label if it is visible within the package.

(i) Proper name of the product.

(ii) Name of the antibody or antibodies present as set forth in paragraph (a)(4) of this section.

(iii) Name, address (including ZIP Code), and license number of the manufacturer.

(iv) Lot number, including sublot designations.

(v) Expiration date.

(vi) Preservative used and its concentration.

(vii) Number of containers, if more than one.

(viii) Volume or equivalent volume for dried products when reconstituted, and precautions for adequate mixing when reconstituting.

(ix) Recommended storage temperature in degrees Celsius.

(x) Source of the product if other than human serum or plasma.

(xi) Reference to enclosed package insert.

(xii) If a dried product, a statement indicating the period within which the product may be used after reconstitution.

(xiii) The statement: "FOR IN VITRO DIAGNOSTIC USE."

(xiv) The statement: "MEETS FDA POTENCY REQUIREMENTS."

(xv) If human blood was used in manufacturing the product, the statement: "CAUTION: ALL BLOOD PRODUCTS SHOULD BE TREATED AS POTENTIALLY INFECTIOUS. SOURCE MATERIAL FROM WHICH THIS PRODUCT WAS DERIVED WAS FOUND NEGATIVE WHEN TESTED IN ACCORDANCE WITH CURRENT FDA REQUIRED TESTS. NO KNOWN TEST METHODS CAN OFFER ASSURANCE THAT PRODUCTS DERIVED FROM HUMAN BLOOD WILL NOT TRANSMIT INFECTIOUS AGENTS."

(xvi) A statement of an observable indication of an alteration of the product, *e.g.,* turbidity, color change, precipitate, that may indicate possible deterioration of the product.

(3) *Package insert.* Each final container of Blood Grouping Reagent shall be accompanied by a package insert meeting the requirements of § 809.10. If two or more final containers requiring identical package inserts are placed in a single package, only one package insert per package is required.

(4) *Names of antibodies.*

BLOOD GROUP DESIGNATION FOR CONTAINER LABEL

Anti-A	Anti-Jk^b
Anti-A$_1$	Anti-Js^a
Anti-A, B	Anti-Js^b
Anti-A and B	Anti-K
Anti-B	Anti-k
Anti-C	Anti-Kp^a
Anti-C^w	Anti-Kp^b
Anti-$\bar{c}$	Anti-Le^a
Anti-CD	Anti-Le^b
Anti-CDE	Anti-Lu^a
Anti-Co^b	Anti-Lu^b
Anti-D	Anti-M
Anti-DE	Anti-M^g
Anti-Di^a	Anti-N
Anti-E	Anti-P$_1$
Anti-e	Anti-S
Anti-Fy^a	Anti-$\bar{s}$
Anti-Fy^b	Anti-U
Anti-I	Anti-Wr^a
Anti-Jk^a	Anti-Xg^a

(b) The applicant may provide the labeling information referenced in paragraph (a) of this section in the form of:

(1) A symbol accompanied by explanatory text adjacent to the symbol;

(2) A symbol not accompanied by adjacent explanatory text that:

(i) Is contained in a standard that FDA recognizes under its authority in section 514(c) of the Federal Food, Drug, and Cosmetic Act;

(ii) Is used according to the specifications for use of the symbol set forth in FDA's section 514(c) recognition; and

(iii) Is explained in a paper or electronic symbols glossary that is included in the labeling for the device and the labeling on or within the package containing the device bears a prominent and conspicuous statement identifying the location of the symbols glossary that is written in English or, in the case of articles distributed solely in Puerto Rico or in a Territory where the predominant language is one other than English, the predominant language may be used; or

(3) A symbol not accompanied by adjacent explanatory text that:

(i) Is established in a standard developed by a standards development organization (SDO);

(ii) Is not contained in a standard that is recognized by FDA under its authority in section 514(c) of the Federal Food, Drug, and Cosmetic Act or is contained in a standard that is recognized by FDA but is not used according to the specifications for use of the symbol set forth in FDA's section 514(c) recognition;

(iii) Is determined by the manufacturer to be likely to be read and understood by the ordinary individual under customary conditions of purchase and use in compliance with section 502(c) of the Federal Food, Drug, and Cosmetic Act;

(iv) Is used according to the specifications for use of the symbol set forth in the SDO-developed standard; and

(v) Is explained in a paper or electronic symbols glossary that is included in the labeling for the device and the labeling on or within the package containing the device bears a prominent and conspicuous statement identifying the location of the symbols glossary that is written in English or, in the case of articles distributed solely in Puerto Rico or in a Territory where the predominant language is one other than English, the predominant language may be used.

(c) The use of symbols in device labeling to provide the labeling information referenced in paragraph (a) of this section which do not meet the requirements in paragraph (b) of this section renders a device misbranded under section 502(c) of the Federal Food, Drug, and Cosmetic Act.

(d) For purposes of paragraph (b) of this section:

(1) An SDO is an organization that is nationally or internationally recognized and that follows a process for standard development that is transparent, (*i.e.*, open to public scrutiny), where the participation is balanced, where an appeals process is included, where the standard is not in conflict with any statute, regulation, or policy under which FDA operates, and where the standard is national or international in scope.

(2) The term "symbols glossary" means a compiled listing of:

(i) Each SDO-established symbol used in the labeling for the device;

(ii) The title and designation number of the SDO-developed standard containing the symbol;

(iii) The title of the symbol and its reference number, if any, in the standard; and

(iv) The meaning or explanatory text for the symbol as provided in the FDA recognition or, if FDA has not recognized the standard or portion of the standard in which the symbol is located or the symbol is not used according to the specifications for use of the symbol set forth in FDA's section 514(c) recognition, the explanatory text as provided in the standard.

[81 FR 38925, June 15, 2016]

Subpart D—Reagent Red Blood Cells

SOURCE: 52 FR 37450, Oct. 7, 1987, unless otherwise noted.

§660.30 Reagent Red Blood Cells.

(a) *Proper name and definition.* The proper name of the product shall be Reagent Red Blood Cells, which shall consist of a preparation of human red blood cells used to detect or identify human blood-group antibodies.

(b) *Source.* Reagent Red Blood Cells shall be prepared from human peripheral blood meeting the criteria of §§660.31 and 660.32 of this chapter, or from umbilical·cord cells which shall be collected and prepared according to the manufacturer's biologics license application.

[52 FR 37450, Oct. 7, 1987, as amended at 64 FR 56454, Oct. 20, 1999]

§660.31 Eligibility of donor.

Donors of peripheral blood for Reagent Red Blood Cells must meet all the criteria for donor eligibility under §§630.10 and 630.15 of this chapter.

[80 FR 29906, May 22, 2015]

§660.32 Collection of source material.

Blood for Reagent Red Blood Cells from donors of peripheral blood shall be collected as prescribed under §640.4 of this chapter, except that paragraphs (c), (d), (g), and (h) of §640.4 shall not apply.

§ 660.33 Testing of source material.

Except as provided in this section, a sample of each blood incorporated into the Reagent Red Blood Cell product shall be individually tested, with no fewer than two donor sources of each antibody specificity employed, to confirm the identification of all blood group antigens specified in the labeling as present or absent. The manufacturer shall perform at least one of the required tests for each factor. The Reagent Red Blood Cell product may be tested with a single donor source of antibody specificity if only one source of antibody is available, and the Director, Center for Biologics Evaluation and Research, has approved the use of a single donor source of antiserum. Each of these tests shall be conducted and interpreted independently, and any discrepancy between the results of these two tests shall be resolved by testing with at least one additional antiserum before concluding that the antigen is present or absent. Where fewer than three donor sources of an antibody specificity are available, test discrepancies shall be resolved in accordance with the manufacturer's biologics license application. Group O Reagent Red Blood Cells used in the detection or identification of unexpected antibodies shall include at least the following common antigens in each lot of the product: D, C, E, c̄, e, K, k̄, Fyᵃ, Fyᵇ, Jkᵃ, Jkᵇ, Leᵃ, Leᵇ, P₁, M, N, S, and s̄.

[52 FR 37450, Oct. 7, 1987, as amended at 55 FR 11013, Mar. 26, 1990; 64 FR 56454, Oct. 20, 1999]

§ 660.34 Processing.

(a) *Processing method.* The processing method shall be one that has been shown to yield consistently a product that is capable of detecting, throughout the dating period, alloantibodies corresponding to all required blood group antigens specified in the labeling as present.

(b) *Products prepared from pooled red blood cells.* If the product is recommended for the detection of unexpected antibodies, the pool shall be prepared by combining equal amounts of cells from no more than two donors. Umbilical cord cells are exempt from this requirement. Pooled cells shall not

be recommended for pretransfusion tests, done in lieu of a major crossmatch, to detect unexpected antibodies in patients' samples.

(c) *Absence of antibodies.* Each lot of final product shall be free of demonstrable antibodies, including anti-A and anti-B, unless the package insert and container lable include instructions to wash the cells before use. The final product shall also be direct antiglobulin test negative when tested with polyspecific anti-human globulin.

(d) *Final container.* The final containers used for each lot of product shall be clean and shall permit observation of the contents for hemolysis or a change in color. The final container label, container cap, and dropper bulb of a Reagent Red Blood Cell product may be color-coded with a visual match to a specific color approved by the Director, Center for Biologics Evaluation and Research.

(e) *Date of manufacture.* The date of manufacture of the product shall be the date that the blood is withdrawn from the donor or obtained from umbilical cords. The period during which the reagent red blood cell source material is kept by the manufacturer in storage in a frozen state at −65 °C or colder is excluded from the dating period. If the product consists of red blood cells from two or more donors, the date of manufacture of the final product shall be the date of withdrawal of blood from the donor of the oldest constituent blood. When a product consists of more than one container, e.g., cell panel, the date of manufacture of each container of the product shall be the earliest date that blood was withdrawn from a donor for any container of the product.

(f) *Retention samples.* Retention samples shall be maintained as required by § 600.13 of this chapter, except that samples must be retained only throughout the dating period of the product.

[52 FR 37450, Oct. 7, 1987, as amended at 55 FR 11013, Mar. 26, 1990; 67 FR 9587, Mar. 4, 2002]

§ 660.35 Labeling.

(a) In addition to the items required by § 809.10 of this chapter and other applicable labeling provisions of this chapter, the following information shall be included in the labeling:

(1)(i) A logo or company name may be placed on the final container label, however, the logo or company name shall be located along the bottom or end of the label, outside of the main panel.

(ii) If washing the cells is required by the manufacturer, the container label shall include appropriate instructions; if the cells should not be washed before use, e.g., if washing will adversely affect the product, the package insert shall explain.

(2) The container label of Group O cells shall state:

"FOR USE IN DETECTION OF UNEXPECTED ANTIBODIES" or "FOR USE IN IDENTIFICATION OF UNEXPECTED ANTIBODIES" or "NOT FOR USE IN DETECTION OR IDENTIFICATION OF UNEXPECTED ANTIBODIES".

(3) Except as provided in this section, the container and package labels shall state the percentage of red blood cells in the suspension either as a discrete figure with a variance of more than [±] 1 percentage unit or as a range the extremes of which differ by no more than 2 percentage units. If the stated red blood cell concentration is less than 2 percent, the variance shall be no more than [±] 0.5 percentage unit.

(4) The words "pooled cells" shall appear on the container and package labels of products prepared from pooled cells. The package label or package insert shall state that pooled cells are not recommended for pre-transfusion tests, done in lieu of a major cross-match, to detect unexpected antibodies in patients' samples.

(5) The package insert of a pooled product intended for detection of unexpected antibodies shall identify the number of donors contributing to the pool. Products designed exclusively for ABO Serum Grouping and umbilical cord cells need not identify the number of donors in the pool.

(6) When the product is a multicontainer product, e.g., a cell panel, the container label and package label shall be assigned the same identifying lot number, and shall also bear a number or symbol to distinguish one container from another. Such number or symbol shall also appear on the antigenic constitution matrix.

(7) The package label or package insert shall state the blood group antigens that have been tested for and found present or absent on the cells of each donor, or refer to such information in an accompanying antigenic constitution matrix. Cells for ABO Serum Grouping are exempt from this requirement. The package insert or antigen constitution matrix shall list each of the antigens tested with only one source of antibody.

(8) The package label or package insert shall bear the cautionary statement: "The reactivity of the product may decrease during the dating period."

(9) The package insert of a product intended for the detection or identification of unexpected antibodies shall note that the rate at which antigen reactivity (e.g., agglutinability) is lost is partially dependent upon individual donor characteristics that are neither controlled nor predicted by the manufacturer.

(10) The package insert shall provide adequate directions for use.

(11) The package insert shall bear the statement:

"CAUTION: ALL BLOOD PRODUCTS SHOULD BE TREATED AS POTENTIALLY INFECTIOUS. SOURCE MATERIAL FROM WHICH THIS PRODUCT WAS DERIVED WAS FOUND NEGATIVE WHEN TESTED IN ACCORDANCE WITH CURRENT FDA REQUIRED TESTS. NO KNOWN TEST METHODS CAN OFFER ASSURANCE THAT PRODUCTS DERIVED FROM HUMAN BLOOD WILL NOT TRANSMIT INFECTIOUS AGENTS."

(12) The package insert or the antigenic constitution matrix for each lot of product shall specify the date of manufacture or the length of the dating period.

(13) Manufacturers shall identify with a permanent donor code in the product labeling each donor of peripheral blood used for detection or identification of unexpected antibodies.

(b) The applicant may provide the labeling information referenced in paragraph (a) of this section in the form of:

(1) A symbol accompanied by explanatory text adjacent to the symbol;

(2) A symbol not accompanied by adjacent explanatory text that:

(i) Is contained in a standard that FDA recognizes under its authority in section 514(c) of the Federal Food, Drug, and Cosmetic Act;

(ii) Is used according to the specifications for use of the symbol set forth in FDA's section 514(c) recognition; and

(iii) Is explained in a paper or electronic symbols glossary that is included in the labeling for the device and the labeling on or within the package containing the device bears a prominent and conspicuous statement identifying the location of the symbols glossary that is written in English or, in the case of articles distributed solely in Puerto Rico or in a Territory where the predominant language is one other than English, the predominant language may be used; or

(3) A symbol not accompanied by adjacent explanatory text that:

(i) Is established in a standard developed by a standards development organization (SDO);

(ii) Is not contained in a standard that is recognized by FDA under its authority in section 514(c) of the Federal Food, Drug, and Cosmetic Act or is contained in a standard that is recognized by FDA but is not used according to the specifications for use of the symbol set forth in FDA's section 514(c) recognition;

(iii) Is determined by the manufacturer to be likely to be read and understood by the ordinary individual under customary conditions of purchase and use in compliance with section 502(c) of the Federal Food, Drug, and Cosmetic Act;

(iv) Is used according to the specifications for use of the symbol set forth in the SDO-developed standard; and

(v) Is explained in a paper or electronic symbols glossary that is included in the labeling for the device and the labeling on or within the package containing the device bears a prominent and conspicuous statement identifying the location of the symbols glossary that is written in English or, in the case of articles distributed solely in Puerto Rico or in a Territory where the predominant language is one other than English, the predominant language may be used.

(c) The use of symbols in device labeling to provide the labeling information referenced in paragraph (a) of this section which do not meet the requirements of paragraph (b) of this section renders a device misbranded under section 502(c) of the Federal Food, Drug, and Cosmetic Act.

(d) For purposes of paragraph (b) of this section:

(1) An SDO is an organization that is nationally or internationally recognized and that follows a process for standard development that is transparent, (*i.e.,* open to public scrutiny), where the participation is balanced, where an appeals process is included, where the standard is not in conflict with any statute, regulation, or policy under which FDA operates, and where the standard is national or international in scope.

(2) The term "symbols glossary" means a compiled listing of:

(i) Each SDO-established symbol used in the labeling for the device;

(ii) The title and designation number of the SDO-developed standard containing the symbol;

(iii) The title of the symbol and its reference number, if any, in the standard; and

(iv) The meaning or explanatory text for the symbol as provided in the FDA recognition or, if FDA has not recognized the standard or portion of the standard in which the symbol is located or the symbol is not used according to the specifications for use of the symbol set forth in FDA's section 514(c) recognition, the explanatory text as provided in the standard.

[81 FR 38926, June 15, 2016]

§ 660.36 Samples and protocols.

(a) The following shall be submitted to the Center for Biologics Evaluation and Research Sample Custodian (see mailing addresses in § 600.2(c) of this chapter), within 30 days after each routine establishment inspection by FDA.

(1) From a lot of final product, samples from a cell panel intended for identification of unexpected antibodies. The sample shall be packaged as for distribution and shall have at least 14 days remaining in the dating period when shipped to the Center for Biologics Evaluation and Research.

(2) A protocol which shall include the following:

(i) Complete test records of at least two donors of the samples submitted, including original and confirmation phenotyping records.

(ii) Bleeding records or receipt records which indicate collection date, volume, and HBsAg test results.

(iii) Manufacturing records which document all steps involved in the preparation of the product.

(iv) Test results which verify that the final product meets specifications.

(v) Identity test results.

(b) A copy of the antigenic constitution matrix specifying the antigens present or absent shall be submitted to the Director, Center for Biologics Evaluation and Research (see mailing addresses in §600.2(c) of this chapter), at the time of initial distribution of each lot of Reagent Red Blood Cells for detection or identification of unexpected antibodies. Products designed exclusively to identify Anti-A, Anti-A₁, and Anti-B, as well as products composed entirely of umbilical cord cells, are excluded from this requirement.

(c) Except for umbilical cord samples, whenever a new donor is used, a sample of red blood cells from each new donor used in a cell panel intended for the identification of unexpected antibodies shall be submitted by the manufacturer to the Director, Center for Biologics Evaluation and Research (see mailing addresses in §600.2(c) of this chapter). The sample should contain a minimum volume of 0.5 milliliter of red blood cells.

[52 FR 37450, Oct. 7, 1987, as amended at 55 FR 11013, 11015, Mar. 26, 1990; 67 FR 9587, Mar. 4, 2002; 70 FR 14985, Mar. 24, 2005; 80 FR 18093, Apr. 3, 2015]

Subpart E—Hepatitis B Surface Antigen

SOURCE: 44 FR 36382, June 22, 1979, unless otherwise noted.

§660.40 Hepatitis B Surface Antigen.

(a) *Proper name and definition.* The proper name of this product shall be Hepatitis B Surface Antigen (HBsAg), which shall consist of a serum or tissue preparation containing one or more subtypes of the Hepatitis B Surface Antigen.

(b) *Source.* The source of the product shall be blood, plasma, serum, or tissue, obtained aseptically from nonhuman primates that have met the applicable requirements of §600.11 of this chapter, or from human donors whose blood is positive for the Hepatitis B Surface Antigen.

§660.41 Processing.

(a) *Method.* The processing method shall be one that has been shown to yield consistently a specific and potent final product, free of properties which would adversely affect the test results when the product is tested by the methods recommended by the manufacturer in the package insert. The product and all ancillary reagents and materials supplied in the package with the product shall be manufactured in a manner that will reduce the risk of transmitting type B viral hepatitis.

(b) *Ancillary reagents and materials.* All ancillary reagents and materials supplied in the package with the product shall meet generally accepted standards of purity and quality and shall be effectively segregated and otherwise manufactured in a manner that will reduce the risk of contaminating the product and other biological products. Ancillary reagents and materials accompanying the product, which are used in the performance of the test as described by the manufacturer's recommended test procedures, shall have been shown not to affect adversely the product within the prescribed dating period.

(c) *Final container.* A final container shall be sufficiently transparent to permit visual inspection of the contents for presence of particulate matter and increased turbidity. The effectiveness of the contents of a final container shall be maintained throughout its dating period.

(d) *Date of manufacture.* The date of manufacture of Hepatitis B Surface Antigen that has been iodinated with radioactive iodine (125I) shall be the day of labeling the antibody with the radionuclide.

[44 FR 36382, June 22, 1979, as amended at 49 FR 1685, Jan. 13, 1984]

§ 660.43 Potency test.

To be satisfactory for release, each filling of Hepatitis B Surface Antigen shall be tested against the Reference Hepatitis B Antiserum Panel and shall be sufficiently potent to be able to detect the antibody in the appropriate sera of the reference panel by all test methods recommended by the manufacturer in the package insert.

§ 660.44 Specificity.

Each filling of the product shall be specific for Hepatitis B Surface Antigen as determined by specificity tests found acceptable to the Director, Center for Biologics Evaluation and Research.

[44 FR 36382, June 22, 1979, as amended at 49 FR 23834, June 8, 1984; 55 FR 11013, Mar. 26, 1990]

§ 660.45 Labeling.

(a) In addition to the requirements of §§ 610.60, 610.61, and 809.10 of this chapter, the labeling shall bear the following:

(1) The "d and y" antigen subtype and the source of the product to follow immediately the proper name on both the final container label and the package label. If the product is intended to identify antibodies to the "r and w" antigen subtype, the antigen subtype designation shall include the "r and w" antigen subtype.

(2) The name of the test method(s) recommended for use of the product on the package label and on the final container label, when capable of bearing a full label (see § 610.60(a) of this chapter).

(3) A warning on the package label and on the final container label stating that the product is capable of transmitting hepatitis and should be handled accordingly.

(4) The package shall include a package insert providing:

(i) Detailed instructions for use,

(ii) An adequate description of all recommended test methods, and

(iii) Warnings as to possible hazards, including hepatitis transmitted in handling the product and any ancillary reagents and materials accompanying the product.

(b) The applicant may provide the labeling information referenced in paragraph (a) of this section in the form of:

(1) A symbol accompanied by explanatory text adjacent to the symbol;

(2) A symbol not accompanied by adjacent explanatory text that:

(i) Is contained in a standard that FDA recognizes under its authority in section 514(c) of the Federal Food, Drug, and Cosmetic Act;

(ii) Is used according to the specifications for use of the symbol set forth in FDA's section 514(c) recognition; and

(iii) Is explained in a paper or electronic symbols glossary that is included in the labeling for the device and the labeling on or within the package containing the device bears a prominent and conspicuous statement identifying the location of the symbols glossary that is written in English or, in the case of articles distributed solely in Puerto Rico or in a Territory where the predominant language is one other than English, the predominant language may be used; or

(3) A symbol not accompanied by adjacent explanatory text that:

(i) Is established in a standard developed by a standards development organization (SDO);

(ii) Is not contained in a standard that is recognized by FDA under its authority in section 514(c) of the Federal Food, Drug, and Cosmetic Act or is contained in a standard that is recognized by FDA but is not used according to the specifications for use of the symbol set forth in FDA's section 514(c) recognition;

(iii) Is determined by the manufacturer to be likely to be read and understood by the ordinary individual under customary conditions of purchase and use in compliance with section 502(c) of the Federal Food, Drug, and Cosmetic Act;

(iv) Is used according to the specifications for use of the symbol set forth in the SDO-developed standard; and

(v) Is explained in a paper or electronic symbols glossary that is included in the labeling for the device and the labeling on or within the package containing the device bears a prominent and conspicuous statement identifying the location of the symbols glossary that is written in English or, in the case of articles distributed solely in Puerto Rico or in a Territory where the predominant language is one other than English, the predominant language may be used.

(c) The use of symbols in device labeling to provide the labeling information referenced in paragraph (a) of this section which do not meet the requirements of paragraph (b) of this section renders a device misbranded under section 502(c) of the Federal Food, Drug, and Cosmetic Act.

(d) For purposes of paragraph (b) of this section:

(1) An SDO is an organization that is nationally or internationally recognized and that follows a process for standard development that is transparent, (*i.e.*, open to public scrutiny), where the participation is balanced, where an appeals process is included, where the standard is not in conflict with any statute, regulation, or policy under which FDA operates, and where the standard is national or international in scope.

(2) The term "symbols glossary" means a compiled listing of:

(i) Each SDO-established symbol used in the labeling for the device;

(ii) The title and designation number of the SDO-developed standard containing the symbol;

(iii) The title of the symbol and its reference number, if any, in the standard; and

(iv) The meaning or explanatory text for the symbol as provided in the FDA recognition or, if FDA has not recognized the standard or portion of the standard in which the symbol is located or the symbol is not used according to the specifications for use of the symbol set forth in FDA's section 514(c) recognition, the explanatory text as provided in the standard.

[81 FR 38928, June 15, 2016]

§660.46 Samples; protocols; official release.

(a) *Samples.* (1) For the purposes of this section, a sample of product not iodinated with ^{125}I means a sample from each filling of each lot packaged as for distribution, including all ancillary reagents and materials; and a sample of product iodinated with ^{125}I or unlyophilized HBsAg-coated red blood cells means a sample from each lot of diagnostic test kits in a finished package, including all ancillary reagents and materials.

(2) Unless the Director, Center for Biologics Evaluation and Research, determines that the reliability and consistency of the finished product can be assured with a smaller quantity of sample or no sample and specifically reduces or eliminates the required quantity of sample, each manufacturer shall submit the following samples to the Director, Center for Biologics Evaluation and Research (see mailing addresses in §600.2(c) of this chapter), within 5 working days after the manufacturer has satisfactorily completed all tests on the samples:

(i) One sample until written notification of official release is no longer required under paragraph (c)(2) of this section.

(ii) One sample of product at periodic intervals of 90 days, beginning after written notification of official release is no longer required under paragraph (c)(2) of this section. The sample submitted at the 90-day interval shall be from the first lot or filling, as applicable, released by the manufacturer, under the requirements of §610.1 of this chapter, after the end of the previous 90-day interval. The sample shall be identified as "surveillance sample" and shall include the date of manufacture.

(iii) Samples may at any time be required to be submitted to the Director, Center for Biologics Evaluation and Research, if the Director finds that continued evaluation is necessary to ensure the potency, quality, and reliability of the product.

(b) *Protocols.* For each sample submitted as required in paragraph (a)(1) of this section, the manufacturer shall send a protocol that consists of a summary of the history of manufacture of the product, including all results of each test for which test results are requested by the Director, Center for Biologics Evaluation and Research. The protocols submitted with the samples at periodic intervals as provided in paragraph (a)(2)(ii) of this section shall be identified by the manufacturer as "surveillance test results."

(c) *Official release.* (1) The manufacturer shall not distribute the product until written notification of official release is received from the Director, Center for Biologics Evaluation and Research, except as provided in paragraph (c)(2) of this section. Official release is required for at least five consecutive lots or fillings, as applicable, manufactured after licensure of the product.

(2) After written notification of official release is received from the Director, Center for Biologics Evaluation and Research, for at least five consecutive lots or fillings manufactured after licensure of the products, and after the manufacturer receives from the Director, Center for Biologics Evaluation and Research, written notification that official release is no longer required, subsequent lots or fillings may be released by the manufacturer under the requirements of § 610.1 of this chapter.

(3) The manufacturer shall not distribute lots or fillings, as applicable, of products that require sample submission under paragraph (a)(2)(iii) of this section until written notification of official release or notification that official release is no longer required is received from the Director, Center for Biologics Evaluation and Research.

[48 FR 20407, May 6, 1983, as amended at 49 FR 23834, June 8, 1984; 51 FR 15611, Apr. 25, 1986; 55 FR 11013, 11014, Mar. 26, 1990; 70 FR 14985, Mar. 24, 2005; 80 FR 18093, Apr. 3, 2015]

Subpart F—Anti-Human Globulin

§ 660.50   Anti-Human Globulin.

(a) *Proper name and definition.* The proper name of this product shall be Anti-Human Globulin which shall consist of one or more antiglobulin antibodies identified in § 660.55(a)(4).

(b) *Source.* The source of this product shall be either serum from animals immunized with one or more human serum globulins or protein-rich fluids derived from stable immunoglobulin-secreting cell lines maintained either in tissue cultures or in secondary hosts.

[50 FR 5579, Feb. 11, 1985, as amended at 65 FR 77499, Dec. 12, 2000; 81 FR 38928, June 15, 2016]

§ 660.51   Processing.

(a) *Processing method.* (1) The processing method shall be one that has been shown to yield consistently a specific, potent final product, free of properties that would adversely affect the product for its intended use throughout its dating period.

(2) Anti-IgG, –C3d (polyspecific) reagents and anti-IgG products may be colored green.

(3) Only that material which has been fully processed, thoroughly mixed in a single vessel, and filtered shall constitute a lot. Each lot shall be identified by a lot number.

(4) A lot may be subdivided into sublots which shall be identified by the lot number to which has been added a distinctive prefix or suffix. If lots are to be subdivided, the manufacturer shall include this information in the license application . The manufacturer shall describe the test specifications to verify that each sublot is identical to other sublots of the lot.

(b) *Final containers and dropper assemblies.* (1) Final containers and dropper assemblies shall be clean.

(2) Final containers and dropper pipettes shall be colorless and sufficiently transparent to permit observation of the contents for presence of particulate matter or increased turbidity.

(c) *Date of manufacture.* The date of manufacture shall be the date the manufacturer begins the last entire group of potency tests.

[50 FR 5579, Feb. 11, 1985, as amended at 50 FR 16474, Apr. 26, 1985; 65 FR 77499, Dec. 12, 2000; 67 FR 9587, Mar. 4, 2002]

§ 660.52   Reference preparations.

Reference Anti-Human Globulin preparations shall be obtained from the Food and Drug Administration, Center for Biologics Evaluation and Research, Reagents and Standards Shipping, 10903 New Hampshire Ave., Bldg. 75, Rm. G704, Silver Spring, MD 20993–0002, and shall be used as described in the accompanying package insert for determining the potency of Anti-Human Globulin.

[50 FR 5579, Feb. 11, 1985, as amended at 50 FR 16474, Apr. 26, 1985; 51 FR 15611, Apr. 25, 1986; 55 FR 11015, Mar. 26, 1990; 67 FR 9587, Mar. 4, 2002; 70 FR 14986, Mar. 24, 2005; 80 FR 18093, Apr. 3, 2015]

§660.53 Controls for serological procedures.

Red blood cells sensitized with complement shall be tested with appropriate positive and negative control antisera. All tests shall be performed in accordance with serological testing procedures approved by the Director, Center for Biologics Evaluation and Research.

[50 FR 5579, Feb. 11, 1985, as amended at 50 FR 16474, Apr. 26, 1985; 51 FR 15611, Apr. 25, 1986; 55 FR 11014, Mar. 26, 1990; 67 FR 9587, Mar. 4, 2002; 70 FR 14986, Mar. 24, 2005]

§660.54 Potency tests, specificity tests, tests for heterospecific antibodies, and additional tests for nonspecific properties.

The following tests shall be performed using test procedures approved by the Director, Center for Biologics Evaluation and Research:

(a) Potency tests for determining anti-IgG and anti-complement activity.

(b) Specificity tests, tests for heterospecific antibodies, and additional tests for nonspecific properties.

[50 FR 5579, Feb. 11, 1985, as amended at 50 FR 16474, Apr. 26, 1985; 51 FR 15611, Apr. 25, 1986; 55 FR 11014, Mar. 26, 1990; 67 FR 9587, Mar. 4, 2002; 70 FR 14986, Mar. 24, 2005]

§660.55 Labeling.

(a) In addition to the applicable labeling requirements of §§610.62 through 610.65 and §809.10 of this chapter, and in lieu of the requirements in §§610.60 and 610.61 of this chapter, the following requirements shall be met:

(1) *Final container label*—(i) *Color coding.* The main panel of the final container label of all Anti-IgG, -C3d (polyspecific) reagents shall be white or colorless and printing shall be solid dark contrasting lettering. The main panel of the final container label of all other Anti-Human Globulin reagents shall be black with solid white lettering. A logo or company name may be placed on the final container label; however, the logo or company name shall be located along the bottom or end of the label, outside of the main panel.

(ii) *Required information.* The proper name "Anti-Human Globulin" need not appear on the final container label provided the final container is distributed in a package and the package label bears the proper name. The final container label shall bear the following information:

(A) Name of the antibody or antibodies present as set forth in paragraph (a)(4) of this section. Anti-Human Globulin may contain one or more antibodies to either immunoglobulins or complement components but the name of each significant antibody must appear on the final container label (*e.g.*, anti-C3b, -C3d, -C4d). The final container labels of polyspecific Anti-Human Globulin are not required to identify antibody specificities other than anti-IgG and anti-C3d but the reactivity of the Anti-Human Globulin shall be accurately described in the package insert.

(B) Name, address, and license number of the manufacturer.

(C) Lot number, including any sublot designations.

(D) Expiration date.

(E) Source of the product.

(F) Recommended storage temperature in degrees Celsius.

(G) Volume of product.

(H) Appropriate cautionary statement if the Anti-Human Globulin is not polyspecific. For example, "DOES NOT CONTAIN ANTIBODIES TO IMMUNOGLOBULINS" or "DOES NOT CONTAIN ANTIBODIES TO COMPLEMENT COMPONENTS."

(I) If the final container is not enclosed in a package, all items required for a package label shall appear on the container label.

(iii) *Lettering size.* The type size for the designation of the specific antibody on the label of a final container shall be not less than 12 point, unless otherwise approved by the Director, Center for Biologics Evaluation and Research. The prefix anti- and other parts of the name such as polyspecific may appear in smaller type.

(iv) *Visual inspection.* When the label has been affixed to the final container, a sufficient area of the container shall remain uncovered for its full length or for no less than 5 millimeters of the lower circumference to permit inspection of the contents.

(2) *Package label.* The following items shall appear either on the package label or on the final container label if see-through packaging is used:

(i) Proper name of the product, and the name of the antibody or antibodies as listed in paragraph (a)(4) of this section.

(ii) Name, address (including ZIP code), and license number of the manufacturer.

(iii) Lot number, including any sublot designations.

(iv) Expiration date.

(v) Preservative(s) used and its concentration.

(vi) Number of containers, if more than one.

(vii) Recommended storage temperature in degrees Celsius.

(viii) Source of the product.

(ix) Reference to enclosed package insert.

(x) The statement: "For In Vitro Diagnostic Use."

(xi) The statement: "Meets FDA Potency Requirements."

(xii) A statement of an observable indication of an alteration of the product, *e.g.,* turbidity, color change, precipitate, that may indicate possible deterioration of the product.

(xiii) Appropriate cautions.

(3) *Package insert.* Each final container of Anti-Human Globulin shall be accompanied by a package insert meeting the requirements of § 809.10 of this chapter. If two or more final containers requiring identical package inserts are placed in a single package, only one package insert per package is required.

(4) *Names of antibodies.* Anti-Human Globulin preparations may contain one or more of the antibody specificities listed in this paragraph as described in paragraph (a)(1)(ii)(A) of this section.

Antibody designation on container label	Definition
(1) Anti-IgG, -C3d; Polyspecific	Contains anti-IgG and anti-C3d (may contain other anticomplement and anti-immunoglobulin antibodies).
(2) Anti-IgG	Contains anti-IgG with no anti-complement activity (not necessarily gamma chain specific).
(3) Anti-IgG; heavy chains	Contains only antibodies reactive against human gamma chains.
(4) Anti-C3b	Contains only C3b antibodies with no anti-immunoglobulin activity. *Note:* The antibody produced in response to immunization is usually directed against the antigenic determinant which is located in the C3c subunit; some persons have called this antibody "anti-C3c." In product labeling, this antibody should be designated anti-C3b.
(5) Anti-C3d	Contains only C3d antibodies with no anti-immunoglobulin activity.
(6) Anti-C4b	Contains only C4b antibodies with no anti-immunoglobulin activity.
(7) Anti-C4d	Contains only C4d antibodies with no anti-immunoglobulin activity.

(b) The applicant may provide the labeling information referenced in this section in the form of:

(1) A symbol accompanied by explanatory text adjacent to the symbol;

(2) A symbol not accompanied by adjacent explanatory text that:

(i) Is contained in a standard that FDA recognizes under its authority in section 514(c) of the Federal Food, Drug, and Cosmetic Act;

(ii) Is used according to the specifications for use of the symbol set forth in FDA's section 514(c) recognition; and

(iii) Is explained in a paper or electronic symbols glossary that is included in the labeling for the device

and the labeling on or within the package containing the device bears a prominent and conspicuous statement identifying the location of the symbols glossary that is written in English or, in the case of articles distributed solely in Puerto Rico or in a Territory where the predominant language is one other than English, the predominant language may be used; or

(3) A symbol not accompanied by adjacent explanatory text that:

(i) Is established in a standard developed by a standards development organization (SDO);

(ii) Is not contained in a standard that is recognized by FDA under its authority in section 514(c) or is contained in a standard that is recognized by FDA but is not used according to the specifications for use of the symbol set forth in FDA's section 514(c) recognition;

(iii) Is determined by the manufacturer to be likely to be read and understood by the ordinary individual under customary conditions of purchase and use in compliance with section 502(c) of the Federal Food, Drug, and Cosmetic Act;

(iv) Is used according to the specifications for use of the symbol set forth in the SDO-developed standard; and

(v) Is explained in a paper or electronic symbols glossary that is included in the labeling for the device and the labeling on or within the package containing the device bears a prominent and conspicuous statement identifying the location of the symbols glossary that is written in English or, in the case of articles distributed solely in Puerto Rico or in a Territory where the predominant language is one other than English, the predominant language may be used.

(c) The use of symbols in device labeling to provide the labeling information referenced in paragraph (a) of this section which do not meet the requirements of paragraph (b) of this section renders a device misbranded under section 502(c) of the Federal Food, Drug, and Cosmetic Act.

(d) For purposes of paragraph (b) of this section:

(1) An SDO is an organization that is nationally or internationally recognized and that follows a process for standard development that is transparent, (i.e., open to public scrutiny), where the participation is balanced, where an appeals process is included, where the standard is not in conflict with any statute, regulation, or policy under which FDA operates, and where the standard is national or international in scope.

(2) The term "symbols glossary" means a compiled listing of:

(i) Each SDO-established symbol used in the labeling for the device;

(ii) The title and designation number of the SDO-developed standard containing the symbol;

(iii) The title of the symbol and its reference number, if any, in the standard; and

(iv) The meaning or explanatory text for the symbol as provided in the FDA recognition or, if FDA has not recognized the standard or portion of the standard in which the symbol is located or the symbol is not used according to the specifications for use of the symbol set forth in FDA's section 514(c) recognition, the explanatory text as provided in the standard.

[81 FR 38928, June 15, 2016]

PART 680—ADDITIONAL STANDARDS FOR MISCELLANEOUS PRODUCTS

Sec.
680.1 Allergenic Products.
680.2 Manufacture of Allergenic Products.
680.3 Tests.

AUTHORITY: 21 U.S.C. 321, 351, 352, 353, 355, 360, 371; 42 U.S.C. 216, 262, 263, 263a, 264.

SOURCE: 38 FR 32100, Nov. 20, 1973, unless otherwise noted.

CROSS REFERENCES: For U.S. Customs Service regulations relating to viruses, serums, and toxins, see 19 CFR 12.21–12.23. For U.S. Postal Service regulations relating to the admissibility to the United States mails see parts 124 and 125 of the Domestic Mail Manual, that is incorporated by reference in 39 CFR part 111.

§ 680.1 Allergenic Products.

(a) *Definition.* Allergenic Products are products that are administered to man for the diagnosis, prevention or treatment of allergies.

(b) *Source materials—*(1) *Criteria for source material.* Only specifically identified allergenic source materials that contain no more than a total of 1.0 percent of detectable foreign materials shall be used in the manufacture of Allergenic Products, except that this requirement shall not apply to molds and animals described under paragraphs (b) (2) and (3) of this section, respectively. Source materials such as pelts, feathers, hairs, and danders shall be collected in a manner that will minimize contamination of the source material.

(2) *Molds.* (i) Molds (excluding rusts and smuts) used as source material in the manufacture of Allergenic Products shall meet the requirements of § 610.18 of this chapter and § 680.2 (a) and (b).

(ii) Mold cultures shall be free of contaminating materials (including microorganisms) prior to harvest, and care shall be taken to minimize contamination during harvest and subsequent processing.

(iii) Mold manufacturers shall maintain written standard operating procedures, developed by a qualified individual, that will ensure the identity of the seed culture, prescribe adequate processing of the mold, and specify the acceptable limits and kinds of contamination. These limits shall be based on results of appropriate tests performed by the manufacturer on at least three consecutive lots of a mold that is a representative species of mold subject to the standard operating procedures. The tests shall be performed at each manufacturing step during and subsequent to harvest, as specified in the standard operating procedures. Before use of the mold as a source material for Allergenic Products, in accordance with 21 CFR 601.2, the standard operating procedures and test data from the three representative lots described above shall be submitted to and approved by the Director, Center for Biologics Evaluation and Research (see mailing address in § 600.2(a) of this chapter).

(3) *Mammals and birds*—(i) *Care of animals.* Animals intended as a source material for Allergenic Products shall be maintained by competent personnel in facilities or designated areas that will ensure adequate care. Competent veterinary care shall be provided as needed.

(ii) *Health of animals.* Only animals in good health and free from detectable skin diseases shall be used as a source material for Allergenic Products. The determination of good health prior to collection of the source material shall be made by a licensed veterinarian or a competent individual under the supervision and instruction of a licensed veterinarian provided that the licensed veterinarian certifies in writing that the individual is capable of determining the good health of the animals.

(iii) *Immunization against tetanus.* Animals of the equine genus intended as a source material for Allergenic Products shall be treated to maintain immunity to tetanus.

(iv) *Reporting of certain diseases.* In cases of actual or suspected infection with foot and mouth disease, glanders, tetanus, anthrax, gas gangrene, equine infectious anemia, equine encephalomyelitis, or any of the pock diseases among animals intended for use or used as source material in the manufacture of Allergenic Products, the manufacturer shall immediately notify the Director, Center for Biologics Evaluation and Research (see mailing address in § 600.2(a) of this chapter).

(v) *Dead animals.* Dead animals may be used as source material in the manufacture of Allergenic Products: *Provided,* That (*a*) the carcasses shall be frozen or kept cold until the allergen can be collected, or shall be stored under other acceptable conditions so that the postmortal decomposition processes do not adversely affect the allergen, and (*b*) when alive, the animal met the applicable requirements prescribed in paragraphs (b)(3) (i), (ii), and (iii) of this section.

(vi) *Mammals and birds inspected by the U.S. Department of Agriculture.* Mammals and birds, subject to inspection by the U.S. Department of Agriculture at the time of slaughter and found suitable as food, may be used as a source material, and the requirements of paragraph (b)(3) (i) through (iv) of this section do not apply in such a case. Notwithstanding U.S. Department of Agriculture inspection, the carcasses of such inspected animals shall be frozen or kept cold until the allergen is collected, or shall be stored under other acceptable conditions so that the postmortal decomposition processes do not adversely affect the allergen.

(c) *Listing of source materials and suppliers.* Each licensed manufacturer shall initially list with the Director, Center for Biologics Evaluation and Research (see mailing address in § 600.2(a) of this chapter), the name and address of each of the manufacturer's source material suppliers. The listing shall identify each source material obtained from each source material supplier. The licensed manufacturers shall update the listing annually to include new source material suppliers or to delete those no longer supplying source materials.

(d) *Exemptions.* (1) Exemptions or modifications from the requirements under paragraph (b) of this section shall be made only upon written approval by the Director, Center for Biologics Evaluation and Research.

(2) Nonlicensed source material suppliers are exempt from drug registration.

[38 FR 32100, Nov. 20, 1973, as amended at 49 FR 25432, June 21, 1984; 49 FR 31395, Aug. 7, 1984; 55 FR 11014, Mar. 26, 1990; 67 FR 9587, Mar. 4, 2002; 70 FR 14986, Mar. 24, 2005; 80 FR 18093, Apr. 3, 2015]

§680.2 Manufacture of Allergenic Products.

(a) *Extraneous allergenic substances.* All manufacturing steps shall be performed so as to insure that the product will contain only the allergenic and other substances intended to be included in the final product.

(b) *Cultures derived from microorganisms.* Culture media into which organisms are inoculated for the manufacture of Allergenic Products shall contain no allergenic substances other than those necessary as a growth requirement. Neither horse protein nor any allergenic derivative of horse protein shall be used in culture media.

(c) *Liquid products for oral administration.* Liquid products intended for oral administration that are filled in multiple dose final containers shall contain a preservative in a concentration adequate to inhibit microbial growth.

(d) *Residual pyridine.* Products for which pyridine is used in manufacturing shall have no more residual pyridine in the final product than 25 micrograms per milliliter.

(e) [Reserved]

(f) *Records.* A record of the history of the manufacture or propagation of each lot of source material intended for manufacture of final Allergenic Products shall be available at the establishment of the manufacturer of the source material, as required by §211.188 of this chapter. A summary of the history of the manufacture or propagation of the source material shall be available at the establishment of the manufacturer of the final product.

[38 FR 32100, Nov. 20, 1973, as amended at 49 FR 25433, June 21, 1984; 67 FR 9587, Mar. 4, 2002]

§680.3 Tests.

(a) *Identity.* When a specific identity test meeting the provisions of §610.14 of this chapter cannot be performed, the manufacture of each lot shall be separated from the manufacture of other products in a manner that will preclude adulteration, and records made in the course of manufacture shall be in sufficient detail to verify the identity of the product.

(b) [Reserved]

(c) *Sterility.* A sterility test shall be performed on each lot of each Allergenic Product as required by §610.12 of this chapter.

(d) [Reserved]

(e) *Potency.* The potency of each lot of each Allergenic Product shall be determined as prescribed in §610.10 of this chapter. Except as provided in this section, the potency test methods shall measure the allergenic activity of the product. Until manufacturers are notified by the Director, Center for Biologics Evaluation and Research, of the existence of a potency test that measures the allergenic activity of an allergenic product, manufacturers may continue to use unstandardized potency designations.

(f) *Records.* The records related to the testing requirements of this section shall be prepared and maintained as required by §§211.165, 211.167, 211.188, and 211.194 of this chapter.

[38 FR 32100, Nov. 20, 1973, as amended at 39 FR 19777, June 6, 1974; 41 FR 4015, Jan. 28, 1976; 52 FR 37607, Oct. 8, 1987; 55 FR 11013, Mar. 26, 1990; 67 FR 9587, Mar. 4, 2002; 77 FR 26175, May 3, 2012; 77 FR 30884, May 24, 2012; 80 FR 37974, July 2, 2015]

SUBCHAPTER G—COSMETICS

PART 700—GENERAL

Subpart A—General Provisions

Sec.
700.3 Definitions.

Subpart B—Requirements for Specific Cosmetic Products

700.11 Cosmetics containing bithionol.
700.13 Use of mercury compounds in cosmetics including use as skinbleaching agents in cosmetic preparations also regarded as drugs.
700.14 Use of vinyl chloride as an ingredient, including propellant of cosmetic aerosol products.
700.15 Use of certain halogenated salicylanilides as ingredients in cosmetic products.
700.16 Use of aerosol cosmetic products containing zirconium.
700.18 Use of chloroform as an ingredient in cosmetic products.
700.19 Use of methylene chloride as an ingredient of cosmetic products.
700.23 Chlorofluorocarbon propellants.
700.25 Tamper-resistant packaging requirements for cosmetic products.
700.27 Use of prohibited cattle materials in cosmetic products.
700.35 Cosmetics containing sunscreen ingredients.

AUTHORITY: 21 U.S.C. 321, 331, 352, 355, 361, 362, 371, 374.

SOURCE: 39 FR 10054, Mar. 15, 1974, unless otherwise noted.

Subpart A—General Provisions

§ 700.3 Definitions.

As used in this subchapter:

(a) The term *act* means the Federal Food, Drug, and Cosmetic Act.

(b) The term *cosmetic product* means a finished cosmetic the manufacture of which has been completed. Any cosmetic product which is also a drug or device or component thereof is also subject to the requirements of Chapter V of the act.

(c) The term *flavor* means any natural or synthetic substance or substances used solely to impart a taste to a cosmetic product.

(d) The term *fragrance* means any natural or synthetic substance or substances used solely to impart an odor to a cosmetic product.

(e) The term *ingredient* means any single chemical entity or mixture used as a component in the manufacture of a cosmetic product.

(f) The term *proprietary ingredient* means any cosmetic product ingredient whose name, composition, or manufacturing process is protected from competition by secrecy, patent, or copyright.

(g) The term *chemical description* means a concise definition of the chemical composition using standard chemical nomenclature so that the chemical structure or structures of the components of the ingredient would be clear to a practicing chemist. When the composition cannot be described chemically, the substance shall be described in terms of its source and processing.

(h) The term *cosmetic raw material* means any ingredient, including an ingredient that is a mixture, which is used in the manufacture of a cosmetic product for commercial distribution and is supplied to a cosmetic product manufacturer, packer, or distributor by a cosmetic raw material manufacturer or supplier.

(i) The term *commercial distribution* of a cosmetic product means annual gross sales in excess of $1,000 for that product.

(j) *Establishment* means a place of business where cosmetic products are manufactured or packaged.

(k) The term *manufacture* of a cosmetic product means the making of any cosmetic product by chemical, physical, biological, or other procedures, including manipulation, sampling, testing, or control procedures applied to the product.

(l) The term *packaging* of a cosmetic product means filling or labeling the product container, including changing the immediate container or label (but excluding changing other labeling) at any point in the distribution of the cosmetic product from the original place of manufacture to the person who makes final delivery or sale to the ultimate consumer.

(m) The term *all business trading names used by the establishment* means any name which is used on a cosmetic product label and owned by the cosmetic product manufacturer or packer, but is different from the principal name under which the cosmetic product manufacturer or packer is registered.

(n) The definitions and interpretations contained in sections 201, 601, and 602 of the act shall be applicable to such terms when used in the regulations in this subchapter.

(o) *System of commercial distribution* of a cosmetic product means any distribution outside the establishment manufacturing the product, whether for sale, to promote future sales (including free samples of the product), or to gage consumer acceptance through market testing, in excess of $1,000 in cost of goods.

(p) *Filed screening procedure* means a procedure that is:

(1) On file with the Food and Drug Administration and subject to public inspection;

(2) Designed to determine that there is a reasonable basis for concluding that an alleged injury did not occur in conjunction with the use of the cosmetic product; and

(3) Which is subject, upon request by the Food and Drug Administration, to an audit conducted by the Food and Drug Administration at reasonable times and, where an audit is conducted, such audit shows that the procedure is consistently being applied and that the procedure is not disregarding reportable information.

(q) *Reportable experience* means an experience involving any allergic reaction, or other bodily injury, alleged to be the result of the use of a cosmetic product under the conditions of use prescribed in the labeling of the product, under such conditions of use as are customary or reasonably foreseeable for the product or under conditions of misuse, that has been reported to the manufacturer, packer, or distributor of the product by the affected person or any other person having factual knowledge of the incident, other than an alleged experience which has been determined to be unfounded or spurious

when evaluated by a filed screening procedure.

[39 FR 10054, Mar. 15, 1974, as amended at 46 FR 38073, July 24, 1981]

Subpart B—Requirements for Specific Cosmetic Products

§700.11 Cosmetics containing bithionol.

(a) Bithionol has been used to some extent as an antibacterial agent in cosmetic preparations such as detergent bars, shampoos, creams, lotions, and bases used to hide blemishes. New evidence of clinical experience and photopatch tests indicate that bithionol is capable of causing photosensitivity in man when used topically and that in some instances the photosensitization may persist for prolonged periods as severe reactions without further contact with sensitizing articles. Also, there is evidence to indicate that bithionol may produce cross-sensitization with other commonly used chemicals such as certain halogenated salicylanilides and hexachlorophene. It is, therefore, the view of the Food and Drug Administration that bithionol is a deleterious substance which may render any cosmetic product that contains it injurious to users. Accordingly, any cosmetic containing bithionol is deemed to be adulterated under section 601(a) of the Federal Food, Drug, and Cosmetic Act.

(b) Regulatory proceedings may be initiated with respect to any cosmetic preparation containing bithionol shipped within the jurisdiction of the act after March 15, 1968.

§700.13 Use of mercury compounds in cosmetics including use as skinbleaching agents in cosmetic preparations also regarded as drugs.

(a) Mercury-containing cosmetic preparations have been represented for many years as skin-bleaching agents or as preparations to remove or prevent freckles and/or brown spots (so-called age spots). Preparations intended for such use are regarded as drugs as well as cosmetics. In addition to such use as skin-bleaching agents, mercury compounds have also been widely used as preservatives in cosmetics such as hand and body creams and lotions; hair shampoos, hair sets and rinses, hair straighteners, hair coloring, and other preparations; bath oils, bubble bath, and other bath preparations; makeup; antiperspirants and deodorants; and eye-area cosmetics.

(b) The toxicity of mercury compounds is extensively documented in scientific literature. It is well known that mercury compounds are readily absorbed through the unbroken skin as well as through the lungs by inhalation and by intestinal absorption after ingestion. Mercury is absorbed from topical application and is accumulated in the body, giving rise to numerous adverse effects. Mercury is a potent allergen and sensitizer, and skin irritation is common after topical application. Cosmetic preparations containing mercury compounds are often applied with regularity and frequency for prolonged periods. Such chronic use of mercury-containing skin-bleaching preparations has resulted in the accumulation of mercury in the body and the occurrence of severe reactions. Recently it has also been determined that microorganisms in the environment can convert various forms of mercury into highly toxic methyl mercury which has been found in the food supply and is now considered to be a serious environmental problem.

(c) The effectiveness of mercury-containing preparations as skin-bleaching agents is questionable. The Food and Drug Administration has not been provided with well controlled studies to document the effectiveness of these preparations. Although mercurial preservatives are recognized as highly effective, less toxic and satisfactory substitutes are available except in the case of certain eye-area cosmetics.

(d) Because of the known hazards of mercury, its questionable efficacy as a skin-bleaching agent, and the availability of effective and less toxic nonmercurial preservatives, there is no justification for the use of mercury in skin-bleaching preparations or its use as a preservative in cosmetics, with the exception of eye-area cosmetics for which no other effective and safe nonmercurial preservative is available. The continued use of mercurial preservatives in such eye-area cosmetics

is warranted because mercury compounds are exceptionally effective in preventing *Pseudomonas* contamination of cosmetics and *Pseudomonas* infection of the eye can cause serious injury, including blindness. Therefore:

(1) The Food and Drug Administration withdraws the opinion expressed in trade correspondence TC–9 (issued May 13, 1939) and concludes that any product containing mercury as a skin-bleaching agent and offered for sale as skin-bleaching, beauty, or facial preparation is misbranded within the meaning of sections 502(a), 502(f)(1) and (2), and 502(j), and may be a new drug without approval in violation of section 505 of the Federal Food, Drug, and Cosmetic Act. Any such preparation shipped within the jurisdiction of the Act after January 5, 1973 will be the subject of regulatory action.

(2) The Food and Drug Administration withdraws the opinion expressed in trade correspondence TC–412 (issued Feb. 11, 1944) and will regard as adulterated within the meaning of section 601(a) of the Act any cosmetic containing mercury unless the cosmetic meets the conditions of paragraph (d)(2) (i) or (ii) of this section.

(i) It is a cosmetic containing no more than a trace amount of mercury and such trace amount is unavoidable under conditions of good manufacturing practice and is less than 1 part per million (0.0001 percent), calculated as the metal; or

(ii) It is a cosmetic intended for use only in the area of the eye, it contains no more than 65 parts per million (0.0065 percent) of mercury, calculated as the metal, as a preservative, and there is no effective and safe nonmercurial substitute preservative available for use in such cosmetic.

§ 700.14 Use of vinyl chloride as an ingredient, including propellant of cosmetic aerosol products.

(a) Vinyl chloride has been used as an ingredient in cosmetic aerosol products including hair sprays. Where such aerosol products are used in the confines of a small room, as is often the case, the level of vinyl chloride to which the individual may be exposed could be significantly in excess of the safe level established in connection with occupational exposure. Evidence indicates that vinyl chloride inhalation can result in acute toxicity, manifested by dizziness, headache, disorientation, and unconsciousness where inhaled at high concentrations. Studies also demonstrate carcinogenic effects in animals as a result of inhalation exposure to vinyl chloride. Furthermore, vinyl chloride has recently been linked to liver disease, including liver cancer, in workers engaged in the polymerization of vinyl chloride. It is the view of the Commissioner that vinyl chloride is a deleterious substance which may render any cosmetic aerosol product that contains it as an ingredient injurious to users. Accordingly, any cosmetic aerosol product containing vinyl chloride as an ingredient is deemed to be adulterated under section 601(a) of the Federal Food, Drug, and Cosmetic Act.

(b) Any cosmetic aerosol product containing vinyl chloride as an ingredient shipped within the jurisdiction of the Act is subject to regulatory action.

[39 FR 30830, Aug. 26, 1974]

§ 700.15 Use of certain halogenated salicylanilides as ingredients in cosmetic products.

(a) Halogenated salicylanilides (tribromsalan (TBS,3,4′,5–tribromosalicylanilide), dibromsalan (DBS,4′5–dibromosalicylanilide), metabromsalan (MBS, 3,5–dibromosalicylanilide) and 3,3′,4,5′–tetrachlorosalicylanilide (TCSA)) have been used as antimicrobial agents for a variety of purposes in cosmetic products. These halogenated salicylanilides are potent photosensitizers and cross-sensitizers and can cause disabling skin disorders. In some instances, the photosensitization may persist for prolonged periods as a severe reaction without further exposure to these chemicals. Safer alternative antimicrobial agents are available.

(b) These halogenated salicylanilides are deleterious substances which render any cosmetic that contains them injurious to users. Therefore, any cosmetic product that contains such a halogenated salicylanilide as an ingredient at any level for any purpose is deemed to be adulterated under section 601(a) of the Federal Food, Drug, and Cosmetic Act.

(c) Any cosmetic product containing these halogenated salicylanilides as an ingredient that is initially introduced into interstate commerce after December 1, 1975, that is not in compliance with this section is subject to regulatory action.

[40 FR 50531, Oct. 30, 1975]

§ 700.16 Use of aerosol cosmetic products containing zirconium.

(a) Zirconium-containing complexes have been used as an ingredient in cosmetics and/or cosmetics that are also drugs, as, for example, aerosol antiperspirants. Evidence indicates that certain zirconium compounds have caused human skin granulomas and toxic effects in the lungs and other organs of experimental animals. When used in aerosol form, some zirconium will reach the deep portions of the lungs of users. The lung is an organ, like skin, subject to the development of granulomas. Unlike the skin, the lung will not reveal the presence of granulomatous changes until they have become advanced and, in some cases, permanent. It is the view of the Commissioner that zirconium is a deleterious substance that may render any cosmetic aerosol product that contains it injurious to users.

(b) Any aerosol cosmetic product containing zirconium is deemed to be adulterated under section 601(a) of the Federal Food, Drug, and Cosmetic Act.

(c) Any such cosmetic product introduced in interstate commerce after September 15, 1977 is subject to regulatory action.

[42 FR 41376, Aug. 16, 1977]

§ 700.18 Use of chloroform as an ingredient in cosmetic products.

(a) Chloroform has been used as an ingredient in cosmetic products. Recent information has become available associating chloroform with carcinogenic effects in animals. Studies conducted by the National Cancer Institute have demonstrated that the oral administration of chloroform to mice and rats induced hepatocellular carcinomas (liver cancer) in mice and renal tumors in male rats. Scientific literature indicates that chloroform is absorbed from the gastrointestinal tract, through the respiratory system, and through the skin. The Commissioner concludes that, on the basis of these findings, chloroform is a deleterious substance which may render injurious to users any cosmetic product that contains chloroform as an ingredient.

(b) Any cosmetic product containing chloroform as an ingredient is adulterated and is subject to regulatory action under sections 301 and 601(a) of the Federal Food, Drug, and Cosmetic Act. Any cosmetic product containing chloroform in residual amounts from its use as a processing solvent during manufacture, or as a byproduct from the synthesis of an ingredient, is not, for the purpose of this section, considered to contain chloroform as an ingredient.

[41 FR 26845, June 29, 1976]

§ 700.19 Use of methylene chloride as an ingredient of cosmetic products.

(a) Methylene chloride has been used as an ingredient of aerosol cosmetic products, principally hair sprays, at concentrations generally ranging from 10 to 25 percent. In a 2-year animal inhalation study sponsored by the National Toxicology Program, methylene chloride produced a significant increase in benign and malignant tumors of the lung and liver of male and female mice. Based on these findings and on estimates of human exposure from the customary use of hair sprays, the Food and Drug Administration concludes that the use of methylene chloride in cosmetic products poses a significant cancer risk to consumers, and that the use of this ingredient in cosmetic products may render these products injurious to health.

(b) Any cosmetic product that contains methylene chloride as an ingredient is deemed adulterated and is subject to regulatory action under sections 301 and 601(a) of the Federal Food, Drug, and Cosmetic Act.

[54 FR 27342, June 29, 1989]

§ 700.23 Chlorofluorocarbon propellants.

The use of chlorofluorocarbons in cosmetics as propellants in self-pressurized containers is prohibited as provided in § 2.125 of this chapter.

[43 FR 11317, Mar. 17, 1978]

§ 700.25 Tamper-resistant packaging requirements for cosmetic products.

(a) *General.* Because most cosmetic liquid oral hygiene products and vaginal products are not now packaged in tamper-resistant retail packages, there is the opportunity for the malicious adulteration of those cosmetic products with health risks to individuals who unknowingly purchase adulterated products and with loss of consumer confidence in the security of cosmetic product packages. The Food and Drug Administration has the authority and responsibility under the Federal Food, Drug, and Cosmetic Act (the act) to establish a uniform national requirement for tamper-resistant packaging of cosmetic liquid oral hygiene products or products used vaginally that will improve the packaging security and help assure the safety of those products. Such a cosmetic product for retail sale that is not packaged in a tamper-resistant package or that is not properly labeled under this section is adulterated under section 601 of the act or misbranded under section 602 of the act, or both.

(b) *Requirement for tamper-resistant package.* Each manufacturer and packer who packages a cosmetic liquid oral hygiene product or vaginal product for retail sale shall package the product in a tamper-resistant package, if this product is accessible to the public while held for sale. A tamper-resistant package is one having an indicator or barrier to entry which, if breached or missing, can reasonably be expected to provide visible evidence to consumers that tampering has occurred. To reduce the likelihood of substitution of a tamper-resistant feature after tampering, the indicator or barrier to entry is required to be distinctive by design (e.g., an aerosol product container) or by the use of an identifying characteristic (e.g., a pattern, name, registered trademark, logo, or picture). For purposes of this section, the term "distinctive by design" means the packaging cannot be duplicated with commonly available materials or through commonly available processes. For purposes of this section, the term "aerosol product" means a product which depends upon the power of a liquified or compressed gas to expel the contents from the container. A tamper-resistant package may involve an immediate-container and closure system or secondary-container or carton system or any combination of systems intended to provide a visual indication of package integrity. The tamper-resistant feature shall be designed to and shall remain intact when handled in a reasonable manner during manufacture, distribution, and retail display.

(c) *Labeling.* Each retail package of a cosmetic product covered by this section, except aerosol products as defined in paragraph (b) of this section, is required to bear a statement that is prominently placed so that consumers are alerted to the specific tamper-resistant feature of the package. The labeling statement is also required to be so placed that it will be unaffected if the tamper-resistant feature of the package is breached or missing. If the tamper-resistant feature chosen to meet the requirement in paragraph (b) of this section is one that uses an identifying characteristic, that characteristic is required to be referred to in the labeling statement. For example, the labeling statement on a bottle with a shrink band could say "For your protection, this bottle has an imprinted seal around the neck."

(d) *Requests for exemptions from packaging and labeling requirements.* A manufacturer or packer may request an exemption from the packaging and labeling requirements of this section. A request for an exemption is required to be submitted in the form of a citizen petition under §10.30 of this chapter and should be clearly identified on the envelope as a "Request for Exemption from Tamper-resistant Rule." The petition is required to contain the following:

(1) The name of the product.

(2) The reasons that the product's compliance with the tamper-resistant packaging or labeling requirements of

this section is unnecessary or cannot be achieved.

(3) A description of alternative steps that are available, or that the petitioner has already taken, to reduce the likelihood that the product will be the subject of malicious adulteration.

(4) Other information justifying an exemption.

This information collection requirement has been approved by the Office of Management and Budget under number 0910–0149.

(e) *Effective date.* Cosmetic products covered by this section are required to comply with the requirements of this section on the dates listed below except to the extent that a product's manufacturer or packer has obtained an exemption from a packaging or labeling requirement.

(1) *Initial effective date for packaging requirements.* (i) The packaging requirement in paragraph (b) of this section is effective on Feburary 7, 1983 for each affected cosmetic product (except vaginal tablets) packaged for retail sale on or after that date, except for the requirement in paragraph (b) of this section for a distinctive indicator or barrier to entry.

(ii) The packaging requirement in paragraph (b) of this section is effective on May 5, 1983 for each cosmetic product that is a vaginal tablet packaged for retail sale on or after that date.

(2) *Initial effective date for labeling requirements.* The requirement in paragraph (b) of this section that the indicator or barrier to entry be distinctive by design and the requirement in paragraph (c) of this section for a labeling statement are effective on May 5, 1983 for each affected cosmetic product packaged for retail sale on or after that date, except that the requirement for a specific label reference to any identifying characteristic is effective on February 6, 1984 for each affected cosmetic product packaged for retail sale on or after that date.

(3) *Retail level effective date.* The tamper-resistant packaging requirement of paragraph (b) of this section is effective February 6, 1984 for each affected cosmetic product held for sale on or after that date that was packaged for retail sale before May 5, 1983. This does

141

not include the requirement in paragraph (b) of this section that the indicator or barrier to entry be distinctive by design. Products packaged for retail sale after May 5, 1983, as required to be in compliance with all aspects of the regulations without regard to the retail level effective date.

[47 FR 50451, Nov. 5, 1982; 48 FR 1707, Jan. 14, 1983; 48 FR 11427, Mar. 18, 1983, as amended at 48 FR 16664, Apr. 19, 1983; 48 FR 37624, Aug. 19, 1983]

EFFECTIVE DATE NOTE: See 48 FR 41579, Sept. 16, 1983, for a document announcing an interim stay of the effective date of certain provisions in paragraph (e)(3) of § 700.25.

§ 700.27 Use of prohibited cattle materials in cosmetic products.

(a) *Definitions.* The definitions and interpretations of terms contained in section 201 of the Federal Food, Drug, and Cosmetic Act (the FD&C Act) apply to such terms when used in this part. The following definitions also apply:

(1) *Prohibited cattle materials* mean specified risk materials, small intestine of all cattle except as provided in paragraph (b)(2) of this section, material from nonambulatory disabled cattle, material from cattle not inspected and passed, or mechanically separated (MS) (Beef). Prohibited cattle materials do not include the following:

(i) Tallow that contains no more than 0.15 percent insoluble impurities, tallow derivatives, gelatin, hides and hide-derived products, and milk and milk products, and

(ii) Cattle materials inspected and passed from a country designated under paragraph (e) of this section.

(2) *Inspected and passed* means that the product has been inspected and passed for human consumption by the appropriate regulatory authority, and at the time it was inspected and passed, it was found to be not adulterated.

(3) *Mechanically separated (MS) (Beef)* means a meat food product that is finely comminuted, resulting from the mechanical separation and removal of most of the bone from attached skeletal muscle of cattle carcasses and parts of carcasses that meets the specifications contained in 9 CFR 319.5, the U.S. Department of Agriculture regula-

tion that prescribes the standard of identity for MS (Species).

(4) *Nonambulatory disabled cattle* means cattle that cannot rise from a recumbent position or that cannot walk, including, but not limited to, those with broken appendages, severed tendons or ligaments, nerve paralysis, fractured vertebral column, or metabolic conditions.

(5) *Specified risk material* means the brain, skull, eyes, trigeminal ganglia, spinal cord, vertebral column (excluding the vertebrae of the tail, the transverse processes of the thoracic and lumbar vertebrae, and the wings of the sacrum), and dorsal root ganglia of cattle 30 months of age and older and the tonsils and distal ileum of the small intestine of all cattle.

(6) *Tallow* means the rendered fat of cattle obtained by pressing or by applying any other extraction process to tissues derived directly from discrete adipose tissue masses or to other carcass parts and tissues. Tallow must be produced from tissues that are not prohibited cattle materials or must contain no more than 0.15 percent insoluble impurities as determined by the method entitled "Insoluble Impurities" (AOCS Official Method Ca 3a–46), American Oil Chemists' Society (AOCS), 5th Edition, 1997, incorporated by reference in accordance with 5 U.S.C. 552(a) and 1 CFR part 51, or another method equivalent in accuracy, precision, and sensitivity to AOCS Official Method Ca 3a–46. You may obtain copies of the method from AOCS (*http://www.aocs.org*) 2211 W. Bradley Ave. Champaign, IL 61821. Copies may be examined at the Food and Drug Administration's Main Library, 10903 New Hampshire Ave., Bldg. 2, Third Floor, Silver Spring, MD 20993, 301–796–2039 or at the National Archives and Records Administration (NARA). For information on the availability of this material at NARA, call 202–741–6030, or go to *http://www.archives.gov/federal_register/ code_of_federal_regulations/ ibr_locations.html.*

(7) *Tallow derivative* means any chemical obtained through initial hydrolysis, saponification, or transesterification of tallow; chemical conversion of material obtained by hydrolysis, saponification, or trans-

esterification may be applied to obtain the desired product.

(8) *Gelatin* means a product that has been obtained by the partial hydrolysis of collagen derived from hides, connective tissue, and/or bone bones of cattle and swine. Gelatin may be either Type A (derived from an acid-treated precursor) or Type B (derived from an alkali-treated precursor) that has gone through processing steps that include filtration and sterilization or an equivalent process in terms of infectivity reduction.

(b) *Requirements.* (1) No cosmetic shall be manufactured from, processed with, or otherwise contain, prohibited cattle materials.

(2) The small intestine is not considered prohibited cattle material if the distal ileum is removed by a procedure that removes at least 80 inches of the uncoiled and trimmed small intestine, as measured from the caeco-colic junction and progressing proximally towards the jejunum, or by a procedure that the establishment can demonstrate is equally effective in ensuring complete removal of the distal ileum.

(c) *Records.* (1) Manufacturers and processors of a cosmetic that is manufactured from, processed with, or otherwise contains, material from cattle must establish and maintain records sufficient to demonstrate that the cosmetic is not manufactured from, processed with, or does not otherwise contain, prohibited cattle materials.

(2) Records must be retained for 2 years after the date they were created.

(3) Records must be retained at the manufacturing or processing establishment or at a reasonably accessible location.

(4) The maintenance of electronic records is acceptable. Electronic records are considered to be reasonably accessible if they are accessible from an onsite location.

(5) Records required by this section and existing records relevant to compliance with this section must be available to FDA for inspection and copying.

(6) When filing entry with U.S. Customs and Border Protection, the importer of record of a cosmetic manufactured from, processed with, or other-

wise containing, cattle material must affirm that the cosmetic was manufactured from, processed with, or otherwise contains, cattle material and must affirm that the cosmetic was manufactured in accordance with this section. If a cosmetic is manufactured from, processed with, or otherwise contains, cattle material, then the importer of record must, if requested, provide within 5 days records sufficient to demonstrate that the cosmetic is not manufactured from, processed with, or does not otherwise contain, prohibited cattle material.

(7) Records established or maintained to satisfy the requirements of this subpart that meet the definition of electronic records in §11.3(b)(6) of this chapter are exempt from the requirements of part 11 of this chapter. Records that satisfy the requirements of this subpart but that are also required under other applicable statutory provisions or regulations remain subject to part 11 of this chapter.

(d) *Adulteration.* Failure of a manufacturer or processor to operate in compliance with the requirements of paragraph (b) or (c) of this section renders a cosmetic adulterated under section 601(c) of the act.

(e) *Process for designating countries.* A country seeking designation must send a written request to the Director, Office of the Center Director, Center for Food Safety and Applied Nutrition, Food and Drug Administration, at the address designated in 21 CFR 5.1100. The request shall include information about a country's bovine spongiform encephalopathy (BSE) case history, risk factors, measures to prevent the introduction and transmission of BSE, and any other information relevant to determining whether specified risk materials, the small intestine of cattle except as provided in paragraph (b)(2) of this section, material from nonambulatory disabled cattle, or MS (Beef) from cattle from the country should be considered prohibited cattle materials. FDA shall respond in writing to any such request and may impose conditions in granting any such request. A country designation granted by FDA under this paragraph will be subject to future review by FDA, and may be revoked if FDA determines that it is no longer appropriate.

[70 FR 53068, Sept. 7, 2005, as amended at 71 FR 59668, Oct. 11, 2006; 73 FR 20794, Apr. 17, 2008; 81 FR 5596, Feb. 3, 2016; 81 FR 14732, Mar. 18, 2016]

§ 700.35 Cosmetics containing sunscreen ingredients.

(a) A product that includes the term "sunscreen" in its labeling or in any other way represents or suggests that it is intended to prevent, cure, treat, or mitigate disease or to affect a structure or function of the body comes within the definition of a drug in section 201(g)(1) of the act. Sunscreen active ingredients affect the structure or function of the body by absorbing, reflecting, or scattering the harmful, burning rays of the sun, thereby altering the normal physiological response to solar radiation. These ingredients also help to prevent diseases such as sunburn and may reduce the chance of premature skin aging, skin cancer, and other harmful effects due to the sun when used in conjunction with limiting sun exposure and wearing protective clothing. When consumers see the term "sunscreen" or similar sun protection terminology in the labeling of a product, they expect the product to protect them in some way from the harmful effects of the sun, irrespective of other labeling statements. Consequently, the use of the term "sunscreen" or similar sun protection terminology in a product's labeling generally causes the product to be subject to regulation as a drug. However, sunscreen ingredients may also be used in some products for nontherapeutic, nonphysiologic uses (e.g., as a color additive or to protect the color of the product). To avoid consumer misunderstanding, if a cosmetic product contains a sunscreen ingredient and uses the term "sunscreen" or similar sun protection terminology anywhere in its labeling, the term must be qualified by describing the cosmetic benefit provided by the sunscreen ingredient.

(b) The qualifying information required under paragraph (a) of this section shall appear prominently and conspicuously at least once in the labeling in conjunction with the term "sunscreen" or other similar sun protection terminology used in the labeling. For example: "Contains a sunscreen—to protect product color."

[64 FR 27693, May 21, 1999]

PART 701—COSMETIC LABELING

Subpart A—General Provisions

Sec.
701.1 Misbranding.
701.2 Form of stating labeling requirements.
701.3 Designation of ingredients.
701.9 Exemptions from labeling requirements.

Subpart B—Package Form

701.10 Principal display panel.
701.11 Identity labeling.
701.12 Name and place of business of manufacturer, packer, or distributor.
701.13 Declaration of net quantity of contents.

Subpart C—Labeling of Specific Ingredients

701.20 Detergent substances, other than soap, intended for use in cleansing the body.
701.30 Ingredient names established for cosmetic ingredient labeling.

AUTHORITY: 21 U.S.C. 321, 352, 361, 362, 363, 371, 374; 15 U.S.C. 1454, 1455.

SOURCE: 39 FR 10056, Mar. 15, 1974, unless otherwise noted.

Subpart A—General Provisions

§ 701.1 Misbranding.

(a) Among representations in labeling of a cosmetic which render such cosmetic misbranded is a false or misleading representation with respect to another cosmetic or a food, drug, or device.

(b) The labeling of a cosmetic which contains two or more ingredients may be misleading by reason (among other reasons) of the designation of such cosmetic in such labeling by a name which includes or suggests the name of one or more but not all such ingredients, even though the names of all such ingredients are stated elsewhere in the labeling.

§ 701.2 Form of stating labeling requirements.

(a) A word, statement, or other information required by or under authority of the Act to appear on the label may lack that prominence and conspicuousness required by section 602(c) of the Act by reason (among other reasons) of:

(1) The failure of such word, statement, or information to appear on the part or panel of the label which is presented or displayed under customary conditions of purchase;

(2) The failure of such word, statement, or information to appear on two or more parts or panels of the label, each of which has sufficient space therefor, and each of which is so designed as to render it likely to be, under customary conditions of purchase, the part or panel displayed;

(3) The failure of the label to extend over the area of the container or package available for such extension, so as to provide sufficient label space for the prominent placing of such word, statement, or information;

(4) Insufficiency of label space (for the prominent placing of such word, statement, or information) resulting from the use of label space for any word, statement, design, or device which is not required by or under authority of the Act to appear on the label;

(5) Insufficiency of label space (for the prominent placing of such word, statement, or information) resulting from the use of label space to give materially greater conspicuousness to any other word, statement, or information, or to any design or device;

(6) Smallness or style of type in which such word, statement, or information appears, insufficient background contrast, obscuring designs or vignettes, or crowding with other written, printed, or graphic matter.

(b)(1) All words, statements, and other information required by or under authority of the Act to appear on the label or labeling shall appear thereon in the English language: *Provided, however,* That in the case of articles distributed solely in the Commonwealth of Puerto Rico or in a Territory where the predominant language is one other than English, the predominant language may be substituted for English.

(2) If the label contains any representation in a foreign language, all words, statements, and other information required by or under authority of the Act to appear on the label shall appear thereon in the foreign language.

(3) If the labeling contains any representation in a foreign language, all words, statements, and other information required by or under authority of the Act to appear on the label or labeling shall appear on the labeling in the foreign language.

§ 701.3 Designation of ingredients.

(a) The label on each package of a cosmetic shall bear a declaration of the name of each ingredient in descending order of predominance, except that fragrance or flavor may be listed as fragrance or flavor. An ingredient which is both fragrance and flavor shall be designated by each of the functions it performs unless such ingredient is identified by name. No ingredient may be designated as fragrance or flavor unless it is within the meaning of such term as commonly understood by consumers. Where one or more ingredients is accepted by the Food and Drug Administration as exempt from public disclosure pursuant to the procedure established in § 720.8(a) of this chapter, in lieu of label declaration of identity the phrase "and other ingredients" may be used at the end of the ingredient declaration.

(b) The declaration of ingredients shall appear with such prominence and conspicuousness as to render it likely to be read and understood by ordinary individuals under normal conditions of purchase. The declaration shall appear on any appropriate information panel in letters not less than $\frac{1}{16}$ of an inch in height and without obscuring design, vignettes, or crowding. In the absence of sufficient space for such declaration on the package, or where the manufacturer or distributor wishes to use a decorative container, the declaration may appear on a firmly affixed tag, tape, or card. In those cases where there is insufficient space for such declaration on the package, and it is not practical to firmly affix a tag, tape, or card, the Commissioner may establish

145

by regulation an acceptable alternate, e.g., a smaller type size. A petition requesting such a regulation as an amendment to this paragraph shall be submitted pursuant to part 10 of this chapter.

(c) A cosmetic ingredient shall be identified in the declaration of ingredients by:

(1) The name specified in § 701.30 as established by the Commissioner for that ingredient for the purpose of cosmetic ingredient labeling pursuant to paragraph (e) of this section;

(2) In the absence of the name specified in § 701.30, the name adopted for that ingredient in the following editions and supplements of the following compendia, listed in order as the source to be utilized:

(i) CTFA (Cosmetic, Toiletry and Fragrance Association, Inc.) Cosmetic Ingredient Dictionary, Second Ed., 1977 (available from the Cosmetic, Toiletry and Fragrance Association, Inc. 1110 Vermont Ave. NW., Suite 800, Washington, DC 20005, or at the National Archives and Records Administration (NARA), which is incorporated by reference, except for the following deletions and revisions. (For information on the availability of this material at NARA, call 202–741–6030, or go to: *http://www.archives.gov/federal_register/code_of_federal_regulations/ibr_locations.html*.)

(a) The following names are not adopted for the purpose of cosmetic ingredient labeling:

Acid Black 58
Acid Black 107
Acid Black 139
Acid Blue 168
Acid Blue 170
Acid Blue 188
Acid Blue 209
Acid Brown 19
Acid Brown 30
Acid Brown 44
Acid Brown 45
Acid Brown 46
Acid Brown 48
Acid Brown 224
Acid Orange 80
Acid Orange 85
Acid Orange 86
Acid Orange 88
Acid Orange 89
Acid Orange 116
Acid Red 131
Acid Red 213

Acid Red 252
Acid Red 259
Acid Violet 73
Acid Violet 76
Acid Violet 99
Acid Yellow 114
Acid Yellow 127
Direct Yellow 81
Solvent Black 5
Solvent Brown 43
Solvent Yellow 63
Solvent Yellow 90

(b) The following names are adopted for the purpose of cosmetic ingredient labeling, provided the respective monographs are revised to describe their otherwise disclosed chemical compositions, or describe their chemical compositions more precisely, and such revised monographs are published in supplements to this dictionary edition by July 18, 1980.

Acid Black 2
Benzophenone-11
Carbomer 934
Carbomer 934P
Carbomer 940
Carbomer 941
Carbomer 960
Carbomer 961
Chlorofluorocarbon 11S
Dimethicone Copolyol
Disperse Red 17
Pigment Green 7
Polyamino Sugar Condensate
SD Alcohol (all 27 alphanumeric designations)
Sodium Chondroitin Sulfate
Synthetic Beeswax

(c) The following names are adopted for the purpose of cosmetic ingredient labeling until January 19, 1981.

Amphoteric (all 20 numeric designations)
Quaternium (all 49 numeric designations)

(ii) United States Pharmacopeia, 19th Ed., 1975, and Second Supplement to the USP XIX and NF XIV, 1976. (Copies are available from the U.S. Pharmacopeial Convention, Inc., 12601 Twinbrook Parkway, Rockville, MD 20852, or at the National Archives and Records Administration (NARA). For information on the availability of this material at NARA, call 202–741–6030, or go to: *http://www.archives.gov/federal_register/code_of_federal_regulations/ibr_locations.html.*).

(iii) National Formulary, 14th Ed., 1975, and Second Supplement to the USP XIX and NF XIV, 1976. (Copies are available from the U.S. Pharmacopeial Convention, Inc., 12601 Twinbrook Parkway, Rockville, MD 20852, or at the National Archives and Records Administration (NARA). For information on the availability of this material at NARA, call 202-741-6030, or go to: *http:// www.archives.gov/federal_register/ code_of_federal_regulations/ ibr_locations.html.*).

(iv) Food Chemicals Codex, 2d Ed., 1972; First Supplement, 1974, and Second Supplement, 1975, which are incorporated by reference. Copies are available from the Center for Food Safety and Applied Nutrition, Food and Drug Administration, 5001 Campus Dr., College Park, MD 20740, or at the National Archives and Records Administration (NARA). For information on the availability of this material at NARA, call 202-741-6030, or go to: *http:// www.archives.gov/federal_register/ code_of_federal_regulations/ ibr_locations.html.*

(v) USAN and the USP dictionary of drug names, USAN 1975, 1961–1975 cumulative list. (Copies are available from the U.S. Pharmacopeial Convention, Inc., 12601 Twinbrook Parkway, Rockville, MD 20852, or at the National Archives and Records Administration (NARA). For information on the availability of this material at NARA, call 202-741-6030, or go to: *http:// www.archives.gov/federal_register/ code_of_federal_regulations/ ibr_locations.html.*)

(3) In the absence of such a listing, the name generally recognized by consumers.

(4) In the absence of any of the above, the chemical or other technical name or description.

(d) Where a cosmetic product is also an over-the-counter drug product, the declaration shall declare the active drug ingredients as set forth in §201.66(c)(2) and (d) of this chapter, and the declaration shall declare the cosmetic ingredients as set forth in §201.66(c)(8) and (d) of this chapter.

(e) Interested persons may submit a petition requesting the establishment of a specific name for a cosmetic ingredient pursuant to part 10 of this chapter. The Commissioner may also propose such a name on his own initiative.

(f) As an alternative to listing all ingredients in descending order of predominance, ingredients may be grouped and the groups listed in the following manner and order:

(1) Ingredients, other than color additives, present at a concentration greater than 1 percent, in descending order of predominance; followed by

(2) Ingredients, other than color additives, present at a concentration of not more than 1 percent, without respect to order of predominance; followed by

(3) Color additives, without respect to order of predominance. Ingredients specified in paragraph (f)(2) of this section may be included with those specified in paragraph (f)(1) of this section and listed in descending order of predominance.

(g) A declaration of ingredients may include an ingredient not in the product if the ingredient is identified by the phrase "may contain" and:

(1) It is a color additive added to some batches of the product for purposes of color matching; or

(2)(i) The same declaration of ingredients is also used for other products similar in composition and intended for the same use, including products which may be assortments of products similar in composition and intended for the same use; and

(ii) Such products are "shaded" products, i.e., those falling within the product categories identified in §720.4 (c)(3), (7) and (8)(v) of this chapter; and

(iii) All products sharing the common declaration of ingredients are sold by the labeler under a common trade name or brand designation, and no trade name or brand designation not common to all such products appears in the labeling of any of them; and

(iv) The ingredient is a color additive.

(h) As an alternative to a declaration of color additive ingredients for each product, the color additives of an assortment of cosmetic products that are sold together in the same package may be declared in a single composite list in a manner that is not misleading and that indicates that the list pertains to all the products.

147

(i) As an alternative to the declaration of ingredients specified in paragraph (b) of this section, the declaration of ingredients may appear in letters not less than ¹⁄₁₆ of an inch in height in labeling accompanying the product, as for example, on padded sheets or in leaflets, if the total surface area of the package is less than 12 square inches. This paragraph is inapplicable to any packaged cosmetic product enclosed in an outer container, e.g., a folding carton. In addition, this paragraph is applicable only to cosmetic products meeting one of the following requirements:

(1) The cosmetic products are held and displayed for sale in tightly compartmented trays or racks of a display unit. The holder of the labeling bearing the declaration of ingredients shall be attached to the display unit; or

(2) The cosmetic products are "shaded" products, i.e., those falling within the product categories identified in § 720.4 (c)(3), (7) and (8)(v) of this chapter, and are held for sale in tightly compartmented trays or racks. The holder of the labeling bearing the declaration of ingredients shall be attached to a display chart bearing samples of the product shades, which is displayed to purchasers. Such a display chart shall be of such construction and design as to permit its continuous use as a display, such as on a counter, and shall be designed for the primary purpose of displaying samples of the shades of the products.

(j) The holder of labeling bearing a declaration of ingredients and used in accordance with paragraph (i) of this section shall be attached to the display unit or chart and shall meet one of the following conditions:

(1) The labeling is on the front of the display unit or chart and can be read in full by a purchaser facing the display unit or chart under customary conditions of retail sale; or

(2) The labeling is on the front of the display unit or chart, is partially visible, and is accompanied by a conspicuous notice on the front of the display unit or chart describing the location of such labeling in letters not less than ³⁄₁₆ of an inch in height, e.g., "Ingredient lists above", that can be read by a purchaser facing the display unit

or chart under customary conditions of retail sale, or by the notice required by provisions in paragraph (k)(3) of this section, if conspicuous at all times; or

(3) The labeling is on a side of the display unit or chart, but not on the top, back, or bottom, and is accompanied by a conspicuous notice on the front of the display unit or chart describing the location of such labeling in letters not less than ³⁄₁₆ of an inch in height, e.g., "Ingredient lists located on right side of display", that can be read by a purchaser facing the display unit or chart under customary conditions of retail sale.

(k) Any use of a display unit or chart bearing labeling under the provisions of paragraph (i) of this section shall meet the following requirements:

(1) All articles of labeling bearing ingredient declarations and used in conjunction with any one display unit or chart shall be identical and shall declare the ingredients of all products sold in conjunction with the display unit or chart for which the ingredient declaration is made pursuant to paragraph (i) of this section.

(2) Any display unit or chart intended for such use shall be shipped together with the labeling intended to be attached to it.

(3) Every display unit or chart and/or labeling system shall be designed so that the words "Federal law requires ingredient lists to be displayed here" in letters not less than ³⁄₁₆ of an inch in height (i) become conspicuous when no ingredient declarations are displayed and when the last list has been taken, or (ii) are conspicuous at all times adjacent to the place where ingredient declarations are to be attached.

(4) Any labeling containing a declaration of ingredients which reflects a formulation change and not shipped accompanying a display unit or chart shall be dated. Whenever any formulation change is made, and the labeling containing the declaration of ingredients is thereby required to be used in conjunction with products of both the old and new formulations, the labeling shall declare the ingredients of both the old and new formulations separately in a way that is not misleading

and in a way that permits the purchaser to identify the ingredient declaration applicable to each package, or which clearly advises the purchaser that the formulation has been changed and that either declaration may be applicable.

(5) Sufficient copies of the declaration of ingredients shall be provided with each shipment of a cosmetic so that a purchaser may obtain a copy of the declaration with each purchase. Display units and replacement labeling for display units shall be accompanied by instructions to the retailer, which when followed will result in compliance with the requirements of this section. Copies of the declaration accompanying refills shall be attached to the specific refill items to which they pertain, or shall be packed with the specific refill items to which they pertain, in a container that does not contain other cosmetic products.

(6) The firm whose name appears on a product pursuant to §701.12 shall promptly mail a copy of the declaration of ingredients to any person requesting it.

(7) The display unit or chart shall be designed and located such that the labeling is easily accessible to a purchaser facing the display unit or chart under customary conditions of retail sale.

(l) The provisions of this section do not require the declaration of incidental ingredients that are present in a cosmetic at insignificant levels and that have no technical or functional effect in the cosmetic. For the purpose of this paragraph, incidental ingredients are:

(1) Substances that have no technical or functional effect in the cosmetic but are present by reason of having been incorporated into the cosmetic as an ingredient of another cosmetic ingredient.

(2) Processing aids, which are as follows:

(i) Substances that are added to a cosmetic during the processing of such cosmetic but are removed from the cosmetic in accordance with good manufacturing practices before it is packaged in its finished form.

(ii) Substances that are added to a cosmetic during processing for their technical or functional effect in the processing, are converted to substances the same as constituents of declared ingredients, and do not significantly increase the concentration of those constituents.

(iii) Substances that are added to a cosmetic during the processing of such cosmetic for their technical and functional effect in the processing but are present in the finished cosmetic at insignificant levels and do not have any technical or functional effect in that cosmetic.

(m) In the event that there is a current or anticipated shortage of a cosmetic ingredient, the declaration required by this section may specify alternatives to any ingredients that may be affected. An alternative ingredient shall be declared either (1) immediately following the normally used ingredient for which it substitutes, in which case it shall be identified as an alternative ingredient by the word "or" following the name of the normally used ingredient and any other alternative ingredient, or (2) following the declaration of all normally used ingredients, in which case the alternative ingredients in the group so listed shall be listed in expected descending order of predominance or in accordance with the provisions of paragraph (f) of this section and shall be identified as alternative ingredients by the phrase "may also contain". This paragraph is inapplicable to any ingredient mentioned in advertising, or in labeling other than in the declaration of ingredients required by this section.

(n) In the event that the shortage of a cosmetic ingredient necessitates a formulation change, packages bearing labels declaring the ingredients of the old formulation may be used if the revised ingredient declaration appears (1) on a firmly affixed tag, tape, card, or sticker or similar overlabeling attached to the package and bearing the conspicuous words "new ingredient list" in letters not less than 1/16 of an inch in height, or (2) on labeling inside an unsealed package and the package bears the conspicuous words, on a sticker or similar overlabeling, "new ingredient list inside" in letters not less than 1/16 of an inch in height.

(o) The ingredients of products that are similar in composition and intended for the same use may be declared as follows:

(1) The declaration of ingredients for an assortment of such products that are sold together in the same package, e.g., eyeshadows of different colors, may declare the ingredients that are common to all the products, in a single list in their cumulative order of predominance or in accordance with the provisions of paragraph (f) of this section, together with a statement, in terms that are as informative as practicable and that are not misleading, declaring the other ingredients and identifying the products in which they are present. The color additive ingredients of all the products in such an assortment, whether or not common to all the products, may be declared in a single composite list following the declaration of the other ingredients without identifying the products in which they are present.

(2) The ingredients of an assortment of such products that are sold together in the same package, e.g., eyeshadows of different colors, may be declared in a single list in their cumulative order of predominance or in accordance with the provisions of paragraph (f) of this section, if the package is designed such that it has a total surface area available to bear labeling of less than 12 square inches. For the purpose of this paragraph, surface area is not available for labeling if physical characteristics of the package surface, e.g., decorative relief, make application of a label impractical.

(3) The declaration of ingredients for such a product that is individually packaged and bears a label that is shared with other products pursuant to the provisions of paragraph (g)(2) of this section, e.g., one lipstick in a line of lipsticks, may declare the ingredients that are common to all such products, in a single list in their cumulative order of predominance or in accordance with the provisions of paragraph (f) of this section, together with a statement, in terms that are as informative as practicable and that are not misleading, declaring the other ingredients in such products, and identifying the products in which they are present. The color additive ingredients shall be declared in accordance with the provisions of paragraph (g) of this section.

(4) The declaration of ingredients for an assortment of such cosmetic products that bears a label that is shared with other products pursuant to the provisions of paragraph (g)(2) of this section, e.g., one of several compacts in a line of compacts, may declare the ingredients that are common to all such products, in a single list in their cumulative order of predominance or in accordance with the provisions of paragraph (f) of this section, together with a statement, in terms that are as informative as practicable and that are not misleading, declaring the other ingredients in such products and identifying the products in which they are present. The color additive ingredients shall be declared in accordance with the provisions of paragraph (g) of this section.

(p) As an alternative to the declaration of ingredients in letters not less than 1/16 of an inch in height, letters may be not less than 1/32 of an inch in height if the package is designed such that it has a total surface area available to bear labeling of less than 12 square inches. For the purpose of this paragraph, surface area is not available for labeling if physical characteristics of the package surface, e.g., decorative relief, make application of a label impractical.

(q) The inside containers in a multiunit or multicomponent retail cosmetic package are not required to bear a declaration of ingredients when the labeling of the multiunit or multicomponent retail cosmetic package meets all the requirements of this section and the inside containers are not intended to be, and are not customarily, separated from the retail package for retail sale.

(r) In the case of cosmetics distributed to the consumers by direct mail, as an alternative to the declaration of ingredients on an information panel, the declaration of ingredients may appear in letters not less than 1/16 of an inch in height in labeling that accompanies and specifically relates to the cosmetic(s) mailed, or in labeling furnished to each consumer for his personal use and from which he orders cosmetics through the mail, e.g., a direct mail sales catalog or brochure, provided all of the following additional requirements are met:

(1) The declarations of ingredients are conspicuous and presented in a way that permits the consumer to identify the declaration of ingredients applicable to each cosmetic.

(2) The package mailed to the consumer is accompanied by a notice located on, or affixed to, the top of the package or on top of the contents inside the package, or on the face of the package platform surrounding and holding the product(s), readily visible to the consumer on opening of the package, and provides the following information in letters not less than ³⁄₁₆ of an inch in height:

(i) The location of the declarations of ingredients, e.g., in an accompanying brochure, or in a sales catalog used for ordering;

(ii) A statement that a copy of the declaration of ingredients will be mailed promptly to any person requesting it; and

(iii) The name and place of business of the mail order distributor,

(3) The mail order distributor promptly mails a copy of the declaration of ingredients to any person requesting it.

[39 FR 10056, Mar. 15, 1974, as amended at 40 FR 8922, Mar. 3, 1975; 40 FR 18426, Apr. 28, 1975; 42 FR 4718, Jan. 25, 1977; 42 FR 15676, Mar. 22, 1977; 42 FR 24255, May 31, 1977; 42 FR 46516, Sept. 16, 1977; 42 FR 61257, Dec. 2, 1977; 45 FR 3577, Jan. 18, 1980; 47 FR 9397, Mar. 5, 1982; 54 FR 24900, June 12, 1989; 64 FR 13297, Mar. 17, 1999; 69 FR 18803, Apr. 9, 2004; 81 FR 49897, July 29, 2016]

§701.9 Exemptions from labeling requirements.

(a) Except as provided by paragraphs (b) and (c) of this section, a shipment or other delivery of a cosmetic which is, in accordance with the practice of the trade, to be processed, labeled, or repacked in substantial quantity at an establishment other than that where originally processed or packed, shall be exempt, during the time of introduction into and movement in interstate commerce and the time of holding in such establishment, from compliance with the labeling requirements of sections 601(a) and 602(b) of the act if:

(1) The person who introduced such shipment or delivery into interstate commerce is the operator of the establishment where such cosmetic is to be processed, labeled, or repacked; or

(2) In case such person is not such operator, such shipment or delivery is made to such establishment under a written agreement, signed by and containing the post office addresses of such person and such operator, and containing such specifications for the processing, labeling, or repacking, as the case may be, of such cosmetic in such establishment as will insure, if such specifications are followed, that such cosmetic will not be adulterated or misbranded within the meaning of the act upon completion of such processing, labeling, or repacking. Such person and such operator shall each keep a copy of such agreement until 2 years after the final shipment or delivery of such cosmetic from such establishment, and shall make such copies available for inspection at any reasonable hour to any officer or employee of the Department who requests them.

(b) An exemption of a shipment or other delivery of a cosmetic under paragraph (a)(1) of this section shall, at the beginning of the act of removing such shipment or delivery, or any part thereof, from such establishment, become void ab initio if the cosmetic comprising such shipment, delivery, or part is adulterated or misbranded within the meaning of the act when so removed.

(c) An exemption of a shipment or other delivery of a cosmetic under paragraph (a)(2) of this section shall become void ab initio with respect to the person who introduced such shipment or delivery into interstate commerce upon refusal by such person to make available for inspection a copy of the agreement, as required by such clause.

(d) An exemption of a shipment or other delivery of a cosmetic under paragraph (a)(2) of this section shall expire:

(1) At the beginning of the act of removing such shipment or delivery, or

any part thereof, from such establishment if the cosmetic comprising such shipment, delivery, or part is adulterated or misbranded within the meaning of the act when so removed; or

(2) Upon refusal, by the operator of the establishment where such cosmetic is to be processed, labeled, or repacked, to make available for inspection a copy of the agreement, as required by such clause.

Subpart B—Package Form

§ 701.10 Principal display panel.

The term *principal display panel* as it applies to cosmetics in package form and as used in this part, means the part of a label that is most likely to be displayed, presented, shown, or examined under customary conditions of display for retail sale. The principal display panel shall be large enough to accommodate all the mandatory label information required to be placed thereon by this part with clarity and conspicuousness and without obscuring designs, vignettes, or crowding. Where packages bear alternate principal display panels, information required to be placed on the principal display panel shall be duplicated on each principal display panel. For the purpose of obtaining uniform type size in declaring the quantity of contents of all packages of substantially the same size, the term "area of the principal display panel" means the area of the side or surface that bears the principal display panel, which area shall be:

(a) In the case of a rectangular package where one entire side properly can be considered to be the principal display panel side, the product of the height times the width of that side;

(b) In the case of a cylindrical or nearly cylindrical container, 40 percent of the product of the height of the container times the circumference; and

(c) In the case of any other shape of container, 40 percent of the total surface of the container: *Provided, however,* That where such container presents an obvious "principal display panel" such as the top of a triangular or circular package, the area shall consist of the entire top surface.

In determining the area of the principal display panel, exclude tops, bottoms, flanges at the tops and bottoms of cans, and shoulders and necks of bottles or jars. In the case of cylindrical or nearly cylindrical containers, information required by this part to appear on the principal display panel shall appear within that 40 percent of the circumference which is most likely to be displayed, presented, shown, or examined under customary conditions of display for retail sale.

§ 701.11 Identity labeling.

(a) The principal display panel of a cosmetic in package form shall bear as one of its principal features a statement of the identity of the commodity.

(b) Such statement of identity shall be in terms of:

(1) The common or usual name of the cosmetic; or

(2) An appropriately descriptive name or, when the nature of the cosmetic is obvious, a fanciful name understood by the public to identify such cosmetic; or

(3) An appropriate illustration or vignette representing the intended cosmetic use.

(c) The statement of identity shall be presented in bold type on the principal display panel, shall be in a size reasonably related to the most prominent printed matter on such panel, and shall be in lines generally parallel to the base on which the package rests as it is designed to be displayed.

§ 701.12 Name and place of business of manufacturer, packer, or distributor.

(a) The label of a cosmetic in package form shall specify conspicuously the name and place of business of the manufacturer, packer, or distributor.

(b) The requirement for declaration of the name of the manufacturer, packer, or distributor shall be deemed to be satisfied in the case of a corporation only by the actual corporate name, which may be preceded or followed by the name of the particular division of the corporation. Abbreviations for "Company," "Incorporated," etc., may be used and "The" may be omitted. In the case of an individual, partnership, or association, the name under which the business is conducted shall be used.

(c) Where the cosmetic is not manufactured by the person whose name appears on the label, the name shall be qualified by a phrase that reveals the connection such person has with such cosmetic; such as, "Manufactured for _____", "Distributed by _____", or any other wording that expresses the facts.

(d) The statement of the place of business shall include the street address, city, State, and ZIP Code; however, the street address may be omitted if it is shown in a current city directory or telephone directory. The requirement for inclusion of the ZIP Code shall apply only to consumer commodity labels developed or revised after the effective date of this section. In the case of nonconsumer packages, the ZIP Code shall appear either on the label or the labeling (including the invoice).

(e) If a person manufactures, packs, or distributes a cosmetic at a place other than his principal place of business, the label may state the principal place of business in lieu of the actual place where such cosmetic was manufactured or packed or is to be distributed, unless such statement would be misleading.

§701.13 Declaration of net quantity of contents.

(a) The label of a cosmetic in package form shall bear a declaration of the net quantity of contents. This shall be expressed in terms of weight, measure, numerical count, or a combination of numerical count and weight or measure. The statement shall be in terms of fluid measure if the cosmetic is liquid or in terms of weight if the cosmetic is solid, semisolid, or viscous, or a mixture of solid and liquid. If there is a firmly established, general consumer usage and trade custom of declaring the net quantity of a cosmetic by numerical count, linear measure, or measure of area, such respective term may be used. If there is a firmly established, general consumer usage and trade custom of declaring the contents of a liquid cosmetic by weight, or a solid, semisolid, or viscous cosmetic by fluid measure, it may be used. Whenever the Commissioner determines for a specific packaged cosmetic that an

existing practice of declaring net quantity of contents by weight, measure, numerical count, or a combination of these does not facilitate value comparisons by consumers, he shall by regulation designate the appropriate term or terms to be used for such cosmetic.

(b) Statements of weight shall be in terms of avoirdupois pound and ounce. Statements of fluid measure shall be in terms of the U.S. gallon of 231 cubic inches and quart, pint, and fluid-ounce subdivisions thereof and shall express the volume at 68 °F. (20 °C.).

(c) When the declaration of quantity of contents by numerical count, linear measure, or measure of area does not give accurate information as to the quantity of cosmetic in the package, it shall be augmented by such statement of weight, measure, or size of the individual units or the total weight or measure of the cosmetic as will give such information.

(d) The declaration may contain common or decimal fractions. A common fraction shall be in terms of halves, quarters, eighths, sixteenths, or thirty-seconds; except that if there exists a firmly established, general consumer usage and trade custom of employing different common fractions in the net quantity declaration of a particular commodity they may be employed. A common fraction shall be reduced to its lowest terms; a decimal fraction shall not be carried out to more than two places. A statement that includes small fractions of an ounce shall be deemed to permit smaller variations than one which does not include such fractions.

(e) The declaration shall be located on the principal display panel of the label; with respect to packages bearing alternate principal display panels, it shall be duplicated on each principal display panel: *Provided*, That:

(1) The principal display panel of a cosmetic marketed in a "boudoir-type" container including decorative cosmetic containers of the "cartridge," "pill box," "compact," or "pencil" variety, and those with a capacity of one-fourth ounce or less, may be considered to be a tear-away tag or tape affixed to the decorative container and bearing the mandatory label information as required by this part, but the type size of

the net quantity of contents statement shall be governed by the dimensions of the decorative container; and

(2) The principal display panel of a cosmetic marketed on a display card to which the immediate container is affixed may be considered to be the display panel of the card, and the type size of the net quantity of content statement is governed by the dimensions of the display card.

(f) The declaration shall appear as a distinct item on the principal display panel, shall be separated (by at least a space equal to the height of the lettering used in the declaration) from other printed label information appearing above or below the declaration and (by at least a space equal to twice the width of the letter "N" of the style of type used in the quantity of contents statement) from other printed label information appearing to the left or right of the declaration. It shall not include any term qualifying a unit of weight, measure, or count (such as "giant pint" and "full quart") that tends to exaggerate the amount of the cosmetic in the container. It shall be placed on the principal display panel within the bottom 30 percent of the area of the label panel in line generally parallel to the base on which the package rests as it is designed to be displayed: *Provided,* That:

(1) On packages having a principal display panel of 5 square inches or less, the requirement for placement within the bottom 30 percent of the area of the label panel shall not apply when the declaration of net quantity of contents meets the other requirements of this part; and

(2) In the case of a cosmetic that is marketed with both outer and inner retail containers bearing the mandatory label information required by this part, and the inner container is not intended to be sold separately, the net quantity of contents placement requirement of this section applicable to such inner containers is waived.

(g) The declaration shall accurately reveal the quantity of cosmetic in the package exclusive of wrappers and other material packed therewith: *Provided,* That:

(1) In the case of cosmetics packed in containers designed to deliver the cos-

metic under pressure, the declaration shall state the net quantity of the contents that will be expelled when the instructions for use as shown on the container are followed. The propellant is included in the net quantity declaration; and

(2) In the case of a package which contains the integral components making up a complete kit, and which is designed to deliver the components in the manner of an application (for example, a home permanent wave kit), the declaration may state the net quantity of the contents in nondeceptive terms of the number of applications available in the kit when the instructions for use as shown on the container are followed.

(h) The declaration shall appear in conspicuous and easily legible boldface print or type in distinct contrast (by typography, layout, color, embossing, or molding) to other matter on the package; except that a declaration of net quantity blown, embossed, or molded on a glass or plastic surface is permissible when all label information is so formed on the surface. Requirements of conspicuousness and legibility shall include the specifications that:

(1) The ratio of height to width (of the letter) shall not exceed a differential of 3 units to 1 unit (no more than 3 times as high as it is wide).

(2) Letter heights pertain to upper case or capital letters. When upper and lower case or all lower case letters are used, it is the lower case letter "o" or its equivalent that shall meet the minimum standards.

(3) When fractions are used, each component numeral shall meet one-half the minimum height standards.

(i) The declaration shall be in letters and numerals in a type size established in relationship to the area of the principal display panel of the package and shall be uniform for all packages of substantially the same size by complying with the following type specifications:

(1) Not less than one-sixteenth inch in height on packages the principal display panel of which has an area of 5 square inches or less.

(2) Not less than one-eighth inch in height on packages the principal display panel of which has an area of more

than 5 but not more than 25 square inches.

(3) Not less than three-sixteenths inch in height on packages the principal display panel of which has an area of more than 25 but not more than 100 square inches.

(4) Not less than one-fourth inch in height on packages the principal display panel of which has an area of more than 100 square inches, except not less than one-half inch in height if the area is more than 400 square inches.

Where the declaration is blown, embossed, or molded on a glass or plastic surface rather than by printing, typing, or coloring, the lettering sizes specified in paragraphs (i)(1) through (4) of this section shall be increased by one-sixteenth of an inch.

(j) On packages containing less than 4 pounds or 1 gallon and labeled in terms of weight or fluid measure:

(1) The declaration shall be expressed both in ounces, with identification by weight or by liquid measure and, if applicable (1 pound or 1 pint or more), followed in parentheses by a declaration in pounds for weight units, with any remainder in terms of ounces or common or decimal fractions of the pound (as set forth in paragraphs (m)(1) and (2) of this section), or in the case of liquid measure, in the largest whole units (quarts, quarts and pints, or pints, as appropriate) with any remainder in terms of fluid ounces or common or decimal fractions of the pint or quart (as set forth in paragraphs (m)(3) and (4) of this section). Net weight or fluid measure of less than 1 ounce shall be expressed in common or decimal fractions of the respective ounce and not in drams.

(2) The declaration may appear in more than one line. The term "net weight" shall be used when stating the net quantity of contents in terms of weight. Use of the terms "net" or "net contents" in terms of fluid measure or numerical count is optional. It is sufficient to distinguish avoirdupois ounce from fluid ounce through association of terms; for example, "Net wt. 6 oz." or "6 oz. net wt." and "Net contents 6 fl. oz." or "6 fl. oz."

(k) On packages containing 4 pounds or 1 gallon or more and labeled in terms of weight or fluid measure, the declaration shall be expressed in pounds for weight units with any remainder in terms of ounces or common or decimal fractions of the pound; in the case of fluid measure, it shall be expressed in the largest whole unit (gallons, followed by common or decimal fractions of a gallon or by the next smaller whole unit or units (quarts or quarts and pints)) with any remainder in terms of fluid ounces or common or decimal fractions of the pint or quart (as set forth in paragraph (m)(5) of this section).

(l) [Reserved]

(m) Examples: (1) A declaration of 1½ pounds weight shall be expressed as "Net wt. 24 oz. (1 lb. 8 oz.)", "Net wt. 24 oz. (1½ lb.)", or "Net wt. 24 oz. (1.5 lb.)".

(2) A declaration of three-fourths pound avoirdupois weight shall be expressed as "Net wt. 12 oz."

(3) A declaration of 1 quart liquid measure shall be expressed as "Net contents 32 fl. oz. (1 qt.)".

(4) A declaration of 1¾ quarts liquid measure shall be expressed as "Net contents 56 fl. oz. (1 qt. 1½ pt.)" or "Net contents 56 fl. oz. (1 qt. 1 pt. 8 oz.)" but not in terms of quart and ounce such as "Net content 56 fl. oz. (1 qt. 24 oz.)".

(5) A declaration of 2½ gallons liquid measure shall be expressed in the alternative as "Net contents 2 gal. 2 qt." and not as "2 gal. 4 pt."

(n) For quantities, the following abbreviations and none other may be employed (periods and plural forms are optional):

weight wt.	inch in.
square sq.	gallon gal.
fluid fl.	quart qt.
yard yd.	pint pt.
feet or foot ft.	ounce oz.
	pound lb.

(o) On packages labeled in terms of linear measure, the declaration shall be expressed both in terms of inches and, if applicable (1 foot or more), the largest whole units (yards, yards and feet, feet). The declaration in terms of the largest whole units shall be in parentheses following the declaration in terms of inches and any remainder shall be in terms of inches or common or decimal fractions of the foot or yard. Examples are "86 inches (2 yd. 1

ft. 2 inches)'', ''90 inches (2½ yd.)'', ''30 inches (2.5 ft.)'', etc.

(p) On packages labeled in terms of area measure, the declaration shall be expressed in terms of square inches and, if applicable (1 square foot or more), the largest whole square unit (square yards, square yards and square feet, square feet). The declaration in terms of the largest whole units shall be in parentheses following the declaration in terms of square inches and any remainder shall be in terms of square inches or common or decimal fractions of the square foot or square yard; for example, ''158 sq. inches (1 sq. ft. 14 sq. inches)'', etc.

(q) Nothing in this section shall prohibit supplemental statements at locations other than the principal display panel(s) describing in nondeceptive terms the net quantity of contents, provided that such supplemental statements of net quantity of contents shall not include any term qualifying a unit of weight, measure, or count that tends to exaggerate the amount of the cosmetic contained in the package; for example, ''giant pint'' and ''full quart.'' Dual or combination declarations of net quantity of contents as provided for in paragraphs (a), (c), and (j) of this section (for example, a combination of net weight plus numerical count) are not regarded as supplemental net quantity statements and shall be located on the principal display panel.

(r) A separate statement of the net quantity of contents in terms of the metric system is not regarded as a supplemental statement and an accurate statement of the net quantity of contents in terms of the metric system of weight or measure may also appear on the principal display panel or on other panels.

(s) The declaration of net quantity of contents shall express an accurate statement of the quantity of contents of the package. Reasonable variations caused by loss or gain of moisture during the course of good distribution practice or by unavoidable deviations in good manufacturing practice will be recognized. Variations from stated quantity of contents shall not be unreasonably large.

Subpart C—Labeling of Specific Ingredients

§ 701.20 Detergent substances, other than soap, intended for use in cleansing the body.

(a) In its definition of the term *cosmetic*, the Federal Food, Drug, and Cosmetic Act specifically excludes soap. The term *soap* is nowhere defined in the act. In administering the act, the Food and Drug Administration interprets the term ''soap'' to apply only to articles that meet the following conditions:

(1) The bulk of the nonvolatile matter in the product consists of an alkali salt of fatty acids and the detergent properties of the article are due to the alkali-fatty acid compounds; and

(2) The product is labeled, sold, and represented only as soap.

(b) Products intended for cleansing the human body and which are not ''soap'' as set out in paragraph (a) of this section are ''cosmetics,'' and accordingly they are subject to the requirements of the act and the regulations thereunder. For example, such a product in bar form is subject to the requirement, among others, that it shall bear a label containing an accurate statement of the weight of the bar in avoirdupois pounds and ounces, this statement to be prominently and conspicuously displayed so as to be likely to be read under the customary conditions of purchase and use.

§ 701.30 Ingredient names established for cosmetic ingredient labeling.

The Commissioner establishes the following names for the purpose of cosmetic ingredient labeling pursuant to paragraph (e) of § 701.3:

Chemical name or description	Chemical formula	Established label name
Trichlorofluoromethane	CCl_3F	Chlorofluorocarbon 11.
Trichlorofluoromethane and 0.3 pct nitromethane	$CCl_3F + CH_3NO_2$	Chlorofluorocarbon 11 S.
Dichlorodifluoromethane	CCl_2F_2	Chlorofluorocarbon 12.
Chlorodifluoromethane	$CHClF_2$	Hydrochlorofluorocarbon 22.
1, 2-dichloro-1, 1, 2, 2-tetrafluoroethane	$CClF_2CClF_2$	Chlorofluorocarbon 114.
1-Chloro-1, 1-difluoroethane	CH_3CClF_2	Hydrochlorofluorocarbon 142 B.

Chemical name or description	Chemical formula	Established label name
1, 1-difluoroethane	CH_3CHF_2	Hydrofluorocarbon 152 A.
Ethyl ester of hydrolyzed animal protein is the ester of ethyl alcohol and the hydrolysate of collagen or other animal protein, derived by acid, enzyme, or other form of hydrolysis.	....	Ethyl ester of hydrolyzed animal protein.

[42 FR 24255, May 13, 1977, as amended at 45 FR 3577, Jan. 18, 1980]

PART 710—VOLUNTARY REGISTRATION OF COSMETIC PRODUCT ESTABLISHMENTS

Sec.
710.1 Who should register.
710.2 Time for registration.
710.3 How and where to register.
710.4 Information requested.
710.5 Amendments to registration.
710.6 Notification, of registrant; cosmetic product establishment registration number.
710.7 Inspection of registrations.
710.8 Misbranding by reference to registration or to registration number.
710.9 Exemptions.

AUTHORITY: 21 U.S.C. 321, 331, 361, 362, 371, 374.

SOURCE: 39 FR 10059, Mar. 15, 1974, unless otherwise noted.

§710.1 Who should register.

The owner or operator of a cosmetic product establishment which is not exempt under §710.9 and engages in the manufacture or packaging of a cosmetic product is requested to register for each such establishment, whether or not the product enters interstate commerce. This request extends to any foreign cosmetic product establishment whose products are exported for sale in any State as defined in section 201(a)(1) of the act. No registration fee is required.

§710.2 Time for registration.

The owner or operator of an establishment entering into the manufacture or packaging of a cosmetic product should register his establishment within 30 days after the operation begins.

§710.3 How and where to register.

Form FD–2511 ("Registration of Cosmetic Product Establishment") is obtainable on request from the Food and Drug Administration, 5001 Campus Dr., College Park, MD 20740, or at any Food and Drug Administration district office. The completed form should be mailed to Cosmetic Product Establishment Registration, Food and Drug Administration, 5001 Campus Dr., College Park, MD 20740.

[39 FR 10059, Mar. 15, 1974, as amended at 68 FR 15355, Mar. 31, 2003; 81 FR 49897, July 29, 2016]

§710.4 Information requested.

Form FD–2511 requests information on the name and address of the cosmetic product establishment, including post office ZIP code; all business trading names used by the establishment; and the type of business (manufacturer and/or packer). The information requested should be given separately for each establishment as defined in §700.3(j) of this chapter.

[39 FR 10059, Mar. 15, 1974, as amended at 46 FR 38073, July 24, 1981; 54 FR 39640, Sept. 27, 1989]

§710.5 Amendments to registration.

Within 30 days after a change in any of the information contained on a submitted Form FD–2511, a new Form FD–2511 should be submitted to amend the registration. This amendment is also necessary when a registration is to be canceled because an establishment has changed its name and no longer conducts business under the original name.

§710.6 Notification of registrant; cosmetic product establishment registration number.

The Commissioner of Food and Drugs will provide the registrant with a validated copy of Form FD–2511 as evidence of registration. This validated copy will be sent only to the location shown for the registering establishment. A permanent registration number will be assigned to each cosmetic

157

product establishment registered in accordance with the regulations in this part.

§ 710.7　Inspection of registrations.

A copy of the Form FD–2511 filed by the registrant will be available for inspection at the Food and Drug Administration, 5001 Campus Dr., College Park, MD 20740.

[39 FR 10059, Mar. 15, 1974, as amended at 68 FR 15355, Mar. 31, 2003; 81 FR 49897, July 29, 2016]

§ 710.8　Misbranding by reference to registration or to registration number.

Registration of a cosmetic product establishment or assignment of a registration number does not in any way denote approval of the firm or its products by the Food and Drug Administration. Any representation in labeling or advertising that creates an impression of official approval because of registration or possession of a registration number will be considered misleading.

§ 710.9　Exemptions.

The following classes of persons are not requested to register in accordance with this part 710 because the Commissioner has found that such registration is not justified:

(a) Beauty shops, cosmetologists, retailers, pharmacies, and other persons and organizations that compound cosmetic products at a single location and administer, dispense, or distribute them at retail from that location and who do not otherwise manufacture or package cosmetic products at that location.

(b) Physicians, hospitals, clinics, and public health agencies.

(c) Persons who manufacture, prepare, compound, or process cosmetic products solely for use in research, pilot plant production, teaching, or chemical analysis, and who do not sell these products.

PART 720—VOLUNTARY FILING OF COSMETIC PRODUCT INGREDIENT COMPOSITION STATEMENTS

Sec.
720.1　Who should file.
720.2　Times for filing.
720.3　How and where to file.
720.4　Information requested about cosmetic products.
720.5　[Reserved]
720.6　Amendments to statement.
720.7　Notification of person submitting cosmetic product ingredient statement.
720.8　Confidentiality of statements.
720.9　Misbranding by reference to filing or to statement number.

AUTHORITY: 21 U.S.C. 321, 331, 361, 362, 371, 374.

SOURCE: 39 FR 10060, Mar. 15, 1974, unless otherwise noted.

§ 720.1　Who should file.

Either the manufacturer, packer, or distributor of a cosmetic product is requested to file Form FDA 2512 ("Cosmetic Product Ingredient Statement"), whether or not the cosmetic product enters interstate commerce. This request extends to any foreign manufacturer, packer, or distributor of a cosmetic product exported for sale in any State as defined in section 201(a)(1) of the Federal Food, Drug, and Cosmetic Act. No filing fee is required.

[57 FR 3129, Jan. 28, 1992]

§ 720.2　Times for filing.

Within 180 days after forms are made available to the industry, Form FDA 2512 should be filed for each cosmetic product being commercially distributed as of the effective date of this part. Form FDA 2512 should be filed within 60 days after the beginning of commercial distribution of any product not covered within the 180-day period.

[57 FR 3129, Jan. 28, 1992]

§ 720.3　How and where to file.

Forms FDA 2512 and FDA 2514 ("Discontinuance of Commercial Distribution of Cosmetic Product Formulation") are obtainable on request from the Food and Drug Administration, 5001 Campus Dr., College Park, MD

20740, or at any Food and Drug Administration district office. The completed form should be mailed or delivered to: Cosmetic Product Statement, Food and Drug Administration, 5001 Campus Dr., College Park, MD 20740, according to the instructions provided with the forms.

[57 FR 3129, Jan. 28, 1992, as amended at 68 FR 15355, Mar. 31, 2003; 81 FR 49897, July 29, 2016]

§720.4 Information requested about cosmetic products.

(a) Form FDA–2512 requests information on:

(1) The name and address, including post office ZIP code of the person (manufacturer, packer, or distributor) designated on the label of the product.

(2) The name and address, including post office ZIP code, of the manufacturer or packer of the product if different from the person designated on the label of the product, when the manufacturer or packer submits the information requested under this paragraph.

(3) The brand name or names of the cosmetic product.

(4) The cosmetic product category or categories.

(5) The ingredients in the product.

(b) The person filing Form FDA–2512 should:

(1) Provide the information requested in paragraph (a) of this section.

(2) Have the form signed by an authorized individual.

(3) Provide poison control centers with ingredient information and/or adequate diagnostic and therapeutic procedures to permit rapid evaluation and treatment of accidental ingestion or other accidental use of the cosmetic product.

(4) Provide ingredient information (and, when requested, ingredient samples) to a licensed physician who, in connection with the treatment of a patient, requests assistance in determining whether an ingredient in the cosmetic product is the cause of the problem for which the patient is being treated.

(c) One or more of the following cosmetic product categories should be cited to indicate the product's intended use.

(1) *Baby products.* (i) Baby shampoos.

(ii) Lotions, oils, powders, and creams.

(iii) Other baby products.

(2) *Bath preparations.* (i) Bath oils, tablets, and salts.

(ii) Bubble baths.

(iii) Bath capsules.

(iv) Other bath preparations.

(3) *Eye makeup preparations.* (i) Eyebrow pencil.

(ii) Eyeliner.

(iii) Eye shadow.

(iv) Eye lotion.

(v) Eye makeup remover.

(vi) Mascara.

(vii) Other eye makeup preparations.

(4) *Fragrance preparations.* (i) Colognes and toilet waters.

(ii) Perfumes.

(iii) Powders (dusting and talcum) (excluding aftershave talc).

(iv) Sachets.

(v) Other fragrance preparations.

(5) *Hair preparations (noncoloring).* (i) Hair conditioners.

(ii) Hair sprays (aerosol fixatives).

(iii) Hair straighteners.

(iv) Permanent waves.

(v) Rinses (noncoloring).

(vi) Shampoos (noncoloring).

(vii) Tonics, dressings, and other hair grooming aids.

(viii) Wave sets.

(ix) Other hair preparations.

(6) *Hair coloring preparations.* (i) Hair dyes and colors (all types requiring caution statement and patch test).

(ii) Hair tints.

(iii) Hair rinses (coloring).

(iv) Hair shampoos (coloring).

(v) Hair color sprays (aerosol).

(vi) Hair lighteners with color.

(vii) Hair bleaches.

(viii) Other hair coloring preparations.

(7) *Makeup preparations (not eye).* (i) Blushers (all types).

(ii) Face powders.

(iii) Foundations.

(iv) Leg and body paints.

(v) Lipstick.

(vi) Makeup bases.

(vii) Rouges.

(viii) Makeup fixatives.

(ix) Other makeup preparations.

(8) *Manicuring preparations.* (i) Basecoats and undercoats.

(ii) Cuticle softeners.

(iii) Nail creams and lotions.

(iv) Nail extenders.

(v) Nail polish and enamel.

(vi) Nail polish and enamel removers.

(vii) Other manicuring preparations.

(9) *Oral hygiene products.* (i) Dentifrices (aerosol, liquid, pastes, and powders).

(ii) Mouthwashes and breath fresheners (liquids and sprays).

(iii) Other oral hygiene products.

(10) *Personal cleanliness.* (i) Bath soaps and detergents.

(ii) Deodorants (underarm).

(iii) Douches.

(iv) Feminine hygiene deodorants.

(v) Other personal cleanliness products.

(11) *Shaving preparations.* (i) Aftershave lotions.

(ii) Beard softeners.

(iii) Men's talcum.

(iv) Preshave lotions (all types).

(v) Shaving cream (aerosol, brushless, and lather).

(vi) Shaving soap (cakes, sticks, etc.).

(vii) Other shaving preparation products.

(12) *Skin care preparations, (creams, lotions, powder, and sprays).* (i) Cleansing (cold creams, cleansing lotions, liquids, and pads).

(ii) Depilatories.

(iii) Face and neck (excluding shaving preparations).

(iv) Body and hand (excluding shaving preparations).

(v) Foot powders and sprays.

(vi) Moisturizing.

(vii) Night.

(viii) Paste masks (mud packs).

(ix) Skin fresheners.

(x) Other skin care preparations.

(13) *Suntan preparations.* (i) Suntan gels, creams, and liquids.

(ii) Indoor tanning preparations.

(iii) Other suntan preparations.

(d) Ingredients in the product should be listed as follows:

(1) A list of each ingredient of the cosmetic product in descending order of predominance by weight (except that the fragrance and/or flavor may be designated as such without naming each individual ingredient when the manufacturer or supplier of the fragrance and/or flavor refuses to disclose ingredient data).

(2) An ingredient should be listed by the name adopted by the Food and Drug Administration (FDA) for the ingredient pursuant to § 701.3(c) of this chapter.

(3) In the absence of a name adopted by FDA pursuant to § 701.3(c) of this chapter, its common or usual name, if it has one, or its chemical or technical name should be listed.

(4) If an ingredient is a mixture, each ingredient of the mixture should be listed in accordance with paragraphs (d)(2) and (d)(3) of this section, unless such mixture is a formulation voluntarily registered on Form FDA 2512, in which case such mixture should be identified as "fragrance," "flavor," "fragrance and flavor" or "base formulation," as appropriate, and by stating its FDA-assigned cosmetic product ingredient statement number.

(5) When the manufacturer or supplier of a fragrance and/or flavor refuses to disclose ingredient data, the fragrance and/or flavor should be listed as such. The nonconfidential listing of the product name and/or trade name or name of the manufacturer or supplier of each proprietary fragrance and/or flavor mixture is optional.

(e) A separate Form FDA-2512 should be filed for each different formulation of a cosmetic product. However, except for the hair coloring preparations listed in paragraph (c)(6) of this section for which a statement for each shade of such product is required, a single Form FDA-2512 may be filed for two or more shades of a cosmetic product where only the amounts of the color additive ingredient used are varied or in the case of flavors and fragrances where only the amounts of the flavors and fragrances used are varied.

(Information collection requirements in this section were approved by the Office of Management and Budget (OMB) and assigned OMB control number 0910-0030)

[39 FR 10060, Mar. 15, 1974, as amended at 46 FR 38073, July 24, 1981; 57 FR 3129, Jan. 28, 1992]

§ 720.5 [Reserved]

§ 720.6 Amendments to statement.

Changes in the information requested under §§ 720.4 (a)(3) and (a)(5) on the ingredients or brand name of a cosmetic product should be submitted by filing an amended Form FDA 2512 within 60 days after the product is entered into commercial distribution. Other changes do not justify immediate amendment, but should be shown by filing an amended Form FDA 2512 within a year after such changes. Notice of discontinuance of commercial distribution of a cosmetic product formulation should be submitted by Form FDA 2514 within 180 days after discontinuance of commercial distribution becomes known to the person filing.

[57 FR 3130, Jan. 28, 1992, as amended at 67 FR 9587, Mar. 4, 2002]

§720.7 Notification of person submitting cosmetic product ingredient statement.

When Form FDA 2512 is received, FDA will either assign a permanent cosmetic product ingredient statement number or a Food and Drug Administration (FDA) reference number in those cases where a permanent number cannot be assigned. Receipt of the form will be acknowledged by sending the individual signing the statement an appropriate notice bearing either the FDA reference number or the permanent cosmetic product ingredient statement number. If the person submitting Form FDA 2512 has not complied with §§720.4 (b)(1) and (b)(2), the person will be notified as to the manner in which the statement is incomplete.

[57 FR 3130, Jan. 28, 1992]

§720.8 Confidentiality of statements.

(a) Data and information contained in, attached to, or included with Forms FDA 2512 and FDA 2514, and amendments thereto are submitted voluntarily to the Food and Drug Administration (FDA). Any request for confidentiality of a cosmetic ingredient submitted with such forms or separately will be handled in accordance with the procedure set forth in this section. The request for confidentiality will also be subject to the provisions of §20.111 of this chapter, as well as to the exemptions in subpart D of part 20 of this chapter and to the limitations on exemption in subpart E of part 20 of this chapter.

(b) Any request for confidentiality of the identity of a cosmetic ingredient should contain a full statement, in a well-organized format, of the factual and legal grounds for that request, including all data and other information on which the petitioner relies, as well as representative information known to the petitioner that is unfavorable to the petitioner's position. The statement of the factual grounds should include, but should not be limited to, scientific or technical data, reports, tests, and other relevant information addressing the following factors that FDA will consider in determining whether the identity of an ingredient qualifies as a trade secret:

(1) The extent to which the identity of the ingredient is known outside petitioner's business;

(2) The extent to which the identity of the ingredient is known by employees and others involved in petitioner's business;

(3) The extent of measures taken by the petitioner to guard the secrecy of the information;

(4) The value of the information about the identity of the claimed trade secret ingredient to the petitioner and to its competitors;

(5) The amount of effort or money expended by petitioner in developing the ingredient; and

(6) The ease or difficulty with which the identity of the ingredient could be properly acquired or duplicated by others.

(c) The request for confidentiality should also be accompanied by a statement that the identity of the ingredient for which confidentiality is requested has not previously been published or disclosed to anyone other than as provided in §20.81(a) of this chapter.

(d) FDA will return to the petitioner any request for confidentiality that contains insufficient data to permit a review of the merits of the request. FDA will also advise the petitioner about the additional information that is necessary to enable the agency to proceed with its review of the request.

(e) If, after receiving all of the data that are necessary to make a determination about whether the identity of an ingredient is a trade secret, FDA tentatively decides to deny the request, the Agency will inform the person requesting trade secrecy of its tentative determination in writing. FDA will set forth the grounds upon which it relied in making this tentative determination. The petitioner may submit, within 60 days from the date of receipt of the written notice of the tentative denial, additional relevant information and arguments and request that the Agency reconsider its decision in light of both the additional material and the information that it originally submitted.

(f) If the petitioner submits new data in response to FDA's tentative denial of trade secret status, the agency will consider that material together with the information that was submitted initially before making its final determination.

(g) A final determination that an ingredient is not a trade secret within the meaning of § 20.61 of this chapter constitutes final Agency action that is subject to judicial review under 5 U.S.C. Chapter 7. If suit is brought within 30 calendar days after such a determination, FDA will not disclose the records involved or require that the disputed ingredient or ingredients be disclosed in labeling until the matter is finally determined in the courts. If suit is not brought within 30 calendar days after a final determination that an ingredient is not a trade secret within the meaning of § 20.61 of this chapter, the records involved will be available for public disclosure in accordance with part 20 of this chapter.

[51 FR 11444, Apr. 3, 1986, as amended at 57 FR 3130, Jan. 28, 1992; 68 FR 25288, May 12, 2003; 87 FR 55914, Sept. 13, 2022]

§ 720.9 Misbranding by reference to filing or to statement number.

The filing of Form FDA 2512 or assignment of a number to the statement does not in any way denote approval by the Food and Drug Administration of the firm or the product. Any representation in labeling or advertising that creates an impression of official approval because of such filing or such number will be considered misleading.

[57 FR 3130, Jan. 28, 1992]

PART 740—COSMETIC PRODUCT WARNING STATEMENTS

Subpart A—General

Sec.
740.1 Establishment of warning statements.
740.2 Conspicuousness of warning statements.

Subpart B—Warning Statements

740.10 Labeling of cosmetic products for which adequate substantiation of safety has not been obtained.
740.11 Cosmetics in self-pressurized containers.
740.12 Feminine deodorant sprays.
740.17 Foaming detergent bath products.
740.18 Coal tar hair dyes posing a risk of cancer.
740.19 Suntanning preparations.

AUTHORITY: 21 U.S.C. 321, 331, 352, 355, 361, 362, 371, 374.

Subpart A—General

§ 740.1 Establishment of warning statements.

(a) The label of a cosmetic product shall bear a warning statement whenever necessary or appropriate to prevent a health hazard that may be associated with the product.

(b) The Commissioner of Food and Drugs, either on his own initiative or on behalf of any interested person who has submitted a petition, may publish a proposal to establish or amend, under subpart B of this part, a regulation prescribing a warning for a cosmetic. Any such petition shall include an adequate factual basis to support the petition, shall be in the form set forth in part 10 of this chapter, and will be published for comment if it contains reasonable grounds for the proposed regulation.

[40 FR 8917, Mar. 3, 1975, as amended at 42 FR 15676, Mar. 22, 1977]

§ 740.2 Conspicuousness of warning statements.

(a) A warning statement shall appear on the label prominently and conspicuously as compared to other words, statements, designs, or devices and in bold type on contrasting background to render it likely to be read and understood by the ordinary individual under customary conditions of purchase and use, but in no case may the letters and/

or numbers be less than ⅟₁₆ inch in height, unless an exemption pursuant to paragraph (b) of this section is established.

(b) If the label of any cosmetic package is too small to accommodate the information as required by this section, the Commissioner may establish by regulation an acceptable alternative method, e.g., type size smaller than ⅟₁₆ inch in height. A petition requesting such a regulation, as an amendment to this section, shall be submitted to the Division of Dockets Management in the form established in part 10 of this chapter.

[40 FR 8917, Mar. 3, 1975, as amended at 42 FR 15676, Mar. 22, 1977; 69 FR 13717, Mar. 24, 2004]

Subpart B—Warning Statements

§ 740.10 Labeling of cosmetic products for which adequate substantiation of safety has not been obtained.

(a) Each ingredient used in a cosmetic product and each finished cosmetic product shall be adequately substantiated for safety prior to marketing. Any such ingredient or product whose safety is not adequately substantiated prior to marketing is misbranded unless it contains the following conspicuous statement on the principal display panel:

Warning—The safety of this product has not been determined.

(b) An ingredient or product having a history of use in or as a cosmetic may at any time have its safety brought into question by new information that in itself is not conclusive. The warning required by paragraph (a) of this section is not required for such an ingredient or product if:

(1) The safety of the ingredient or product had been adequately substantiated prior to development of the new information;

(2) The new information does not demonstrate a hazard to human health; and

(3) Adequate studies are being conducted to determine expeditiously the safety of the ingredient or product.

(c) Paragraph (b) of this section does not constitute an exemption to the adulteration provisions of the Act or to any other requirement in the Act or this chapter.

[40 FR 8917, Mar. 3, 1975]

§ 740.11 Cosmetics in self-pressurized containers.

(a)(1) The label of a cosmetic packaged in a self-pressurized container and intended to be expelled from the package under pressure shall bear the following warning:

Warning—Avoid spraying in eyes. Contents under pressure. Do not puncture or incinerate. Do not store at temperature above 120 °F. Keep out of reach of children.

(2) In the case of products intended for use by children, the phrase "except under adult supervision" may be added at the end of the last sentence in the warning required by paragraph (a)(1) of this section.

(3) In the case of products packaged in glass containers, the word "break" may be substituted for the word "puncture" in the warning required by paragraph (a)(1) of this section.

(4) The words "Avoid spraying in eyes" may be deleted from the warning required by paragraph (a)(1) of this section in the case of a product not expelled as a spray.

(b)(1) In addition to the warning required by paragraph (a)(1) of this section, the label of a cosmetic packaged in a self-pressurized container in which the propellant consists in whole or in part of a halocarbon or a hydrocarbon shall bear the following warning:

Warning—Use only as directed. Intentional misuse by deliberately concentrating and inhaling the contents can be harmful or fatal.

(2) The warning required by paragraph (b)(1) of this section is not required for the following products:

(i) Products expelled in the form of a foam or cream, which contain less than 10 percent propellant in the container.

(ii) Products in a container with a physical barrier that prevents escape of the propellant at the time of use.

(iii) Products of a net quantity of contents of less than 2 ozs. that are designed to release a measured amount of product with each valve actuation.

(iv) Products of a net quantity of contents of less than ½ oz.

(c) Labeling requirements for cosmetics packaged in a self- pressurized container containing or manufactured with a chlorofluorocarbon propellant or other ozone-depleting substance designated by the Environmental Protection Agency (EPA) are set forth in 40 CFR part 82.

[40 FR 8917, Mar. 3, 1975, as amended at 42 FR 22033, Apr. 29, 1977; 54 FR 39640, Sept. 27, 1989; 61 FR 20101, May 3, 1996]

§ 740.12 Feminine deodorant sprays.

(a) For the purpose of this section, the term "feminine deodorant spray" means any spray deodorant product whose labeling represents or suggests that the product is for use in the female genital area or for use all over the body.

(b) The label of a feminine deodorant spray shall bear the following statement:

Caution—For external use only. Spray at least 8 inches from skin. Do not apply to broken, irritated, or itching skin. Persistent, unusual odor or discharge may indicate conditions for which a physician should be consulted. Discontinue use immediately if rash, irritation, or discomfort develops.

The sentence "Spray at least 8 inches from skin" need not be included in the cautionary statement for products whose expelled contents do not contain a liquified gas propellant such as a halocarbon or hydrocarbon propellant.

(c) Use of the word "hygiene" or "hygienic" or a similar word or words renders any such product misbranded under section 602(a) of the Federal Food, Drug, and Cosmetic Act. The use of any word or words which represent or suggest that such products have a medical usefulness renders such products misbranded under section 502(a) of the Act and illegal new drugs marketed in violation of section 505 of the Act.

[40 FR 8929, Mar. 3, 1975]

§ 740.17 Foaming detergent bath products.

(a) For the purpose of this section, a foaming detergent bath product is any product intended to be added to a bath for the purpose of producing foam that contains a surface-active agent serving as a detergent or foaming ingredient.

(b) The label of foaming detergent bath products within the meaning of paragraph (a) of this section, except for

those products that are labeled as intended for use exclusively by adults, shall bear adequate directions for safe use and the following caution:

Caution—Use only as directed. Excessive use or prolonged exposure may cause irritation to skin and urinary tract. Discontinue use if rash, redness, or itching occurs. Consult your physician if irritation persists. Keep out of reach of children.

(c) In the case of products intended for use by children, the phrase "except under adult supervision" may be added at the end of the last sentence in the caution required by paragraph (b) of this section.

[51 FR 20475, June 5, 1986]

§ 740.18 Coal tar hair dyes posing a risk of cancer.

(a) The principal display panel of the label and any labeling accompanying a coal tar hair dye containing any ingredient listed in paragraph (b) of this section shall bear, in accordance with the requirements of § 740.2, the following:

Warning—Contains an ingredient that can penetrate your skin and has been determined to cause cancer in laboratory animals.

(b) Hair dyes containing any of the following ingredients shall comply with the requirements of this section: (1) 4-methoxy-m-phenylenediamine (2,4-diaminoanisole) and (2) 4-methoxy-m-phenylenediamine sulfate (2,4-diaminoanisole sulfate).

[44 FR 59522, Oct. 16, 1979]

EFFECTIVE DATE NOTE: At 47 FR 7829, Feb. 23, 1982, § 740.18 was stayed until further notice, effective Sept. 18, 1980.

§ 740.19 Suntanning preparations.

The labeling of suntanning preparations that do not contain a sunscreen ingredient must display the following warning: "Warning—This product does not contain a sunscreen and does not protect against sunburn. Repeated exposure of unprotected skin while tanning may increase the risk of skin aging, skin cancer, and other harmful effects to the skin even if you do not burn." For purposes of this section, the term "suntanning preparations" includes gels, creams, liquids, and other topical products that are intended to provide cosmetic effects on the skin while tanning through exposure to UV radiation (e.g., moisturizing or conditioning products), or to give the appearance of a tan by imparting color to the skin through the application of approved color additives (e.g., dihydroxyacetone) without the need for exposure to UV radiation. The term "suntanning preparations" does not include products intended to provide sun protection or otherwise intended to affect the structure or any function of the body.

[64 FR 27693, May 21, 1999]

PARTS 741–799 [RESERVED]

FINDING AIDS

A list of CFR titles, subtitles, chapters, subchapters and parts and an alphabetical list of agencies publishing in the CFR are included in the CFR Index and Finding Aids volume to the Code of Federal Regulations which is published separately and revised annually.

Table of CFR Titles and Chapters
Alphabetical List of Agencies Appearing in the CFR
List of CFR Sections Affected

Table of CFR Titles and Chapters

(Revised as of April 1, 2023)

Title 1—General Provisions

I   Administrative Committee of the Federal Register (Parts 1—49)
II   Office of the Federal Register (Parts 50—299)
III Administrative Conference of the United States (Parts 300—399)
IV   Miscellaneous Agencies (Parts 400—599)
VI   National Capital Planning Commission (Parts 600—699)

Title 2—Grants and Agreements

SUBTITLE A—OFFICE OF MANAGEMENT AND BUDGET GUIDANCE FOR GRANTS AND AGREEMENTS

I   Office of Management and Budget Governmentwide Guidance for Grants and Agreements (Parts 2—199)
II   Office of Management and Budget Guidance (Parts 200—299)

SUBTITLE B—FEDERAL AGENCY REGULATIONS FOR GRANTS AND AGREEMENTS

III   Department of Health and Human Services (Parts 300—399)
IV   Department of Agriculture (Parts 400—499)
VI   Department of State (Parts 600—699)
VII   Agency for International Development (Parts 700—799)
VIII Department of Veterans Affairs (Parts 800—899)
IX   Department of Energy (Parts 900—999)
X   Department of the Treasury (Parts 1000—1099)
XI   Department of Defense (Parts 1100—1199)
XII   Department of Transportation (Parts 1200—1299)
XIII Department of Commerce (Parts 1300—1399)
XIV   Department of the Interior (Parts 1400—1499)
XV   Environmental Protection Agency (Parts 1500—1599)
XVIII National Aeronautics and Space Administration (Parts 1800—1899)
XX   United States Nuclear Regulatory Commission (Parts 2000—2099)
XXII Corporation for National and Community Service (Parts 2200—2299)
XXIII Social Security Administration (Parts 2300—2399)
XXIV Department of Housing and Urban Development (Parts 2400—2499)
XXV   National Science Foundation (Parts 2500—2599)
XXVI National Archives and Records Administration (Parts 2600—2699)

Title 2—Grants and Agreements—Continued

Title 3—The President

Title 4—Accounts

Title 5—Administrative Personnel

171

172

Title 7—Agriculture—Continued

Title 7—Agriculture—Continued

Title 8—Aliens and Nationality

Title 9—Animals and Animal Products

Title 10—Energy

Title 11—Federal Elections

Title 12—Banks and Banking

Title 12—Banks and Banking—Continued

Title 13—Business Credit and Assistance

Title 14—Aeronautics and Space

Title 15—Commerce and Foreign Trade

175

Title 15—Commerce and Foreign Trade—Continued
Chap.

Title 16—Commercial Practices

Title 17—Commodity and Securities Exchanges

Title 18—Conservation of Power and Water Resources

Title 19—Customs Duties

Title 20—Employees' Benefits

Title 21—Food and Drugs

Title 22—Foreign Relations

180

181

Title 34—Education

Title 35 [Reserved]

Title 36—Parks, Forests, and Public Property

Title 37—Patents, Trademarks, and Copyrights

182

Title 45—Public Welfare

Title 46—Shipping

Title 47—Telecommunication

Title 48—Federal Acquisition Regulations System

Title 49—Transportation

Title 50—Wildlife and Fisheries

Title 50—Wildlife and Fisheries—Continued

Alphabetical List of Agencies Appearing in the CFR
(Revised as of April 1, 2023)

Agency	CFR Title, Subtitle or Chapter
Administrative Conference of the United States	1, III
Advisory Council on Historic Preservation	36, VIII
Advocacy and Outreach, Office of	7, XXV
Afghanistan Reconstruction, Special Inspector General for	5, LXXXIII
African Development Foundation	22, XV
Federal Acquisition Regulation	48, 57
Agency for International Development	2, VII; 22, II
Federal Acquisition Regulation	48, 7
Agricultural Marketing Service	7, I, VIII, IX, X, XI; 9, II
Agricultural Research Service	7, V
Agriculture, Department of	2, IV; 5, LXXIII
Advocacy and Outreach, Office of	7, XXV
Agricultural Marketing Service	7, I, VIII, IX, X, XI; 9, II
Agricultural Research Service	7, V
Animal and Plant Health Inspection Service	7, III; 9, I
Chief Financial Officer, Office of	7, XXX
Commodity Credit Corporation	7, XIV
Economic Research Service	7, XXXVII
Energy Policy and New Uses, Office of	2, IX; 7, XXIX
Environmental Quality, Office of	7, XXXI
Farm Service Agency	7, VII, XVIII
Federal Acquisition Regulation	48, 4
Federal Crop Insurance Corporation	7, IV
Food and Nutrition Service	7, II
Food Safety and Inspection Service	9, III
Foreign Agricultural Service	7, XV
Forest Service	36, II
Information Resources Management, Office of	7, XXVII
Inspector General, Office of	7, XXVI
National Agricultural Library	7, XLI
National Agricultural Statistics Service	7, XXXVI
National Institute of Food and Agriculture	7, XXXIV
Natural Resources Conservation Service	7, VI
Operations, Office of	7, XXVIII
Procurement and Property Management, Office of	7, XXXII
Rural Business-Cooperative Service	7, XVIII, XLII
Rural Development Administration	7, XLII
Rural Housing Service	7, XVIII, XXXV
Rural Utilities Service	7, XVII, XVIII, XLII
Secretary of Agriculture, Office of	7, Subtitle A
Transportation, Office of	7, XXXIII
World Agricultural Outlook Board	7, XXXVIII
Air Force, Department of	32, VII
Federal Acquisition Regulation Supplement	48, 53
Air Transportation Stabilization Board	14, VI
Alcohol and Tobacco Tax and Trade Bureau	27, I
Alcohol, Tobacco, Firearms, and Explosives, Bureau of	27, II
AMTRAK	49, VII
American Battle Monuments Commission	36, IV
American Indians, Office of the Special Trustee	25, VII
Animal and Plant Health Inspection Service	7, III; 9, I
Appalachian Regional Commission	5, IX
Architectural and Transportation Barriers Compliance Board	36, XI

Agency	CFR Title, Subtitle or Chapter
Arctic Research Commission	45, XXIII
Armed Forces Retirement Home	5, XI; 38, II
Army, Department of	32, V
Engineers, Corps of	33, II; 36, III
Federal Acquisition Regulation	48, 51
Benefits Review Board	20, VII
Bilingual Education and Minority Languages Affairs, Office of	34, V
Blind or Severely Disabled, Committee for Purchase from People Who Are	41, 51
Federal Acquisition Regulation	48, 19
Career, Technical, and Adult Education, Office of	34, IV
Census Bureau	15, I
Centers for Medicare & Medicaid Services	42, IV
Central Intelligence Agency	32, XIX
Chemical Safety and Hazard Investigation Board	40, VI
Chief Financial Officer, Office of	7, XXX
Child Support Enforcement, Office of	45, III
Children and Families, Administration for	45, II, III, IV, X, XIII
Civil Rights, Commission on	5, LXVIII; 45, VII
Civil Rights, Office for	34, I
Coast Guard	33, I; 46, I; 49, IV
Coast Guard (Great Lakes Pilotage)	46, III
Commerce, Department of	2, XIII; 44, IV; 50, VI
Census Bureau	15, I
Economic Affairs, Office of the Under-Secretary for	15, XV
Economic Analysis, Bureau of	15, VIII
Economic Development Administration	13, III
Emergency Management and Assistance	44, IV
Federal Acquisition Regulation	48, 13
Foreign-Trade Zones Board	15, IV
Industry and Security, Bureau of	15, VII
International Trade Administration	15, III; 19, III
National Institute of Standards and Technology	15, II; 37, IV
National Marine Fisheries Service	50, II, IV
National Oceanic and Atmospheric Administration	15, IX; 50, II, III, IV, VI
National Technical Information Service	15, XI
National Telecommunications and Information Administration	15, XXIII; 47, III, IV
National Weather Service	15, IX
Patent and Trademark Office, United States	37, I
Secretary of Commerce, Office of	15, Subtitle A
Commercial Space Transportation	14, III
Commodity Credit Corporation	7, XIV
Commodity Futures Trading Commission	5, XLI; 17, I
Community Planning and Development, Office of Assistant Secretary for	24, V, VI
Community Services, Office of	45, X
Comptroller of the Currency	12, I
Construction Industry Collective Bargaining Commission	29, IX
Consumer Financial Protection Bureau	5, LXXXIV; 12, X
Consumer Product Safety Commission	5, LXXI; 16, II
Copyright Royalty Board	37, III
Corporation for National and Community Service	2, XXII; 45, XII, XXV
Cost Accounting Standards Board	48, 99
Council on Environmental Quality	40, V
Council of the Inspectors General on Integrity and Efficiency	5, XCVIII
Court Services and Offender Supervision Agency for the District of Columbia	5, LXX; 28, VIII
Customs and Border Protection	19, I
Defense, Department of	2, XI; 5, XXVI; 32, Subtitle A; 40, VII
Advanced Research Projects Agency	32, I
Air Force Department	32, VII
Army Department	32, V; 33, II; 36, III; 48, 51
Defense Acquisition Regulations System	48, 2
Defense Intelligence Agency	32, I

Agency	CFR Title, Subtitle or Chapter
Defense Logistics Agency	32, I, XII; 48, 54
Engineers, Corps of	33, II; 36, III
National Imagery and Mapping Agency	32, I
Navy, Department of	32, VI; 48, 52
Secretary of Defense, Office of	2, XI; 32, I
Defense Contract Audit Agency	32, I
Defense Intelligence Agency	32, I
Defense Logistics Agency	32, XII; 48, 54
Defense Nuclear Facilities Safety Board	10, XVII
Delaware River Basin Commission	18, III
Denali Commission	45, IX
Disability, National Council on	5, C; 34, XII
District of Columbia, Court Services and Offender Supervision Agency for the	5, LXX; 28, VIII
Drug Enforcement Administration	21, II
East-West Foreign Trade Board	15, XIII
Economic Affairs, Office of the Under-Secretary for	15, XV
Economic Analysis, Bureau of	15, VIII
Economic Development Administration	13, III
Economic Research Service	7, XXXVII
Education, Department of	2, XXXIV; 5, LIII
Bilingual Education and Minority Languages Affairs, Office of	34, V
Career, Technical, and Adult Education, Office of	34, IV
Civil Rights, Office for	34, I
Educational Research and Improvement, Office of	34, VII
Elementary and Secondary Education, Office of	34, II
Federal Acquisition Regulation	48, 34
Postsecondary Education, Office of	34, VI
Secretary of Education, Office of	34, Subtitle A
Special Education and Rehabilitative Services, Office of	34, III
Educational Research and Improvement, Office of	34, VII
Election Assistance Commission	2, LVIII; 11, II
Elementary and Secondary Education, Office of	34, II
Emergency Oil and Gas Guaranteed Loan Board	13, V
Emergency Steel Guarantee Loan Board	13, IV
Employee Benefits Security Administration	29, XXV
Employees' Compensation Appeals Board	20, IV
Employees Loyalty Board	5, V
Employment and Training Administration	20, V
Employment Policy, National Commission for	1, IV
Employment Standards Administration	20, VI
Endangered Species Committee	50, IV
Energy, Department of	2, IX; 5, XXIII; 10, II, III, X
Federal Acquisition Regulation	48, 9
Federal Energy Regulatory Commission	5, XXIV; 18, I
Property Management Regulations	41, 109
Energy, Office of	7, XXIX
Engineers, Corps of	33, II; 36, III
Engraving and Printing, Bureau of	31, VI
Environmental Protection Agency	2, XV; 5, LIV; 40, I, IV, VII
Federal Acquisition Regulation	48, 15
Property Management Regulations	41, 115
Environmental Quality, Office of	7, XXXI
Equal Employment Opportunity Commission	5, LXII; 29, XIV
Equal Opportunity, Office of Assistant Secretary for	24, I
Executive Office of the President	3, I
Environmental Quality, Council on	40, V
Management and Budget, Office of	2, Subtitle A; 5, III, LXXVII; 14, VI; 48, 99
National Drug Control Policy, Office of	2, XXXVI; 21, III
National Security Council	32, XXI; 47, II
Presidential Documents	3
Science and Technology Policy, Office of	32, XXIV; 47, II
Trade Representative, Office of the United States	15, XX

191

Agency	CFR Title, Subtitle or Chapter
Federal Management Regulation	41, 102
Federal Property Management Regulations	41, 101
Federal Travel Regulation System	41, Subtitle F
General	41, 300
Payment From a Non-Federal Source for Travel Expenses	41, 304
Payment of Expenses Connected With the Death of Certain Employees	41, 303
Relocation Allowances	41, 302
Temporary Duty (TDY) Travel Allowances	41, 301
Geological Survey	30, IV
Government Accountability Office	4, I
Government Ethics, Office of	5, XVI
Government National Mortgage Association	24, III
Grain Inspection, Packers and Stockyards Administration	7, VIII; 9, II
Great Lakes St. Lawrence Seaway Development Corporation	33, IV
Gulf Coast Ecosystem Restoration Council	2, LIX; 40, VIII
Harry S. Truman Scholarship Foundation	45, XVIII
Health and Human Services, Department of	2, III; 5, XLV; 45, Subtitle A
Centers for Medicare & Medicaid Services	42, IV
Child Support Enforcement, Office of	45, III
Children and Families, Administration for	45, II, III, IV, X, XIII
Community Services, Office of	45, X
Family Assistance, Office of	45, II
Federal Acquisition Regulation	48, 3
Food and Drug Administration	21, I
Indian Health Service	25, V
Inspector General (Health Care), Office of	42, V
Public Health Service	42, I
Refugee Resettlement, Office of	45, IV
Homeland Security, Department of	2, XXX; 5, XXXVI; 6, I; 8, I
Coast Guard	33, I; 46, I; 49, IV
Coast Guard (Great Lakes Pilotage)	46, III
Customs and Border Protection	19, I
Federal Emergency Management Agency	44, I
Human Resources Management and Labor Relations Systems	5, XCVII
Immigration and Customs Enforcement Bureau	19, IV
Transportation Security Administration	49, XII
HOPE for Homeowners Program, Board of Directors of	24, XXIV
Housing and Urban Development, Department of	2, XXIV; 5, LXV; 24, Subtitle B
Community Planning and Development, Office of Assistant Secretary for	24, V, VI
Equal Opportunity, Office of Assistant Secretary for	24, I
Federal Acquisition Regulation	48, 24
Federal Housing Enterprise Oversight, Office of	12, XVII
Government National Mortgage Association	24, III
Housing—Federal Housing Commissioner, Office of Assistant Secretary for	24, II, VIII, X, XX
Housing, Office of, and Multifamily Housing Assistance Restructuring, Office of	24, IV
Inspector General, Office of	24, XII
Public and Indian Housing, Office of Assistant Secretary for	24, IX
Secretary, Office of	24, Subtitle A, VII
Housing—Federal Housing Commissioner, Office of Assistant Secretary for	24, II, VIII, X, XX
Housing, Office of, and Multifamily Housing Assistance Restructuring, Office of	24, IV
Immigration and Customs Enforcement Bureau	19, IV
Immigration Review, Executive Office for	8, V
Independent Counsel, Office of	28, VII
Independent Counsel, Offices of	28, VI
Indian Affairs, Bureau of	25, I, V
Indian Affairs, Office of the Assistant Secretary	25, VI
Indian Arts and Crafts Board	25, II

194

List of CFR Sections Affected

All changes in this volume of the Code of Federal Regulations (CFR) that were made by documents published in the FEDERAL REGISTER since January 1, 2018 are enumerated in the following list. Entries indicate the nature of the changes effected. Page numbers refer to FEDERAL REGISTER pages. The user should consult the entries for chapters, parts and subparts as well as sections for revisions.

For changes to this volume of the CFR prior to this listing, consult the annual edition of the monthly List of CFR Sections Affected (LSA). The LSA is available at *www.govinfo.gov.* For changes to this volume of the CFR prior to 2001, see the "List of CFR Sections Affected, 1949–1963, 1964–1972, 1973–1985, and 1986–2000" published in 11 separate volumes. The "List of CFR Sections Affected 1986–2000" is available at *www.govinfo.gov.*

2018

21 CFR   83 FR
                                                    Page

Chapter I
600.21 Amended; eff. 6-11-18 3589
   Regulation at 83 FR 3589 with-
      drawn 19936
600.22 Removed; eff. 6-11-18 3589
   Regulation at 83 FR 3589 with-
      drawn 19936

2019

21 CFR   84 FR
                                                    Page

Chapter I
600   Authority citation revised 12508
600.21 Amended............................ 12508
600.22 Removed............................ 12508

2020

21 CFR   85 FR
                                                    Page

Chapter I
600.3 (h) introductory text re-
      vised; (h)(6) added 10063
610.30 (Subpart D) Removed 51639

2021

21 CFR   86 FR
                                                    Page

Chapter I
610.40   (h)(2)(vii) revised................ 49922

2022

21 CFR   87 FR
                                                    Page

Chapter I
720.8   (e) and (g) revised 55914

2023

(No regulations published from
January 1, 2023, through April 1, 2023)

○

199

Table of Contents

Cite this Code: CFR

To cite the regulations in this volume use title, part and section number. Thus, 21 CFR 600.2 refers to title 21, part 600, section 2.

Explanation

The Code of Federal Regulations is a codification of the general and permanent rules published in the Federal Register by the Executive departments and agencies of the Federal Government. The Code is divided into 50 titles which represent broad areas subject to Federal regulation. Each title is divided into chapters which usually bear the name of the issuing agency. Each chapter is further subdivided into parts covering specific regulatory areas.

Each volume of the Code is revised at least once each calendar year and issued on a quarterly basis approximately as follows:

Title 1 through Title 16...as of January 1
Title 17 through Title 27 ....as of April 1
Title 28 through Title 41 ....as of July 1
Title 42 through Title 50 ....as of October 1

The appropriate revision date is printed on the cover of each volume.

LEGAL STATUS

The contents of the Federal Register are required to be judicially noticed (44 U.S.C. 1507). The Code of Federal Regulations is prima facie evidence of the text of the original documents (44 U.S.C. 1510).

HOW TO USE THE CODE OF FEDERAL REGULATIONS

The Code of Federal Regulations is kept up to date by the individual issues of the Federal Register. These two publications must be used together to determine the latest version of any given rule.

To determine whether a Code volume has been amended since its revision date (in this case, April 1, 2023), consult the "List of CFR Sections Affected (LSA)," which is issued monthly, and the "Cumulative List of Parts Affected," which appears in the Reader Aids section of the daily Federal Register. These two lists will identify the Federal Register page number of the latest amendment of any given rule.

EFFECTIVE AND EXPIRATION DATES

Each volume of the Code contains amendments published in the Federal Register since the last revision of that volume of the Code. Source citations for the regulations are referred to by volume number and page number of the Federal Register and date of publication. Publication dates and effective dates are usually not the same and care must be exercised by the user in determining the actual effective date. In instances where the effective date is beyond the cutoff date for the Code a note has been inserted to reflect the future effective date. In those instances where a regulation published in the Federal Register states a date certain for expiration, an appropriate note will be inserted following the text.

OMB CONTROL NUMBERS

The Paperwork Reduction Act of 1980 (Pub. L. 96–511) requires Federal agencies to display an OMB control number with their information collection request.

Many agencies have begun publishing numerous OMB control numbers as amendments to existing regulations in the CFR. These OMB numbers are placed as close as possible to the applicable recordkeeping or reporting requirements.

PAST PROVISIONS OF THE CODE

Provisions of the Code that are no longer in force and effect as of the revision date stated on the cover of each volume are not carried. Code users may find the text of provisions in effect on any given date in the past by using the appropriate List of CFR Sections Affected (LSA). For the convenience of the reader, a "List of CFR Sections Affected" is published at the end of each CFR volume. For changes to the Code prior to the LSA listings at the end of the volume, consult previous annual editions of the LSA. For changes to the Code prior to 2001, consult the List of CFR Sections Affected compilations, published for 1949-1963, 1964-1972, 1973-1985, and 1986-2000.

"[RESERVED]" TERMINOLOGY

The term "[Reserved]" is used as a place holder within the Code of Federal Regulations. An agency may add regulatory information at a "[Reserved]" location at any time. Occasionally "[Reserved]" is used editorially to indicate that a portion of the CFR was left vacant and not dropped in error.

INCORPORATION BY REFERENCE

What is incorporation by reference? Incorporation by reference was established by statute and allows Federal agencies to meet the requirement to publish regulations in the Federal Register by referring to materials already published elsewhere. For an incorporation to be valid, the Director of the Federal Register must approve it. The legal effect of incorporation by reference is that the material is treated as if it were published in full in the Federal Register (5 U.S.C. 552(a)). This material, like any other properly issued regulation, has the force of law.

What is a proper incorporation by reference? The Director of the Federal Register will approve an incorporation by reference only when the requirements of 1 CFR part 51 are met. Some of the elements on which approval is based are:

(a) The incorporation will substantially reduce the volume of material published in the Federal Register.

(b) The matter incorporated is in fact available to the extent necessary to afford fairness and uniformity in the administrative process.

(c) The incorporating document is drafted and submitted for publication in accordance with 1 CFR part 51.

What if the material incorporated by reference cannot be found? If you have any problem locating or obtaining a copy of material listed as an approved incorporation by reference, please contact the agency that issued the regulation containing that incorporation. If, after contacting the agency, you find the material is not available, please notify the Director of the Federal Register, National Archives and Records Administration, 8601 Adelphi Road, College Park, MD 20740-6001, or call 202-741-6010.

CFR INDEXES AND TABULAR GUIDES

A subject index to the Code of Federal Regulations is contained in a separate volume, revised annually as of January 1, entitled CFR INDEX AND FINDING AIDS. This volume contains the Parallel Table of Authorities and Rules. A list of CFR titles, chapters, subchapters, and parts and an alphabetical list of agencies publishing in the CFR are also included in this volume.

An index to the text of "Title 3—The President" is carried within that volume.